THE OTHERS WITHIN US

Dan Bar-On's psychosocial approach sees identity as dynamic, constructed in contradistinction to various "Others." Drawing parallels to other societies, he looks most closely at identity formation among Israelis or, more precisely, among the largely secular Jews from European lands who formed the hegemonic backbone of Israeli society. The Others in question, Diaspora Jews, Jews from Muslim countries, and Arabs, represent repressed aspects of the collective self.

Case studies and analysis depict various stages in identity formation, as do "personal windows" onto the author as he experienced these stages. Monolithic identity construction characterized Israel's early years, but this began to disintegrate with the passing of time, in ways that were often painful and confusing, though necessary in the view of Bar-On and others. A neo-monolithic backlash has been the response to the disintegration stage in recent years. Yet the book holds out the possibility of a constructive dialogue, internal and among groups in society, that will give rise to a better-integrated and more inclusive identity construction.

Dan Bar-On is a professor of psychology in the department of behavioral sciences at Ben-Gurion University of the Negev. He is also the co-director of PRIME (Peace Research Institute in the Middle East) near Beit Jala in the West Bank. He is the author of several books, among them *Legacy of Silence: Encounters with Children of the Third Reich, Fear and Hope: Three Generations of Holocaust Survivors' Families, The Indescribable and the Undiscussable,* and *Tell Your Life Story.* In 1996, he was awarded the David Lopatie Chair for Post-Holocaust Psychological Studies. In 2001, he received the Bundesverdienstkreuz First Class from German President Dr. Johannes Rau. In 2003, he received the Eric Maria Remarque Peace Prize in Osnabrück, Germany. In 2005, he and Professor Sami Adwan, with whom he co-directs PRIME, received the Victor J. Goldberg IIE Prize for Peace in the Middle East and the EAEA Third Out-of-Europe Grundtvig Award on Active Citizenship in a Democratic Society. In 2007, they received a Fulbright scholarship at Monmouth University in New Jersey, U.S.A.

THE OTHERS WITHIN US

Constructing Jewish-Israeli Identity

Dan Bar-On

Ben-Gurion University of the Negev
Translated by Noel Canin

CAMBRIDGE UNIVERSITY PRESS
Cambridge, New York, Melbourne, Madrid, Cape Town, Singapore, São Paulo, Delhi

Cambridge University Press
32 Avenue of the Americas, New York, NY 10013-2473, USA

www.cambridge.org
Information on this title: www.cambridge.org/9780521708289

First published 2008

Printed in the United States of America

A catalog record for this publication is available from the British Library.

Library of Congress Cataloging in Publication Data

Bar-On, Dan, 1938–
['Al ha-'aherim' be-tokhenu. English]
The others within us : constructing Jewish-Israeli identity / Dan Bar-On.
p.   cm.
Includes bibliographical references and index.
ISBN 978-0-521-88187-6 (hardback)
1. National characteristics, Israeli.   2. Jews – Israel – Identity.   3. Self-perception – Israel.   I. Title.
DS113.3.B3513   2008
305.892′4–dc22   2007045444

ISBN   978-0-521-88187-6 hardback
ISBN   978-0-521-70828-9 paperback

To our children: Yariv, who did not live to see all the changes, and Yaarah, Oren, Shani, Nirit, Erez, and Haran. They have accompanied me quite a distance during my transition from monolithic identity to dialogue, while I have taken part in their own transitions.

Contents

Acknowledgments

This book is dedicated to our children. When, about six months ago, I was suddenly diagnosed with cancer, our adult children – along with my wife Tammy – became a committed support group, helping me to go on in spite of the difficult diagnosis, operation, and treatments. Our family had been cancer-stricken before – Yariv and Tammy were diagnosed at intervals of about ten years. But never before did I experience its members as so committed, assisting me in my difficult moments, supporting me to move on, so that I could reach the point that I am at now, on my Fulbright scholarship in New Jersey, with my Palestinian friend and colleague, Professor Sami Adwan. I am indebted to him and to Professor Saliba Sarsar, Associate Vice President for Academic Initiatives at Monmouth University, who helped this fellowship materialize. I am these days trying to find my way among the healthy and the less healthy. Finally publishing this book in English is part of the struggle.

There are many colleagues in Israel and abroad who are faithful partners in my way of thinking, research, and writing, and I am grateful for their support and love and also for the controversy that helped me develop this path. I owe this book to them, as well as the earlier writings in which I detail the names. Among my colleagues at home, I would like in particular to thank Dr. Ifat Maoz of the Hebrew University of Jerusalem, who was the co-author of the first chapter of the first version of this book in Hebrew. Among my colleagues abroad, I want to especially thank Elisabeth Nyffenegger from Geneva, who persisted in her demand that this book appear in English (Hebrew editions were published by Ben-Gurion University of the Negev Press and Mossad Bialik in 1999 and 2005, and the Koerber Foundation in Hamburg brought out the German editions in 2001 and 2005). To these publishers I am grateful as well, and especially Susanne Kutz and Ulrike Fritzsching of the Koeber Foundation and Professor Daniel Sivan of Ben-Gurion University Press. I also want to thank Noel Canin, who translated the manuscript from Hebrew, and Chaia Beckerman who edited it. Finally, I wish to thank Eric Schwartz of Cambridge University Press.

Dan Bar-On
Long Branch, New Jersey, May 2007

Introduction

THE INTERNAL AND EXTERNAL OTHER IN ISRAELI IDENTITY

This book sees the construction of Israeli-Jewish collective identity as an ongoing process rather than as the route already traveled to a definite and permanent structure. My analysis will focus on the secular Ashkenazi (European) Jews who arrived in the land called Palestine and later Israel during the twentieth century, whether out of necessity (as refugees fleeing persecutors) or to fulfill their ideological Zionist aspirations.[1] My argument will be that collective identity construction among this sector of the population has gone through several phases and the transformation has not yet ended.

The process started off with a monolithic identity constructed in opposition to the Diaspora Jew and to gentile enemies. "Monolithic" is a geological expression describing one piece of stone made of a single material. Monolithic identity construction in Israel served a positive function by creating a social entity out of different groups and tribes. During the 1970s, when Israel saw itself as stronger militarily, socially, and politically, a deconstruction of the monolithic structure began. Parts of the Israeli society and leadership, caught up in a nostalgic, idealized view of the past, saw deconstruction as regressive, while other parts of the society and some of its leadership viewed it as progress – toward a realization of internal differences and a more complex self-definition. The deconstruction or disintegration of the monolithic collective identity was painful and energy consuming, and this

---

[1] Although similar processes of identity construction can also be identified within other sectors of Israeli society, this book will focus on the hegemonic group to which I belong, as I do not wish to speak in the name of others.

accounts for the later rise of neo-monolithic constructions, especially vis-
à-vis external enemies, after the new outburst of violence in October 2000.
Today the ascent of neo-monolithic constructions and the disintegration
of previous monolithic constructions continue simultaneously. The whirlwind[2] that ensues makes it very difficult for the average citizen to answer
such basic questions as "who am I?" (as part of this collective) "where do I
come from" and "where am I heading?"

After reviewing these phases, I will try to show that a positive way out can
be found in the development of dialogues among the bits and pieces of the
disintegrated construction that do not fit together anymore (and perhaps
never fit well in the first place). Such dialogue happens now only in small
natural experiments or in planned laboratory settings, but there may be
ways to expand such social opportunities, as I discuss in the postscript.

Changes in Israeli-Jewish identity have not taken place in a vacuum.
This period has seen the world shifting from one kind of political polar-
ity, that of good versus evil (the "enlightened" world as opposed to Nazi
fascism), to another based on warring economic visions (free world capi-
talism as opposed to totalitarian Communism). The polarities created the
need for monolithic constructions all over the world. Only after the fall of
Communism in Eastern Europe in 1989 did the world face a new option of
moving out of polarization. The hope, or illusion, was that the complexities
of democratic political systems, which would allow a reshuffling of power
through dialogue between the West and the rest of the world, would be
recognized as positive. Alas, after 9/11, a neo-monolithic tendency developed in the United States. Fear of immigrants was already widespread in
European countries. It is probable that U.S. citizens who were used to a collective identity constructed monolithically, first against the Nazis during
World War II and later against the Communist USSR, found themselves
quite anxious without an "enemy" and impelled to redefine who they were
as a collective. The neo-monolithic trend became a refuge, helping them

---

[2] In the desert, especially during the fall, strong winds from different directions collide,
whirling around the yellow and dry plains, filling up everything with dust, and blurring
the sense of direction of anyone caught in it. The whirlwind is a central metaphor in my
recent book, *Tell Your Life Story: Creating Dialogue among Jews and Germans, Israelis
and Palestinians* (2006 in German, 2004).

overcome their fears after the vicious terrorist attacks. Yet, in their case as well, disintegration of monolithic constructions continued, catching them between two opposing forces, so that they found difficulty in placing and redefining themselves.

In addition, it is not only national, political drama that leads to disintegration of monolithic construction. Gender, religious, and ethnic issues too have evoked changes in collective identities, particularly in the Western world. After the monolithic phase ended in the Western world, those who had been considered Others often searched desperately for a "voice" long suppressed by the traditional hegemonic system of representation (Gur-Zeev, 2003). "Multiculturalism" is more an aspiration than a reality in many modern societies. They have their difficulties creating a significant dialogue between the "voices," particularly when power relations are asymmetrical. When disparate voices begin to ring out at the same time, struggling to replace the traditional hegemony of power, they sound like a choir off-key, each striving to be heard rather than to listen or blend in with other voices in creation of a meaningful dialogue.

Terms used for recent developments – for example, "postmodernism," "globalization," and "multiculturalism" – be they positive, neutral, or derogatory, can be contrasted with older descriptions such as "modernism" and "divided world," and with previous hegemonic names (Ram, 1993). The question is whether these are only terminological changes or whether they reflect a meaningful transition toward dialogue and containment of complexities. In the United States, for instance, we find multiculturalism in the form of public school classes taught in pupils' mother tongues, such as Spanish or Russian, rather than in English. This was inconceivable in the fifties or the sixties, even in a democratic land populated mainly by the descendants of immigrants. In parallel, political correctness became a test of virtue in the daily use of language (Taub, 1997). In Israel, feminist, Oriental, Haredi (ultra-Orthodox), and Russian voices compete today for political power, although Ashkenazi hegemony still holds sway in politics, the military, and the economic center. These could all be signs of moving toward multiculturalism and dialogue. Nonetheless, there are always those (usually belonging to the traditional hegemony) who view these changes as negative, longing for the good old monolithic days.

In examining current neo-monolithic tendencies, the role of renewed religious and nationalistic fundamentalism deserves special attention. A powerful backlash is especially noticeable in countries evincing a deep sensitivity to threats of the previous monolithic constructions disintegrating. For example, Iran's backlash to fundamental Islam was a reaction to the fast move into modernization initiated by the Shah during the 1960s. In certain fundamentalist Muslim movements, the Americans and Jews are now the personification of total evil, as oppressors of the Arabs or the Palestinians. In parallel, the Palestinians represent total evil to Jewish fundamentalist and racist groups. To the extremists, the evil is genetic rather than a result of any particular act they commit. Therefore, anyone who compromises or gives up any part of the Land of Israel is in the category of *din rodef.* This religious construct permits one to kill in order not to be killed by another. Because the late prime minister favored making peace with the Other, some ultra-nationalist Jewish rabbis declared that judgment against him shortly before Rabin was assassinated by Yigal Amir, a member of an extremist group.

On one hand, extreme neo-monolithic constructions paradoxically support the disintegration of old monolithic constructions. Yet, at the same time, they present the illusion of an alternative that is even more solid, one that beckons to those who are afraid and unable to cope with the ambiguity of the disintegration process. In chaotic times, many people seek an anchor, support, or authority. The possibility of dialogue between the various components of identity is not perceived as a strong counterweight to chaos that can achieve results quickly enough – particularly when groups that consider the Western Other absolute evil, such as Al-Qaeda, hammer away in the background.

IDENTITY FORMATION

The sociopsychological approach to identity construction distinguishes between two different processes (if we momentarily ignore intermediate possibilities): Either identity takes shape in opposition to an "Other" or it is formed through an internal dialogue among the various components of the identity that do not fit together (Gergen, 1991; Sarup, 1996). The first process requires minimal energy, as the perceived characteristics of the Other supply the necessary contrast for defining one's own superior monolithic "self." Sherif's idea of an overriding goal (1966) is part of the literature that shows how it is easier at first to unite under a collective construction of identity, faced by an enemy. Nonetheless, in the long run, considerable energy may be needed to preserve a monolithic construction when, inevitably, conflicting components of the identity cannot be held together anymore. A dialogue process is then necessary to bring together various components of the identity that became incompatible over time. At such a stage, the quality of the dialogue rather than one of the components determines how the collective identity is reconstructed.

According to mid-twentieth-century American concepts of social psychology, social identity stems from one's personal identity (Allport, 1985). In contrast, the European notion identified representation of the collective as a dominant component of personal identity and a prerequisite to understanding the behavior of the individual (Moscovici, 1976; Potter and Wetherell, 1990; Tajfel, 1982). Recently, the concept of identity has become increasingly complex. Identity seems to be composed of contrasts and fragments that are not easily reconcilable. This may not be always obvious, as people try hard to present themselves in a consistent and coherent way (Goffman, 1959). Postmodern thinking has led to relinquishing the concept of identity in favor of "biography" (Fischer-Rosenthal, 1995). Instead of an ostensibly objective and stable *structure* that persists within the individual, a fluid *process* is described. Our biographies are being rewritten constantly, as events and changes in the present – those occurring within us as well as within the external reality – influence our perceptions of past and future (Fischer-Rosenthal, 1995).

According to Anthony Giddens (1991, p. 73), in "societies where modernity is well developed," individuals must make decisions about who they are and how to enact that understanding. It is an ongoing process, a "continuous reflexive endeavor."[3] We create, maintain, and amend sets of narratives to conform to our perceptions of events. This provides continuity between

---

[3] Thanks to an anonymous reviewer not only for this turn of phrase but for the references and clarifications provided.

what we experience and what we expect from the future. In traditional societies, self-image tends to be stable. The pace of change is slower and social structures are less complex, with clear delineation of roles. Those who come to Israel from such societies find themselves plunged into a modern social order, often with few tools and little preparation for radical revision of their biographies. They have incentive to latch onto the monolithic Zionist narrative, even as it is disintegrating. Many immigrants from the West, inclined to come for ideological reasons and ready to construct identities anew, also identify with the hegemonic social narrative.

Longtime residents too may hold tenaciously to its monolithic identity construction. Upheaval challenges the ability to integrate new experiences, and Israel is not only a society of immigrants but turbulent in its own right. The monolithic construction is fostered through ritual and custom, literature and song, in schools, public settings, and in some cases family lore. Beliefs and behaviors of individuals are affected when they identify with the collective (Kimmerling and Moore, 1997). Given a meaningful social and cultural identity to hold on to, identification extends to its successes and failures, privileges and lack of privileges (Tajfel & Turner, 1986).

When stability and calm prevail in modern society, there is more freedom to express aspects of identity that derive from personal biography, whether or not they are valued by the collective. One aspect or another may dominate at any given time, depending on time, place, and the nature of a social interaction. Some social identities are mutually exclusive (one is either female or male), while others may be clustered (white Anglo-Saxon Protestant) or ordered hierarchically – competition of these identities within the individual leads to construction of a hierarchy that differs from one member of a collective to another (Stryker & Serpe, 1994). Threat and turmoil to a society impinge upon the flexibility of this process.

Representations of Other and self play a central role in the personal and collective biographical process, with all its changes. The Other can be constructed in a monolithic way, in opposition to a stable, integrated self. Or, the Other can be perceived as dynamic, undergoing changes in the same way that the self changes throughout its personal and collective life. Furthermore, the Other can be perceived as an *infinity* that cannot ever be fully represented within the *totality* of self-representation: the self tries to build its representation as a fixed structure, while the "Other-ness" of the Other is infinite (Lévinas, 1990). Edward Said (1979), following Arendt (1958), points out the component of power relationships between the self and the Other: The Other and self are fictitious representations intended to legitimize the elitism and hegemony of the collective self in order to continue to oppress and control the Other. Said's concept of orientalism dealt with the manner in which representation of the Arab Other was defined by *Eurocentrism* that sought to control and maintain the elitism and hegemony of Western society. Henriette Dahan Kalev (1997) maintained that Zionism is a private case of this Eurocentric approach, especially as concerns its attitude toward the Oriental ethnic groups of Jews within Israeli society.

Considering the changes that have taken place in Israeli society and its environment, how has representation of the Other expressed itself in Israeli-Jewish identity, as opposed to previous Jewish identity constructions? This question is addressed here through examining the representation of the Other in Jewish-Israeli identity from a sociopsychological perspective, while choosing to depart from quantitative research approaches in favor of a focus on biographical qualitative studies (Bar-On, 1995). Jewish tradition has attributed many meanings to the Other, beginning with the interpretation of Holy Scriptures, Jewish law, and the Kabbalah,[4] through the social-community tradition, to sociological and political conceptualization. This work will focus on the sociopsychological aspect of representation of the Other without undermining the significance of other aspects. I examine the internal and interpersonal emotional processes involved in constructing personal and collective identities, while addressing the social and historic context in which these processes have taken place. There will be an attempt to show how, in Israeli-Jewish society, and especially among its Western-oriented secular members, the representation of the Other has undergone significant changes during recent decades. The four main phases described in this context are also the subject matter of the book's four chapters.

[4] Two different ways of interpreting the Holy Scriptures, the *halachah* [law] represents more institutionalized Jewish rabbinical thinking, while the Kabbalah represents more of the Gnostic and mystic thinking that evolved in opposition to *halachah*.

The chapters show the transition from one generation to the next. Israeli monolithic identity, with its black-and-white contrasting of self and Other, changes in the disintegration phase and later reverts to the neo-monolithic phase. This phase may yet lead in the future to dialogue among the various components of the disintegrated identity.

1. The past: Monolithic identity construction

The monolithic phase was, first of all, an internal Jewish construction. The Zionist movement sought to differentiate itself from traditional religious and Diaspora Jewish identity constructions, emphasizing the new, emerging collective-Zionist self. We will soon see that initially the Zionist hegemonic identity construction internalized anti-Semitic images of the Diaspora Jew and promised to create a "new" Jew who would "heal" the negative attributes through strength, economic self-sufficiency, and willingness to fight for personal and collective independence in the Old-New Land (Raz-Krakotzkin, 1994). Later, with the establishment of the State of Israel, the new Jew was redefined as the *sabra*[5] who was born in Israel and fought for its independence. When massive numbers of Jews emigrated from the Arab countries in the 1940s and 1950s, another threatening Other was identified, albeit Jewish. These Jewish arrivals had to assimilate totally to the new *sabra* identity, which, paradoxically, became a continuation of European, Western Jewish identity construction (Shenhav, 2003).

Secondarily, the monolithic construction was based on the definition of threatening gentile Others. The perception of these external Others was shaped by generations of experiencing persecution, especially within Christian Europe of the Middle Ages. To the familiar gentile Christian Other, two new Others were added during the twentieth century. The Nazi was rightfully perceived as an existential threat to the personal and collective Jewish self. Later, the Middle Eastern Arabs were perceived as a continuation of the German Nazis, trying to annihilate the Jews in their region. In the emerging

---

[5] The *sabra* (prickly pear) is a cactus fruit, common in Arab lands but originally from Mexico, that has thorns on the outside and is soft inside. This became the nickname for the "new" Israeli, who conceals a kind heart with brusque manners that successfully disassociate him or her from the Diaspora Jew.

Israeli society, the self was mobilized in an existential struggle against those Others. Thus collective Israeli identity construction was mobilized mono-lithically against the threat of internal Jewish and external gentile Others. The multiplicity of Others reinforced monolithic construction of Zion-ist hegemonic identity as an "absolute good," in opposition to the "total evil" represented most clearly by Nazi Germany and the Holocaust (Hadar, 1991).

2. The present I: Disintegration of the monolithic construction

The past four decades have seen a gradual disintegration of the monolithic construction of hegemonic Zionist and Jewish-Israeli identities. The dis-integration process slowly revealed internal contradictions that may have existed from the outset within Jewish-Israeli identity, in terms of multiple ethnicities, internal conflicts around the roles of religion and gender, and the like. The monolithic construction was functional during the early years of the State of Israel. At a time of massive hardships, it helped bind Jews who came from all over the world and had very little in common beyond fulfilling a two-thousand-year-old dream of return to their homeland. But as the situation became more relaxed, objectively speaking, the energy and effort invested in preserving a monolithic construction became more evi-dent and more questionable. It became impossible to continue to construct an Israeli-Jewish identity totally different from the identity of the Dias-pora Jew. With significant cultural, ethnic, religious, and gender diversity within the Jewish-Israeli population, correlations involving social stratifi-cation and political power differentiation could no longer be covered up. Neither was it possible to continue to define the external Other only on the basis of what had happened during the *Shoah* (Holocaust) (Segev, 1992). The Likud party took over the government after the elections of 1977, a sign of new voices emerging from within Israeli-Jewish society to question the initial hegemonic power structure. The monolithic identity construc-tion had bolstered this structure's dominance over other parts of the Israeli society for the state's first three decades.

Jewish Others who were once perceived as threatening or opposing Zion-ist identity construction could now also be seen as part of a complex, more multicultural system. Israeli Jews acknowledged that certain aspects of their collective "self" contained elements of the Diaspora itself.[6] Even the kibbutz no longer seemed so different from the Jewish *shtetl* in Poland. In the early years, kibbutz members had perceived their settlements as a complete antithesis of such villages, which they viewed as old-fashioned and decadent.

The disintegration of monolithic construction did not happen at once or in a linear and systematic way. There were ups and downs. Certain parts of the monolithic identity construction survived while others were disintegrating. For example, the military retained its initial monolithic prestige into the late eighties and nineties, in spite of some cracks that dated back to the 1973 war (Kimmerling, 1993).

3. The present II: The neo-monolithic construction

The peace process with Egypt in 1977 and the Oslo Accord of 1993 brought new possibilities to the forefront of the Israeli-Jewish agenda. Each substantial step encouraged people to dispel notions of the external Other as the enemy. Now it seemed realistic to imagine previous enemies as partners in a future peaceful coexistence. Disintegration of the monolithic perception of the Jewish Other, already in progress, could now accompany disintegration of the monolithic construction around external Others.

Much of Israeli society perceived total disintegration of the monolithic construction as a threat to the identity of Israeli Jews, however. Who were they if not defined through those threatening Others? The process of disintegration provoked pain, confusion, and even existential fear. Even when the process was well under way, the illusion prevailed that it would be possible at some point to reestablish the monolithic construction anew. The outbreak of violence in October 2000, like the vicious 9/11 attacks in the United States the next year, established a neo-monolithic construction in Israel and among Jews and non-Jews in other countries. The old fear of the external Other who could not be trusted was awakened; apparently this Other was, after all, just waiting for the right moment to annihilate the Jews.

---

[6] In this context, Amnon Raz-Krakotzkin coined the phrase "negating the negation of the Diaspora" (1994).

What differentiates the neo-monolithic construction from a mere return to the original monolithic phase? During the neo-monolithic phase, the *internal* monolithic construction continues to disintegrate. This combination of disintegration and neo-monolithic construction leads to painful disorientation. The disharmonious bits and pieces of the collective try to gain ascendancy over one another. The impulse is to replace the old hegemony with new ones, not through a dialogue but through a power struggle. The individual is caught in a whirlwind as the dynamic of disintegration pulls in one direction while the neo-monolithic dynamic pulls away. Thus, this phase is characterized by confusion and despair. Lost in the various power struggles, people struggle to define themselves as part of the collective.

4. The future: A dialogue between disintegrated aspects of identity
Ongoing disintegration of the monolithic construction, coupled with the exposure of disintegrated parts of identity, is undeniably disorienting. In addition, the power struggle over hegemony increases the frustration. Nonetheless, these processes may slowly lead competing segments of the society to an awareness that what we have at present is a no-win situation. Awareness creates an opportunity for a deeper and more open dialogue. Instead of a well-bounded and defined Other and self, embodying absolute evil and good, a complex world picture develops that contains conflicting aspects of the identity (in both the collective self and the Other). Though these conflicting aspects are not easily reconciled – either in the present or when reflecting on their suppression in the past – a slowly ripening acknowledgment of their mutual existence may lead to the beginning of a dialogue to replace the endless power struggles.

As mentioned previously, this process is perceived as complex, weak, and even "soft" in comparison to the monolithic or neo-monolithic representations because it tries to encompass internal contradictions and contrasts. The dialogue among the parts is also energy consuming. It is a process that may be seen as unstructured and even chaotic, and the outcomes are neither predictable nor guaranteed. Therefore, there will always be a tension between the option of developing dialogue, with all its complexity, and a kind of atrophy or atavistic desire to re-embrace a simpler and seemingly "tougher" worldview. The neo-monolithic phase therefore does not vanish by itself, even if the interpretation it offers of internal and external realities is inadequate.

METHODOLOGY

Qualitative research methods help demonstrate the four phases described here. As noted, qualitative social research focuses on narrative or biographical analysis reflecting processes within or between individuals in society that can be compared with broader social processes (Rosenthal, 1998). Our examples were developed in micro social settings, but we see them as illustrating current macro social processes.

This kind of presentation is admittedly problematic. First of all, may a personal case indeed represent a broader social process, or does it merely reflect limited phenomena? And can a personal case, even if representative of broad social processes, reflect the greater complexity that exists in society over and above single aspects as represented by certain individuals? I discuss the question of representation elsewhere (Bar-On, 1995, 2004/2006). I contend that the personal case, to the extent that it represents a face of an identified segment of the population, provides insight. A precise mirroring of the society by the individual cannot be expected. The test is whether the personal case raises important theoretical questions that should be addressed, even if they are not the only questions possible with regard to the entire social process.

This kind of research makes no claim that narratives lead to generalizations that can be compared in the manner we expect from statistical analysis. Yet, we do expect an understanding of the social process as it is perceived by the individual and through the analysis of the individual biographical story and narrative.

The research presented here is exploratory in nature and opens a window onto processes that Israeli society has undergone in recent years. The examples emphasize situations of social crisis with personal significance to our interviewees. They are "normal" interviewees and not individuals who have been defined as pathological. We will attempt to understand these situations through an analysis of interviewees' narratives about how they coped. Their words represent the "private language" of people; even they are occasionally fragile and fragmented. (I discuss the fragility of laypeople's language in my 1995 book *Fear and Hope*.)

In this kind of research, the researcher – as interviewer or analyst – is part of the phenomena he or she tries to study. Thus, personal "windows" appear in the different chapters of the book. They represent some of my own transformations from monolithic identity construction, through disintegration of this identity, and on to a beginning of a dialogue among the bits and pieces that no longer fit together.

Interviews conducted with Holocaust survivors and their children and grandchildren at the beginning of the 1990s provide examples of several of the phases (Bar-On, 1995). The monolithic construction of identity in a survivor and his grandson are presented in the first chapter. In the second chapter, an interview with Alon, the son of a Holocaust survivor, illustrates the process of the monolithic construction's disintegrating. Others who demonstrate the disintegration of monolithic Israeli-Jewish identity construction include a man who suffered shell shock in the 1948 war and a soldier who served during the first *Intifada* (1987–92). Also relevant is an analysis of interviews conducted in Germany between 1985 and 1988 with the children of Holocaust perpetrators.

Examples from my work at PRIME (Peace Research Institute in the Middle East) during the second *Intifada* and another interview with a soldier from the first *Intifada* were chosen to illustrate the neo-monolithic stage. Analysis of a confrontation between two students, an Israeli Jew and an Israeli Palestinian who met at a workshop at Ben-Gurion University of the Negev, demonstrates the possibilities of a beginning of a dialogue between components of identity. A postscript suggests how some of the concepts developed in this book in the Israeli-Palestinian context could be applied also to other societies that struggle with similar issues. It also shows how a group process was initiated on the micro level to develop a dialogue between parties in conflict around their identity reconstruction.

ONE The Past: Monolithic Identity Construction[1]

In the beginning God created the heaven and the earth.
And the earth was without form, and void;
and darkness was upon the face of the deep.
And the Spirit of God moved upon the face of the waters.
And God saw the light, that it was good:
And God called the light Day, and the darkness he called Night.
And the evening and the morning were the first day. (Genesis 1:1–5)

The beginnings of collective identity formation, defining the collective self in opposition to the Other, can be characterized in "day and night" terms. This is especially true if the self has to separate from earlier identities that were rooted in the collective for hundreds of years. Such a process was intrinsic to Zionist identity formation, as it defined itself apart from earlier Jewish identities, whether religious, territorial, or social ones. Each of these identities had their own relevant Others. The perceptions of the Others developed and changed (as did the Others themselves) with the shifts that took place both within the Jewish collective and in its environment.

Part of my work is investigating what we do with the Others within us – in the Lévinas tradition: that the otherness of Others is infinite, while we are a closed totality and therefore never can represent in ourselves the full spectrum of that infinity. I learned through my studies that we developed different strategies of dealing with the Others within us: In the case of past Jewish Others, we mostly tried to distance ourselves from them, believing that this provides a larger space, within ourselves, as Israeli Jews. In the

[1]This chapter was written together with Dr. Ifat Maoz.

14

case of Nazism, we demonized them and excluded them from humanity. In the case of the Palestinians, we looked mostly through them, as if they did not exist. Such strategies may be helpful, as long as they correspond to some aspect of reality, but at some point, using them only creates an illusion of a bigger space for us in our social environment. Usually, the next step is that we try to recognize some of these Others, at the price of firmly excluding the rest. This is shortsighted – recognition does not function that way, psychologically speaking. As long exclusion is at work, dialogue cannot work into the deeper levels of self.

It was with the establishment of the Zionist movement in Europe that the Zionist self (and, later on, the Israeli self) was defined in opposition to previous Jewish Others, by setting itself apart from them. The process of identity construction was characterized first by the revival of Hebrew as a spoken language. For two thousand years of Diaspora, following the destruction of the Second Temple, Jews spoke the language of their host countries. Hebrew had been preserved mainly in written form, in sacred texts. Now the languages of Diaspora were rejected as Other. New collective expressions in Hebrew created a clear distinction between "light" and "darkness." For example, one "ascends" to Israel ("makes *aliyah*"), rather than merely immigrating. Conversely, someone who leaves Israel to live in the Diaspora "descends." Likewise, language was co-opted to denigrate the "Diaspora Jew." By resettling the Promised Land and defending himself[2] there, this figure could be transformed into the Israeli-Jewish hero, upright and physically strong. Nourished by the fruits of his labors, he would make the land fertile again, reviving the ancient Hebrew culture that had deteriorated with the destruction of the Temple and the dispersion of the nation of Israel.

Max Nordau, a Zionist physician, wrote around the turn of the century: "We shall therefore renew the connection with our ancient tradition: We will again be broad-chested, vigorous and fearless men" (Nordau, 1960: 187). These expressions reveal almost a frightening similarity to Nazi rhetoric.

---

[2] There is a clear masculine component to this rebirth, elaborated on by Michael Gluzman (1998) and Daniel Boyarin (1997). As opposed to the new masculine Israeli, the European from the Diaspora and, later on, the Eastern Jew, were presented as weak, primitive, and "feminine." Witztum prefers the expression "heroic" to that of "monolithic" to describe this stage in the development of Israeli identity.

But they are also an expression of the rebirth of the ancient as new and good, countering Jewish internalization of anti-Semitic expressions in the Diaspora. Liberal and secular Central European Zionist circles were able to use this revival of ancient biblical heroic images to oppose the deployment of anti-Semitic images that had prevailed in Christian Europe of the Middle Ages. We are more familiar with relatively later denigration of the Jewish Diaspora, such as David Ben-Gurion's referring to Jewish immigrants from Arab countries as "human dust" and Yitzhak Tabenkin, who said, "they are non-existent" (Kimmerling, 1993. But the first Zionist ideologists – Nordau and Herzl, for example – expressed such sentiments much earlier. A truly violent fantasy aimed at the Diaspora Jewish Other appears in an 1887 article in which Herzl referred to Friedrich von Schiller's play, *Wilhelm Tell*:

> When Wilhelm Tell prepares to shoot the apple on his son's head, he has a second arrow ready. Should the first arrow miss its target, the second arrow will take revenge. Friends, the second Zionist arrow is intended for Moishel's chest. (Herzl, 1928: 155)

Moishel is a derogatory name for a Jew stigmatized as a notorious moneylender in Europe.[3] The Arabs almost never appeared at all in these early writings, and when they did (as in Herzl's *Altneuland*), they were romanticized, as in other colonial descriptions of "natives" (Comaroff, 1993). The actual Arab population of Palestine was basically "looked through" rather than recognized.

Though the first Other from which Israeli identity actively tried to disassociate was the Diaspora European Jewish Other, this took great effort. Strong ties still drew most Jews toward a Diaspora center of gravity. In those early days, language, culture – every sense of mimesis – social, economic, and political characteristics all exerted a pull. Creating the momentum to overcome these gravitational forces required a clear definition of the Diaspora Jew as an Other and an unequivocal energy of the new as "good and different." For emigrants to say of those who remained behind, "*I hate the Diaspora Jew and I am very different,*" exacted a high psychological price.

---

[3] I am grateful to Michael Gluzman (1998) for directing my attention to this quotation. See also Shmuel Almog (1984).

This process of *severance* can be contrasted with the process of psychological *separation*, which is characterized by the ability to move back and forth between the new and the old until the choice of the new is made (Bar-On, Sadeh, & Triester, 1995).

In the course of managing this difficult process of severance, symbiotic relations developed between two focuses of power and legitimization. On one hand, the newly established Zionist had strong family ties with parents and siblings who remained behind. In addition, the Diaspora supplied the financial resources for building the settlements in Palestine. Throughout the early Zionist revival, there prevailed an economic and political dependence upon those who were regarded as the Other in the Diaspora. On the other hand, disassociation from that Other required negativity. Meanwhile, those in the Diaspora (although not accepting the Zionist definition as Other) had a paradoxical interest in and need for the continuation of the Zionist endeavor. Therefore, the distinction between the Diaspora Other and the Zionist self never fully succeeded in terms of psychological severance and absolute disconnection. The symbiotic dependencies were a subtext to the clear distinctions that formed in the Zionist discourse between the self and the Jewish Diaspora Other.

With the establishment of the State of Israel, close to a million people emigrated from Arab countries. Almost overnight, Zionists already living there found they needed to clarify the relationship with this new Jewish Other, whose different cultural background and historical proximity to the Arabs was perceived as threatening (Shenhav, 2003). By now, the Israeli self had gained political legitimization and the Jewish hegemonic Zionist had a new image: the native-born *sabra* (Almog, 1997; Kimmerling, 2001). It was impossible to define the Jews from the Arab countries as "Diaspora" Jews in the previous Eurocentric sense. Arriving in the country en masse, with almost no ideological Zionist period of acculturation, they came out of necessity and out of traditional, almost messianic belief in the fulfillment of the promise of return to their religious homeland. The distinction between the Zionist self and the Diaspora Other that attracted the European Jewish pioneers was foreign to them.

The timing of this influx shortly after the Holocaust was the most extreme expression of an attempt by the gentile Other to annihilate the Jewish self. Nazis were represented as monsters, externalizing them from humanity. As the perception grew of hostile Arabs trying to annihilate Israel, they were absorbed into this role of an external demonized Other. (The quiescent Arab population in Israel found its existence largely ignored.) The new Jewish Other seemed to emerge from within that Other, the "absolute evil" (Shenhav, 2003), with which Israel was at war, struggling for its existence. And for many hegemonic European Israeli Jews, the traumatic end of the Holocaust entailed learning of the loss of most family members, while the families that suddenly arrived from the Arab world were mostly large and intact. That must have created envy among the European Jews, who lost large parts of their families during the Holocaust.

The "Oriental" Jews, then, were perceived as different in more than one respect from those who had created the original Zionist-Israeli self. These differences were found in a sense of extended family, ethnic community, religion as tradition, and certain closeness to the Muslim society and culture. It was no accident that the absorption of this collective was and still is very problematic (Dahan Kalev, 1997). Just finding a label for them was a problem. Identifying the immigrants as Oriental when, in fact, Morocco is more Western than Poland, illustrates Edward Said's important critique of the orientalism that characterized the Eurocentric approach (1979). To label the arrivals as a Sephardic ethnic community (as opposed to the Ashkenazi norm) did not solve the problem either. For what about the Sephardic Jews who were living in Palestine before the first waves of the Zionist emigration or those who arrived from Greece and Bulgaria rather than from Arabic-speaking countries? (And what about the German emigrants who were not part of the hegemonic Eastern European Ashkenazi culture?) A new Jewish Other had to be constructed, the "ethnic" Jew who had to assimilate totally. Dahan Kalev asserts that all definitions painted this new, Jewish ethnic Other as inferior to the European Diaspora Other, while maintaining the clear distinction between it and the new hegemonic Israeli self. She stresses that the new Others were never asked what it thought or felt about the way the hegemony defined them. In contrast to the "Diaspora" Ashkenazi, with whom symbiotic relations developed, the ethnic Other was supposed to vanish altogether. Zionist rhetoric claimed that there was no reason for the continuation of Jewish communities in Morocco, Yemen, or Iraq. Even though some of these communities in fact persisted, the emigrants were pressured to blend in with the hegemonic, Zionist self, thereby relinquishing their "inferior" identity. The Zionist self saw no need for a symbiotic relationship with the Arabic-speaking Diaspora as it had in the case of Diaspora Jews from America, South Africa, or Argentina.

The rise of Nazism, the Second World War, and the annihilation of European Jewry had more or less overturned the state of relations between the Jews in Israel and the Diaspora in Europe. The European Other's position as a center of gravity came to a sudden and violent end. Thus, a new center of gravity in Israel emerged, and with it, an external, unexpected justification for the Zionist story (Segev, 1992). It took rather a long time for the Zionist community in Israel to absorb fully the horrifying meaning of this severance of their roots and their collective Other: the loss of family members, the destruction of mother-communities, and in fact, the destruction of most of the Jewish cultures under Nazi occupation. Only afterward did a process of "forced severance" begin, overtaking the voluntary severance that had occurred earlier (Bar-On, Sadeh, & Triester, 1995).

Over the years, depiction of the Holocaust changed and became a meeting point for the two representations of the Jewish Other in Israeli identity. In the first years following the establishment of the State of Israel, the Holocaust was perceived in terms of the Jewish Other – the Diaspora Jews who failed to fight for their lives. The Israeli Jew regarded only the ghetto fighters and partisans in a positive light. Educated by the Zionist movements "there," these figures were embraced by the Israeli self. Particularly jarring was the accusation by Israeli Jews that the survivors *"went like lambs to the slaughter!"* A demeaning program by this name was even promulgated during the fifties by the Ministry of Education. This blame, combined with the guilt and anguish of the survivors themselves, gave rise to a process of silence and silencing that profoundly affected many of their families. Some of the emotional burden was wordlessly passed on to the second generation, and it has taken many years to decipher the social and psychological reasons for the silence (Bar-On, 1995). After the Eichmann trial[4] – and perhaps more

[4] Israel's secret services forcibly brought Eichmann from Argentina in 1960 and he was put on trial in Jerusalem. Charged as one of the architects of the Nazi extermination process, he was sentenced to death and executed in 1961.

so after the 1973 Yom Kippur War (when there were soldiers who were unable to fight but were regarded as heroes for surviving) – new insight brought a retrospective understanding of the challenge of simply surviving during the Holocaust, even without the combat or sacrifice characterizing the primary Israeli wars (Segev, 1992). Appreciation of this challenge was already part of the disintegration of the monolithic construction that we will discuss in Chapter 2.

This change perhaps stemmed from the maturing political awareness of second-generation survivors as well. With political upheaval in 1977 (the Labour Party, in power since the establishment of the state, lost the elections to Menahem Begin and the Likud party) and the rising political power of the ethnic Other, there came a change in the definition of the Holocaust Other. The perception of Other now focused on the external threat of destruction and the attitude of the outside world. Prime Minister Begin used "siege mentality" rhetoric (Bar-Tal & Antebi, 1992) when, in Beirut in 1982, he compared Arafat to Hitler. We cannot trust others with regard to our security, he maintained, "as then, too, the world stood by." With this, in the context of the Holocaust, the circle of the monolithic Other was completed, a circle that had opened with the silencing and delegitimization of the voice of survivors during the forties and fifties. Its completion was in the turning of the Holocaust into a political tool in order to justify Israeli political stands and actions toward the Middle Eastern – particularly Arab and Palestinian – Other (Segev, 1992).

To characterize the monolithic construction of the Diaspora Jewish Other as opposed to the Zionist self, I have chosen to present the voice of a Holocaust survivor and partisan fighter, Ze'ev (a pseudonym), and that of his grandson, Yoav. As a partisan, Ze'ev was less affected than most other survivors by the delegitimizing process of the fifties, for his wartime actions were perceived as consonant with the hegemonic Israeli-Jewish self. Not only did he combat the Nazis, but he also took revenge in his village immediately after the war. Even if he did not tell his children or grandchildren about this, they undoubtedly sensed that he represented the "positive" face of the Holocaust in Israeli society: physical struggle against the Nazi aggressor. Thus, we see in both the grandfather's stories and those of the grandson a positive concept of self. Yoav's narrative expresses much pride, in his grandfather and in anticipation of his own future, joining the army and the fighting Israeli self. In between, we find Hannah, Ze'ev's daughter and Yoav's mother, who silenced her own life story. Painfully, she feels less part of the Israeli "self" as a woman between these two strong male figures.

PERSONAL WINDOW 1

All writing of this nature includes a personal element. It is easy to describe the monolithic phase in each of our identities. Who among us did not believe as a child in a world with sharply drawn boundaries between good and evil? It is harder to describe the disintegration of this innocent phase. Perhaps for me this is because it took place relatively late in life and I experienced it as the disintegration of my personality; a sense that what had been was no longer there and that I had nothing real or continuous to hang onto or that I could confidently call "myself" or, speaking communally, "us." I particularly remember one such period in 1989, after I had completed my research in Germany, where I interviewed the descendants of Holocaust perpetrators. Invited by a colleague from Osnabrück University to stay in his hometown in northern Germany, I spent about three weeks there. I had long-postponed writing assignments to do and looked forward to this quiet time. But I found the atmosphere of Osnabrück depressing: clean, small, and conservative, it was a prosperous German town, but one that concealed and denied its past. And so, within a few days, my writing came to a stop and I found myself spending many hours in bed, in the hotel, wondering what I was doing there. Professionals might have given this various names, from a psychotic breakdown to emotional stress. Under different circumstances, I would probably have tried to escape this situation as fast as possible. But there, within the fiercest alienation as far as I was concerned, I allowed myself to flow with the sensations for a while. What I experienced for some days was a strong sense that who I understood myself to be was disintegrating. As a Jew, an Israeli, a father, and husband, and as other identities I had hitherto "owned," my self was under internal assault. There were of course external explanations for this process. The interviews with the offspring of Nazis were in themselves an attack on my Jewish-Israeli self. In addition, I was affected by tragedies within and outside of the family as well as by previous events I thought I had already processed. I apparently needed a place that was distant and cut off, as well as sufficient time, in order to work out how these events affected me. At present, it suits me to describe this as a disintegration of my "monolithic self" that touched profound components of my "personality."[5]

Essentially, I needed the ability to recognize that, for a long time, I had made attempts to patch over or conceal from myself the incompatibility between the way I thought about myself and described myself to others (positively, of course) and what I actually found. There was another element beyond this incompatibility between self-image and new discovery: aspects of personality that seemed to be in conflict with each other. I have no need to describe this process in heroic terms. It was difficult and unpleasant, and those days in the hotel were rather awful. I was glad when they were over and I could return to my family and ongoing work. But in retrospect I believe this to have been an important time in my inner examination of "where have I come from and where am I going?"

ZE'EV: "WE GREW UP NICE, STRAIGHT, AND HEALTHY"[6]

Ze'ev was born in a village in Byelorussia in 1922, to a large, traditional family that was almost obliterated in the Holocaust. He lost nearly everyone and everything that had been dear to him before the war. He survived as a result of his resourcefulness. Ze'ev's story during the war differs from many other stories of Holocaust survivors. Rather than being a camp survivor, Ze'ev represents resistance fighters. He escaped and joined the partisans, fighting with them until they were liberated by the Russians.

Camp survivors had to confront the memories of hunger, sickness, and helplessness in such places as Majdanek and Auschwitz. Are Ze'ev's memories more positive because he enjoyed relative freedom of action? What part of his life history dictates or colors the construction of his life story? Is it the loss (similar to other survivors) or the war experience (largely different)? Which of these similarities or differences has been passed on to the following generations? And in terms of these similarities and differences, are there

---

[5] I write "personality" with quotation marks as today I suspect that it is a comfortable illusion for us to describe an inner structure that allows us to think of ourselves as integrative, coherent, and continuous but may in fact not exist.

[6] This interview was analyzed together with Bosmat Dvir-Malka. All names are pseudonyms (Bar-On, 1995).

perhaps aspects of his life story that go without self-reflection? In search of answers to these questions, we turn to our interviews with Ze'ev, Hannah, and Yoav.

Ze'ev

"What do I remember of my childhood? I was born in 1922. Are you taping already? [He laughs.] I was born in a small place in Byelorussia. It's near Minsk, midway on the road that leads to Russia. Yes. And I grew up there in a family of six children, father, mother, grandfather and grandmother, cousins, and a big family in a big house. In the middle of it was – how can I explain it? – it was like a hall. But this hall was bigger, let's say, than this entire house [Ze'ev gestures with his hands]. We lived on one side – father, mother, and the children – and on the other side my grandmother – my father's mother – and her sister lived with their big family.

"It's a small place; let's say about 150 to 200 Jewish families. I'm not talking about the gentiles, just about the Jews. I finished elementary school. I would go to the rabbi, the learned man, you know, in a type of *cheder* [religious school]. We learned the *chumash* [Pentateuch], a little Hebrew, and a little Yiddish. Yes, my house wasn't Orthodox; it bordered on being traditional. Shabbat [Sabbath] is Shabbat; on Friday you go to the synagogue. There was a synagogue and occasionally we went to services during the week. We had kosher dishes, you know, some for milk, some for meat. How can I put it? We weren't very rich, but we weren't poor. There was bread, potatoes; there was enough to eat, the basics, as I said. The rest – there were no luxuries. And we grew up. It was a small house: This child" [points at himself] "grew up on a sofa with very wide wooden boards without a foam rubber mattress and without all the extras. And we all grew up, each one of us, nice, straight, and healthy.

"And the war came. The war came and then this small house was pulled apart, the house that I loved – it was not luxurious, but it was loved so much. That is, everything that was dear to me. Everything was made from scratch, with love. In my mother's house, we used to make bread. Every Sunday morning we made bread. And what I remember is that each loaf of bread was like half a table. Six loaves of bread for six days and each Sunday we would make more bread for another week. And that's how it was until . . . the Russians came. The Russians came on the eve of Rosh Hashanah, 1939. Can that be? When did the war start? The Russians came and . . . with that my studies came to an end. There were those who tried to continue, but it was very hard. It wasn't an organized, regular life."

"Everything was handmade, with love" – the warm memory of his childhood home. Ze'ev is well prepared to tell this story. He builds it slowly and gradually. Yet I am tense. His intonation reminds me of my own family from the same generation.

"And we began to work at home, helping the family. And I did all kinds of jobs, whatever there was. This child worked and he didn't get tired of it. The main thing was that the home have what it needed. Ever since my childhood, I've – how do you say it, what's it called in simple Hebrew? I've had it in my head – I need to do things, to hold things together, do maintenance work. And I did everything. I would go to a factory in the town where they cut timber. And they needed to make apple crates. There was a forest where they cut wood in the winter to get it ready for cooking in the summer. Whatever was lacking, we made. The main thing was to have enough to live on. And the Russians came from '39 till '41. And, in '41 the Germans arrived. The Germans, aahh . . . [as if shouting and sighing simultaneously], they came and started killing Jews, each time some more. And later on, entire families, until they killed all the . . . they killed the whole town. Not one Jew was left. Whoever ran away, ran away. Whoever didn't escape was killed. In a mass grave: The grave is still there, a mass grave, in the town. If you were to take me there today, I would be able to find the exact place. It's something you can't forget, not till you die [there is a fierce look in his eyes]. I ran away from there and wandered around all kinds of places, hungry, troubled, no shoes. You know, separated from your home; mother and three sisters murdered, father and three sons still alive. After the war was over, my father and eldest brother died. My younger brother and I remained alive. I live in Israel and my younger brother lives in Montreal, Canada. That's the family background. That's chapter one."

"That's chapter one." I shudder: How is it possible to summarize what was left of an entire family in three words?!

"The second chapter: I wandered about until I got to the Vilna ghetto. In the Vilna ghetto, I worked in all kinds of places. God knows how I got out of there alive. There's a place called Ponar, it's well known; they dug ditches everywhere. Each ditch was, let's say, fifteen meters by fifteen meters, in order to kill Jews. And they would bring Jews there. That's where I worked. I worked on the railroad tracks in the winter. In short, I worked there for a few months, and one day I left the Vilna Ghetto and never went back.

"I got to the forest and joined the partisans – gentiles – and was a partisan until [the end] of the war."

"That's where I worked." The Nazis made it possible to term clearing the tracks for the murder of one's people "work."

"The war ended, there were episodes, you'd need a book. No, you'd need to sit with me day and night. It's not a short story, I'm just telling you everything briefly. The war ended. I met a girl whose family I had known in the forest. How did I meet the family in the forest? On a mission with the *goyim* [gentile partisans], I saw a fire in the distance, far into the forest. I went toward it and saw maybe eight or ten people sitting there, women and small children among them. One of the girls lives in Rishon LeZion today. What can I tell you; I saw they were making soup – soup as black as car oil. Why? There was a hole in the bucket and it was stuffed up with a rag and so when it was on the fire the fire would burn the rag, and the water would run out and so they would add more water. I went there, saw them; it was a very frightening picture. I couldn't help them in the forest, but I made them a promise. I said, 'I am going out on a mission. I'll be gone two or three weeks. It depends on how successful we are getting there. But I promise I will come back and I will bring you a bucket.' And getting a bucket then was like getting a house today. Understand, with that bucket you washed, made soup, and . . . and it's a family.

"Yes, I did what I promised, and the *goyim* laughed at me. 'What a Jew. Why are you dragging that bucket along?' Go tell them I had made a promise. I asked my commander if we could return the way we had come. And I gave them the bucket. So, one of them – she died later on in Israel – she said to me: 'We have cousins, pretty girls. If we stay alive, come to us and I will introduce you to a girl, my cousin.' And as fate would have it, after the war, the army took me to Minsk, and there I heard it was possible to get to Israel through Poland. On the way, I said I would go to their town. Perhaps I would find [them].

"I went there and I found all those who had returned to the town. So she told me, 'Come on, I'll introduce you to my cousin.' And I went into the house where I found a girl and three sisters. The youngest one was ten; my wife was the fourth, the eldest. I met her and I married her. So I took a wife, and her three sisters were ready to come at once [laughs]. Yes, and not long after, we went to Germany and from Germany to Israel. And three sisters live here; they are all married, live near each other, in the northern part of the country."

I am completely immersed in the story. "With the bucket . . . and it's a family." When Ze'ev talks, I find myself reading a new Bible, where only the benign stories are told, the rest described only briefly.

"I raised a family. I have two daughters, two successful daughters, and I have no complaints about them. And I have a grandson and four grand-daughters. One daughter has a son and two girls and the other has two girls. My grandson went into the army two weeks ago. He went into an elite unit [said proudly]. He is very talented and yesterday was his first day in uniform. When he came to see me, there was great happiness. We made a meal and he went back today.

"I came to Israel. Came with money and lost it all here, to the last dime. It didn't work out, not that I didn't want it to; I wasn't lazy. I decided to go to America; my wife has a big family in Texas, a very rich family. And they sent us papers to go there. In the end, I changed my mind; I said, 'I came here, this is where I want to be.' And just as things were going downhill, the wheel turned. And I had all kinds of jobs, whatever came along. I brought a big welding shop from Germany. We were four partners. And I worked in steel construction. I did it all and, in the end, I threw it all away and bought a laundry. Forty girls worked there, in the bay, near Kfar Ata. I was successful there, and that's the way I live. Now we live here in Romema. This is our third apartment.

"How can I say it – it's not luxury, but it's good to say: 'It's good to be alive.' How do you say it? 'Happy with what you've got.' If you can say the shirt you're wearing is the best there is, then you've done well. I have a good wife, I have good daughters. They both finished university. I enjoyed raising them. A great family and that's how we live. That is, I've no complaints against anyone. And, how to say it . . . I didn't like Israel when I got here. When I arrived, I didn't like Israel. I didn't adjust; for me everything was different. Now everything has turned around. When I'm driving down the street for instance, and I see someone hurting a tree, I'll stop and say, 'Sir, why are you doing that? Why are you breaking it?' I mean, over the years everything has turned around. That's all. I don't get involved in politics. And it makes no difference who's in charge or who isn't. There are problems; it hurts that things aren't done properly. There is a lot of corruption, thievery, and things happen. But I've seen that that's how it is, nothing you can do about it. Whoever is strong is in control. That's how it is, nothing to be done. What else do you want to know?"

"Whoever is strong is in control." Ze'ev has a life philosophy that was formed during the war. It doesn't seem to mesh with caring about a tree being damaged. I try to bring him back to his childhood.

"What happened at home? To begin with, we had a piece of land and apart from that we lived [far away] from any big place: a hundred kilometers from Vilna. It's not like today: you get in your car and get to Tel Aviv very quickly. An hour there and an hour back. It wasn't like that then. Then, there was a horse and cart, and getting to Vilna to fetch merchandise for the stores would take a week. And there we had fall and winter. A difficult winter, forty degrees below zero, and the bathroom was outside. And all kinds of tasks – it was a hard life, you might say; not like today. The roads here are wonderful [in comparison] with what we had there.

"Anyway, a lot of young people from Jewish families came to Israel. They are here today; today they are old. When they went to Israel, I was a boy of six. So today they are already eighty. You have to understand, they live in Nahalal, in Haifa, all over. But they all know me and I know all of them. I was at home, knew it, I was very mischievous. Never still. If a gentile boy hit me, I didn't let it go by, I needed to hit him back, let him know that, with me, he couldn't get away with it. And that's how I got to the partisans. And I went back to my birthplace and I burned the place" [his voice is tense]. "And I settled the account with the *goyim* who killed the Jews. I settled the account properly. That is, I have had experiences that I don't want . . . no, I'm not sorry for what I did to them, it was justice!"

Ze'ev's expression hardens when he remembers his revenge. The pain shows in the way he holds his mouth, though his description is brief.

"And that's that. Now my cousin wants to go back to our hometown. He's from Bat Yam and he was back there. He made a movie. He took a video camera and made a movie so you can turn on the television and see a movie. I promise to give it to you when it's ready, I'll give it to you so you can see it. He went back to the town where we were born. He told us that the only thing left is the well in the middle of the village, the well where we got our water. From that well . . . [he chokes]. I have another cousin, his brother. I met them in the forest when they were little children. It was exactly when the Germans arrived. Not one German; they brought thousands of soldiers from the front, and they searched the forest to catch Jews. And the boys had to move from one place to another, and I met them. I was already with the partisans and I saw that child. They couldn't walk another kilometer. I walked with them all day, let's say, like from here to Tivon. They walked a hundred meters and sat down. They had no strength [Ze'ev is very agitated].

"I put that boy in a sack on my back. I told the child, 'Stop crying! If you cry, I'll put you down. I'll leave you here.' Then he stopped crying. He was four or five. He had the sense to stop crying. I brought him to another place. No, no, I didn't leave him. My uncle and aunt had already died, but all the children were alive. The one who lives here in Israel is the one I carried on my back. The rest are in America. That is, the family remained a family. What can I tell you! To this day, when I want to visit him, I don't have to phone, there's no need. I go and see him. There are no barriers between us. That is, the family is very close and we stayed that way – what can I tell you?

"There are no barriers between us." The family here knows no barriers – does this compensate for what has been lost? The richness of what Ze'ev has said makes it difficult to identify what he does not feel inclined to tell. In remembering the town well or the boy he carried on his back, he finds it difficult to express the feelings accompanying these places and moments.

"For example, I am very close to my brother who lives in Canada. He can pick up the phone, talk to me for an hour, an entire hour. In the forest he would go and look for bread. He stayed alive in the forest. At night, he would go to the gentiles and ask for bread to bring to his family, to his aunt who saved him. During the war he was little. He is nine years younger than I am. He went to Canada, got married, and he's doing well. He's doing better than I am, but I don't envy him [laughs]. He was here in the summer. He didn't say he was coming, he just showed up with his wife. He was here for a week and then he went back. He came to talk to the family [looks at me and smiles].

"What else do you remember from the beginning of the war?" I ask.

"The Russians arrived and the place stayed the same. The worst was when the Germans arrived. The Germans arrived, and then the gentiles, the neighbors; they were worse than the Germans. They had always hated the Jews having anything, but they kept quiet about it. It was quiet as long as the Russians were around, but when the Nazis gave them the freedom to act the Jews were sacrificed."

"What do you remember from when the Germans arrived? What did you know?"

"We didn't know what they would do. But, I don't want to go into great detail. We wrote a book, I wrote part of it. I don't want to talk about that a lot, but the moment that I got a rifle, whatever I could do, I did. I did, and my children know now that my cousin was there and he made a movie, so the villagers asked him if I was still alive . . . they remember me all right; I burned down all of their houses. No, not the Jews' houses . . . the Jews were no longer alive. I didn't want the *goyim* to use our houses. There were a few of us who remained alive and we did enough. Enough, enough."

"How did the Jewish partisans get along with the non-Jewish partisans?"

"There were no problems. Look, during the two years I was in the forest with the partisans, I was always in action. I was always leaving the camp. Once with ten people, once with eight. There, you needed to go out at night and to sleep during the day. I was in the bomb unit. I would walk along the railroad tracks at night and lay bombs. Later on, I was moved to the convoy. We got close to the town where I was born and I knew the places. I was in the convoy for a while, but I was always in action. I mean, I didn't have time to think. Time passed quickly. And it was a time . . . when nothing had any value. We were alive then . . . nobody knew what tomorrow would bring.

"And I can tell you, I lived in the forest with those partisans. I lived through it by drinking; I was always half drunk. No, not enough to make me lose my head. I mean, let's say that when I had to go and lay bombs on the railroad tracks, it wasn't because I was Jewish. There were six of us. Each time someone else would go. There was somebody who would carry the bombs and someone who would carry the explosives. The bombs wouldn't work without the explosives. Then, I couldn't go without something to drink. I had a tin bottle at my side, as if I had two grenades. That's the way I held it. I would drink some and things went well. When a person is alone and he knows that he has no family . . . I didn't know then that my father and my older brother were still alive. I escaped by myself to the Vilna ghetto. We didn't see each other. We met when the war ended."

"When did you find out what had happened to them?"

"When they came, when the Jews started coming in '45, they brought my little brother to me when they went to Poland. Then I sent my younger brother to Canada. My mother once said – we were sitting together at home – that she had sisters in Canada and when he got older we should send him to Canada. I remembered that. There was the Joint [Distribution Committee]. We wrote and they replied and he went there. He was eleven and they took him into their family as if he were their own son. And he grew up and studied and later on he married. They opened up a factory for children's clothes and did very well."

"How did you find out about your mother?"

"I already knew about that when I ran away. I knew my mother and sisters had been killed when the whole thing began. I escaped. They caught [them] and immediately brought them to some sort of movie theater, and they burned them alive. They brought them there and they killed the rest. They took my father and my older brother somewhere else, to work, and that child, my younger brother – my younger brother was taken out of the movie house by my aunt, who was a good seamstress; the aunt whose son I carried in the forest. Then the Germans took her out – they knew she could be useful, and they took the entire family. They knew she had six children. However, one of the six was missing; he had run away and was hiding somewhere. So, she grabbed my brother's hand and took him out of there, and that is how he stayed alive."

Ze'ev, perspiring profusely, moves uncomfortably in his chair. I imagine him running away while all of this was happening. Fear and anger still well up inside him.

"None of these things have been written down, they're all impossible to believe, impossible to evaluate. What can I tell you? There was a time when people took reparations from the Germans. I didn't. I refused to sign. What I went through . . . I paid my dues to them. I don't want their reparations. I don't want the good or the bad. I'll manage. As long as I'm young, I'll manage. It's good to have work, to have a country, and everything will be all right."

Ze'ev looks tired and I suggest we take a short break. He willingly agrees.

"I don't sleep very well now. The boy, Yoav, my grandson, went to the army. What can you do? – things aren't quiet and I don't sleep. He was here yesterday and he wasn't feeling very well. I told him to ask for a day off and stay home. Really, he had a fever. He said no, his group sticks together. 'If I don't go back, others will suffer.' He went back this morning."

"Did you tell him your story?"

"He knows, he knows. The children know, my daughter knows, the daughter passes it on to the grandchildren. They both speak Yiddish. They learned it at home. And they pass it on to their children. The children, the grandchildren, don't speak Yiddish anymore, but there are expressions. Let's say, *'Volfi, kum tzim tish.'* Do you know what that means? 'Grandpa, come to the table.' They learned it then, they learned something. And they know where I was born. I went to visit and I took both girls. It was fun with the girls. The whole trip took two weeks. We just talked about keeping the family together. They know everything."

"When did you start talking about the war? Did your children ask or did you start telling?"

"They are very thirsty to know everything. But the things, what I think about the Holocaust, I didn't tell them. I didn't want to. My children said the Germans came and killed the Jews. But the roots of the problem, the troubles the family went through, and what the Nazis did with little children – they [my daughters] don't need to know the details. I didn't want to tell them everything. And they are so pedantic, they write everything down. And my girls already managed by themselves to find out what they wanted to know. There was a different kind of discipline there [during my childhood] for children. I mean, children wouldn't go out and wouldn't take things without permission. I think that they are very talented. They are on the right path, the whole family [he looks at me proudly].

"When I began my immigration to Israel and I came here, it was '49. We came on the ship Negba and arrived in Haifa. We stayed in immigrants' houses, *Sha'ar Ha'aliyah* [the immigration gate, a transit camp]. We stayed there for a month and a half. The mayor gave us a piece of land and we bought barracks from Germany. We were four partners. We brought the barracks to the country and we set them up in the town. I didn't do so well with that, as I told you. And thank heavens, I never gave up, I looked for something else. Then I found the right thing and I went into the laundry [business]. The laundry served a hospital and from then on things went really well. I managed. My wife raised the two girls. Why? I'll tell you. When I left in the morning they were sleeping and when I returned in the evening they were sleeping. And it wasn't like that for one day, it was like that for a number of years. To say 'Enough, I won't do it anymore' – I didn't do that. I always went on.

"We are close to one another in this family, I have no complaints. Now I, I could pick up the phone and tell both girls, 'I want you to come over now.' They wouldn't ask why, they would both be here fifteen minutes later. During the Passover holidays we don't leave the house. There is food, there are festivities, and everybody sits together, that's all. If you let yourself be a part of it, it's festive [coughs]. Rachel's cousin is coming from Russia. We are waiting; he should be arriving soon, in November. She is already excited. We are looking for a house. He is coming with his family. We wrote them. They are from Minsk. First they need to learn Hebrew, right?

"Both my girls grew up with silver spoons in their mouths. I didn't have a car. It was my dream, but I paid five Israeli pounds an hour so my girls could learn English. They speak English, America is nothing. I gave them everything. There are families, you know, that leave home. Here, they didn't leave home. They got married and had children.

"I have a childhood friend who lives in Canada, and his grandson came. He is in Israel now and speaks Hebrew. I took him to where my grandson is doing his preparatory army course. There are tents there, in some remote place near Jerusalem. Yoav said, 'Let's go home, it's hot here.' I told him,

'This is hot! You will have to live in this heat for three years!' I taught him something [laughs].

"I taught him something." Ze'ev talks about Yoav as if he were his youngest son. I think to myself: He was a partisan, but he didn't have a son whose army experience could be a "redemptive" experience for himself.

"I have given you a small picture of our family – how can I explain it – we have no demands; for us, things are good the way they are. That is, one can only do so much. This is a hard country and the weather isn't good, the people come from all over the world and they're nervous. And it hurts me that our youth run away from here. The best run away from here. They have no foundations here. Once he finishes the army, can't he go and live with his parents? They all want to leave because buying a house here is very difficult. It's a lot of money and this [political] regime is no good. These children, they are our wealth. We need to keep them here. Do we lack land? The Jewish National Fund has as much land as you need. But they want money for it. What for? Is it theirs? Give it to these children. Give it to them! They've finished the army. If they go to school here, they won't run away. In Europe we would say, 'a bird in the hand is worth two in the bush.'

Ze'ev sounds more frightened than he did at the beginning of the interview. Is he afraid that Yoav will want to leave Israel when he finishes his army service? Is he afraid of being alone again? After all, he no longer controls what young people do with their lives. This is in contrast to the wonderful story of the child in the forest that led to the meeting with his wife, Rachel. With Ze'ev the difference between description and story is clear: The first is brief, replacing the emotion that is hard for him to feel or express. The second expresses the life truth with which he has come to terms. But there are unresolved questions with regard to this truth: Is solitude the lesson of heroism? Is togetherness strength (as in the idyllic childhood) or weakness because sometimes one must find the resolve to run away)? Ze'ev has undergone a difficult transition from a harsh, prolonged crisis situation to the building of a daily routine in a strange, foreign country; a country where heroism also has meaning, but where you have no real place because you are preoccupied with making a living, with raising daughters, with memories from the past.

MONOLITHIC CONSTRUCTION IN ZE'EV'S STORY

The Other's appearance in Ze'ev's story is circumspect but patent, from the *goy* who lived in the village, to the invasion by the Russians when he had to stop school (though the place remained intact and the Jews remained there), to the Germans who encouraged the murderous acts of local gentiles:

> They wiped out the whole town. Not one Jew was left. Whoever ran away, ran away, whoever didn't was killed. In a mass grave... If you took me there now, I would be able to find the exact place. These are things you can't forget, not till you die.

For Ze'ev, the gentile Other and the Nazi embody absolute evil:

> The Germans entered, and then the gentiles, neighbors; they were worse than the Germans. They had a lot, you know. The gentiles always hated the Jews having anything, but they kept quiet about it. It was quiet as long as the Russians were around, but when the Nazis gave them freedom to act, the Jews were sacrificed."

And after the war he decided to take revenge: "They remember me all right, I burned down all their houses." Later he add, "I settled the account completely. That is... I'm not sorry for what I did to them, it was justice!"

The partisan gentile was a more positive figure – on the side of the fighting self and an aggressor. Ze'ev drinks with the partisans before each mission and doesn't feel they exploit or ridicule him. On the other hand, they sneer at him when, after a mission, he drags a bucket along for a Jewish family in the forest, the family of his future wife. What a wonderful story unfolds in the midst of the valley of the shadow of death! As opposed to these Others, the family unit is presented in an ideal light – both at the time of the Holocaust and in present-day Israel. All along, Ze'ev emphasizes action as a part of family experience. An example is his description of baking bread: "Everything was made from scratch, with love." And, naturally, when external hardship came, action meant survival: "What we didn't have, we made, as long as we survived."

He and his wife almost emigrated from Israel, but "in the end... I said – I came here, I'm staying here." The Zionist self was foreign to him (it isn't clear whether he felt foreign among the Israelis who took him in), but a change took place in him, whether because of the growing children or his improved financial success, and now he feels that it belongs to him. He can make a difference, as in the symbolic description of his intervention to save the tree. Nonetheless, the encounter with Israel has not changed his worldview based on earlier experience that might is power:

> I have nothing to do with politics. And it makes no difference who's in charge or who isn't. There are problems; it hurts that things aren't done properly. There's a lot of corruption, thievery, and things happen. But I've seen that that's how it is, nothing you can do about it. The strong are in control.

Ze'ev has a simple, black-and-white worldview. The contrast to the evil of the Other builds the positive image of self. In this context, the family unit is "absolute good," the haven from the evil going on in the world – evil that reached extreme proportions during the Holocaust. When he is asked if he has told his children and grandchildren what happened to him during the war, we find ambiguity: On one hand, they know and ask, and on the other hand, there is also silence:

> What I think about the Holocaust, I haven't told them. I didn't want to. They said the Germans came and killed the Jews. But the root of the troubles they endured, and what they did with little children – they don't need to know so much. I didn't want to tell them everything.

He probably means details of his revenge and perhaps also the helplessness he felt in the face of the enemy and the hardships endured there. In the interview, it is also easier for Ze'ev to tell about situations in which he acted successfully, and he has a great deal to tell.

A SYNOPSIS OF THE INTERVIEW WITH ZE'EV'S DAUGHTER HANNAH

The interview with Ze'ev's daughter, Hannah, opened with her declaration that she had no life story to tell. Only after my colleague Bosmat insisted that she was sure Hannah had a life story of her own, and an interesting one, did Hannah begin to tell and to cry. Of course, she had a very special story to tell, of her struggle for independence from her parents; of the hardships of growing up in an immigrant family, looked down on by the Israeli kids around her. Only lately had she finally started creating a professional life of her own. Working with new Russian immigrant families, she draws on her experience as a child, and it seems that she is very successful in her new job.

In analyzing the interview, we assumed that Hannah felt that alongside her father's heroic stories, her own life story had no meaning. This assumption was confirmed. She tended to belittle her life story in comparison with that of her parents. Neither did she say very much about her role as mother. It could be that in this family women's stories were less important than men's. Did Hannah feel pushed aside as a woman in the heroic world of her men?

This world is supposedly egalitarian. The Zionist narrative stresses Israeli women's role as pioneers and their service in the army. But in an embattled society defining itself in opposition to perceived Diaspora passivity, the heroic ideal is a male monolithic construct with membership extended to women. Thus, we see Hannah feeling diminished because it does not fit her, and she is unaware that a different identity construction is possible. Women identify with the hegemonic Zionist ideal but they seldom embody it.[7]

We were very curious about the upcoming interview with Hannah's son Yoav, Ze'ev's grandson. Would we find a continuation of her self-denigration in her son or traces of Ze'ev's way of structuring the past in the mirror of the present, as a story of heroism and action? Would the monolithic Other appear in him too, or would we find in him a beginning of the disintegration of the Other and acknowledgment of its various components? These beginnings were evident in what his mother expressed, telling of the difficulties of her life in Israel rather than covering them up. Perhaps such an interview became possible only in the spirit of the 1990s, when such criticism became more legitimate.

[7] Authors who have shed light on the myths and realities concerning women in early Zionist society include Deborah Bernstein (1992), Dafna Izraeli et al. (1999), and more recently, Bat-Sheva Margalit-Stern (2006).

YOAV, ZE'EV'S GRANDSON: "LIFE ISN'T THE TIME YOU ARE ALIVE, BUT WHAT YOU DO WITH IT"

I meet the eighteen-year-old Yoav in his room. He is in between a shower and a friend's party. His room is a mess – typical of a boy his age – with giant posters and a model F-16 airplane that looks as if it is about to land on us at any moment. He is tall, with a full head of hair, warm eyes, and a mischievous look. "Can I offer you something to drink?" He echoes his mother's tone of voice, but he is also trying to create an easygoing atmosphere for the beginning of the interview.

Yoav fluently describes his life from an early age, including the transitions from one home to another. He does so engagingly and humorously, with side remarks about himself and his environment. I listen attentively and wonder to myself how many youngsters of eighteen could so accurately identify a seventh-grade crisis during a move, as Yoav does. He speaks of male and female friends. How did he see the crisis then and how does he see it today?

"Here there are more possibilities, because at a certain stage, in eighth and ninth grade, people feel suffocated in Upper Nazareth [where he lived formerly]. I went to high school in the tenth grade. In terms of studies – I continued playing handball with great intensity – it was simply a waste of three years. So I didn't do anything in school. Every now and then I would become motivated over some test because of my parents, but, on the whole, I didn't study for tests. I didn't go to classes that I didn't think were important, like Arabic, which I quit in the middle of the year. I would go and play handball."

"Were you pressured at home to study?"

"No; that is, my report card wasn't bad, because there were a lot of kids like me and the pace was very slow and there wasn't a problem making up missed work. So I didn't have a terrible report card and my parents didn't think that I was mixed up in a bad crowd or anything like that. They simply didn't bother me. Every now and then they threw out something and I related to what they said. They more or less directed me; they didn't allow me to really mess up in school. I was a pretty good student. Perhaps I could have gotten better grades, but it wasn't that important. In addition, I was on the All Stars handball team at one stage. It was one of the highlights for me. Now, it doesn't seem important any more, but then it interested me a lot, the fact that I was in the Hapoel All Stars. That is the name of the National Youth Handball All Stars Team. At one point I was taken out. There was supposed to be a trip abroad at the end of the year. And the All Stars coach didn't let me go. He had very different theories than my coach here. And I admired my coach here and I admired the other one less."

For the first time, Yoav seems to be searching for words.

"I liked it a lot. I thought it was an honor, and I wanted to be there, but I guess I wasn't good enough and I thought up all sorts of excuses. It heightened my motivation to play, to train. All in all, handball became the most important thing and I played it all day long. For me, it was a highlight because we got into the national play-offs and then . . . I think that was also a highlight in comparison to what you will find in this family. In short, these are the sort of things that I was busy with in my childhood, all connected with sport.

"Girls, I always had girlfriends, but never anything serious. Every now and then I had girlfriends and every now and then something short-term would develop with someone, but it was never really serious. Perhaps I didn't want to be obligated. I was once in love with a girl who was also in love with me. That was also one of my highlights, because I was in love with her for a long time. At some point, she asked me to go out with her. I got excited and made a lot of blunders on the date. To this day, that girl has a lot of very funny stories about that date. In the end, after two or three dates, she made it clear to me that it had no future." He gives me an embarrassed look.

"I've had a girlfriend now for a year and a half, and I love her very much and I think that she has given me relative peace. She affects my life. She's calmed me down a lot in terms of my hyperactivity. It's as if, when you are nervous or something like that, instead of going to play handball or getting irritated, you sit quietly and talk to someone. You know that if you get annoyed at her she'll get annoyed with you and that's not good. Somehow or other I learned to control myself. Perhaps it's also a matter of maturity, perhaps both. And . . . that's it."

Yoav returns to his fluent speech and the warm expression returns to his eyes.

"In terms of school, I made an important decision at the end of the tenth grade to go into the sciences. It is hard for me to remember why I decided to do that; I think it was because I thought it would be easy for me. They gave us psychometric tests and directed me to that program, the science program, based on the results. But I don't think it is an indication. If I had thought about it in advance, I'd have gotten higher grades. I would also have had an easier time if I'd studied biology. I thought I might have a head for mathematics. I'm still not sure about that today. I was with the kids in the science program and it's hard for me to compare myself with them because I didn't work as hard. But in the end my grades were pretty good. I went to the science program with great enthusiasm and slowly my enthusiasm dampened and disappeared.

"When the matriculation exams came – and it was clear that they would come – a lot of damage had already been done, and it was hard to correct it. In any case, it was hard to correct it in the twelfth grade. I really tried hard, I studied a lot harder – didn't know I was capable of it – I tried to make up for all the gaps left from the eleventh grade [sighs]. When I summarize my twelve years of studying – I think I got a lot from the school in Nazareth from an educational perspective. There were some important teachers there. They shaped my character in terms of the atmosphere they created and all kinds of values that they gave me. Later on, from the eighth to the tenth grade, actually through eleventh grade, I didn't do a thing. It was a waste of four years. The State of Israel spent money on me and it was wasted. I think that twelfth grade was one of maturing. First of all, I needed to see how I stood up to the pressure. How I managed with the schedule and all kinds of things like that. I think I improved. I'm sure that if I were to redo my matriculation exams now, I would get better grades, just from the lessons I have learned.

"In addition, in the middle of twelfth grade, the army began calling me for interviews. I think that it's an important thing in life. Should I tell you how things went? I was accepted into a certain unit and I really didn't know what I wanted to do. At a certain point, the idea came up that I would go into a pre-army academic program. But I rejected the idea because I knew I couldn't decide what I wanted to study. Perhaps, unconsciously, I didn't have the desire to work for good grades. I was in eleventh grade when I had to make the decision, in the middle of my bad grades. I wondered what sort of change I should make. Perhaps I decided not to go into the program out of laziness, perhaps due to lack of belief in myself.

"I don't know what I want to be today either. I passed up all kinds of invitations. The air force and the radio station passed me up. Later on, I got invited to the reconnaissance unit, to what is called an orientation course. During the orientation, they filter out people mostly on the basis of your physical ability to cope with pressure. They try to break you and see how you stand up to it. If you are in really good physical shape and you have some ability to withstand pain, you pass. So I passed the orientation. In retrospect, the orientation seemed easy. There were some pretty hard parts, but I never thought for one second that I would quit. I knew I would finish. It's like a handball game where you need to run a little and you suddenly know you won't stop running.

"Later on, they sort you into three reconnaissance groups. The first one is thought of as the best and the other two are made up of those who passed but who, for some reason or another, aren't suitable for the first. That is, some are accepted straight away. Most were dropped and didn't last out the day. Approximately half didn't last out the day and many got an invitation to the other two groups. The rest went to a psychologist. The psychologist was supposed to weed out those who were crazy or unsuitable. Now, I had an "anti" approach to the first group. They seemed like fanatics to me. It's nonsense, I just didn't try to find out anything and, like an idiot, I went and told the psychologist that I was against it. They gave me a questionnaire and told me to list what I thought my good and bad points were. I thought I was pretty disorganized. I don't know whether it's easy to know but I don't always think about things and I don't always manage with time. And organization as well, I mean organizing things...I don't know how to explain it to you, even drawing a picture. You see, there's no order in my head.

"I wrote all that and he understood it. Had I wanted to get into the first group, I could have written down other characteristics that would have helped me get in. I would have made up something, the way a lot of people do. He asked me about these things: 'What do you mean when you say you are disorganized?' I told him that I don't manage well with time. After all, I didn't want to lose out on everything; I wanted to get into the third group. I had heard a lot about this unit. I was also a bit unwilling to take responsibility. I thought that I was in good shape and that it wouldn't be hard for me there. So I told him that I would overcome these faults with willpower if he would send me to the specific unit I wanted to get into. So he took me out of the first; he didn't throw me out altogether. He gave me the other two as options. I was sure I would get what I wanted, I mentioned that unit with every third word. After a while, I was called to the orientation for the second unit. I was depressed for two days and then decided to try and see what it was like. And I went.

"At the beginning of the orientation, I felt great. I don't like giving up on challenges, I mean, I can't stop something [I've started] – even a game. For example, I can play tennis with someone who will tear me apart. And let's say I know that person will go and tell everyone that he did that. I can't stop and say that I don't feel well. I have to finish the game. So I said, I have to finish the orientation and see what it's like.

"At first I felt really good and I enjoyed everything. At a certain point they tried to tear us apart; I mean, push us to the limit of our physical endurance and see how we coped. On the first day, those who weren't in good shape dropped out and I felt good about it. Later on, I began to have a hard time. The hardest part was when I got dehydrated. It was a bit disappointing because I thought it was near the end. After the first two days, each time that I had a hard time, I looked back at what I had achieved up till then; I was in good shape, and I was going to finish the orientation. I thought that if I didn't fail in the middle, when about two-thirds quit, I would get through it.

"And then I got dehydrated. I had a few tears in my eyes and I said that it was a shame if all that effort was for nothing. They gave me intravenous hydration and I tried to get back in. It was hard for me to return and I think that they saw the tears. The leaders there were really something special! I have all kinds of reasons for joining that unit, but if I try to be honest with myself, one reason is they simply personified perfection. In reconnaissance as well, you couldn't see a meter in front of your face and the leaders ran. You run behind them. But the thing that amazed me the most was that they took such good care of us. On one hand, they pushed us to the limits of our ability and, on the other, you felt taken care of, you felt they were paying attention to you. At a certain point I didn't know I was dehydrated, because this had never happened to me before. You feel shitty, excuse the word. You don't know – whether you are just being self-indulgent or whether you really are sick – that something isn't right.

"They also looked for leadership, and the leader gave me some things to do. He gives someone responsibility for some activity and, at first, I was pretty good at it. Later, he gave me an activity and I didn't really hear what he said, and I didn't really see him when he was talking to me. He saw I wasn't . . . that I was confused. So he sat me down on the side. I didn't know what was happening with me at that moment. I don't really remember, I don't remember a lot of it. He sat me down in the shade for about twenty minutes. My pulse was 110; they got worried and took me to the clinic right away. I got an "infusion" and that's it.

"I tried to get back into it afterward. I didn't think about whether I was going to finish or not. I said I had to try and go on. I still didn't feel well, and I didn't know what to tell them because I didn't know that's the way you feel after you've been dehydrated. They asked me if I wanted to continue and I yelled yes, but I really wanted to yell no. At a certain point I demanded to see a doctor because I felt that if I took three more steps I would die. I'm not saying that in order to make an impression; I'd just never felt like that before.

"Let's say I'd fall in handball and get hurt; here it wasn't pain, it was a kind of . . . I had no strength, no mental strength either: I simply couldn't think, I felt nothing. I felt that something wasn't right, something was going on. I guess I had a high fever, so they brought me back and in the end they admired me because I passed.

"I got a bit carried away in the description of the orientation, because it was terrible, terrible. There was a lot more, I cut out a few bits. They also asked us not to talk about it. I got a bit carried away anyway.

"I got a bit carried away," Yoav apologizes again. Then he looks at me proudly.

"I see everything differently now. I mean, the orientation was a turning point. After I got back, I felt really good about myself. It's impossible to describe, simply a kind of exaltation. It wasn't arrogance; I didn't feel I was any better than they were. But I felt as if I didn't care about the others: I didn't care what they said. A lot of things seemed so unimportant. Maybe I'm exaggerating, maybe the orientation wasn't so hard. But it seemed to me to be an effort and I was capable of it. You can ask my parents about me at that time. For example, I'd get up in the morning; I wouldn't go back to sleep. I'd wash the car, work in the garden, things like that.

"On one hand, I want to enlist now, and not because I like it. It's just worthwhile getting started, because I can't really enjoy anything else. I was on holiday at Achziv beach on the Mediterranean. It was a feeling of complete vacation, of independence. But it wasn't quite right. It's as if there is something that is coloring all my pleasures and disappointments. Because I know it's all nothing in comparison to what I'll be going through, the difficulty as well as what I'll gain from military service.

"The course is very difficult, but I'm going because I know I'll get a lot out of it; they invest a lot in each soldier there. And I'll have a chance to work on my character in a way that other people won't have. I'll acquire all kinds of military traits and skills. These are things that other people won't know how to do, that I simply wouldn't have a chance to do if I were to go and be a lawyer or something like that. Parachuting and things like that.

"What do you live for, after all? I look at life differently from other people, and not only in relation to the army. In general, I don't think that I make a big deal out of life. I mean, I don't want to die or anything like that; I love life a lot. But I don't think that life is the time you are alive, but rather what you do with it. Because you can live for thirty years and be a nobody. It's not that I'm belittling it, but every person has his own emotional experiences, his ups and downs. You can even be a respected lawyer who has this case or that case. It's a kind of perspective.

"To go back, I wanted to say: It makes me tense, I'm afraid of the difficulty. I'm not all that energetic; I mean, I was better than average in sports due to natural ability. During a game or training session when things were hard for me, there were always people who broke before I did, and we had to stop the practice because of them. It was also hard for me, but I never exceeded my limits. This is the reason why there generally aren't any athletes in units like those, they're not used to making such effort. It was actually the ones who weren't such good athletes who tried harder, who are more emotionally used to trying hard. It's the effort I'm afraid of, not the other things.

"I have a friend who is enlisting the same day I am. It seems that he is going into the parachute unit. He was also in the orientation. He's a very good person and he broke at one point. He's still sorry about that. He says that at some point he simply got up and said he couldn't go on. I also had moments like those. There is a very thin line between deciding to stop or go on. Almost by chance I went beyond that thin line, and he didn't. He went back home, but he thinks a lot about the army.

"One night we talked about the army until morning because I had found someone who understood me. He was just as nervous as I was. For, as close as people are to me, I see they don't understand. I tell them, for instance, that I'm afraid of the unit . . . that is, I'm nervous about it. 'You've got nothing to be nervous about, you'll get through it, you'll be accepted, you'll finish the course.' Things like that. They don't understand that that is not the problem."

Yoav turns to me.

"Do you understand what I'm talking about? I'm afraid that once again I'll go beyond the point of my endurance. It's a terrible feeling, a feeling that you can't take another step and you do it anyway. I don't know how to explain it. It's just, the first time I ever felt it [was] in the orientation. Perhaps people who have been through more things will make sense of what I am saying. I think about it all the time . . . I get up in the morning and go brush my teeth, so go faster! It's like a test, or something, and you have no strength, and I want to go slowly, then go faster. It's like you are always being tested. I set myself small willpower tests. This goes on all the time; it doesn't leave me, doesn't allow me to really enjoy my freedom. I can't call it freedom; it's more of a short break. I'm talking too much because these are things that are hard to express in words or numbers. I was a pretty mischievous child and I was curious and did all kinds of stuff, but, as yet, nothing big has ever happened to me."

"And how is your relationship with your grandparents?" I ask.

"Which grandparents? I never tried to analyze it, but I can't take them separately, it's just that the Holocaust has to come up. Because my grand-mother and grandfather on my mother's side – it's as if they need to help us. It's as if they are obligated to us, they need to come and take care of us, Grandma needs to come and clean and she needs to come and cook, she needs to send us food. The other grandma doesn't need to. We visit them [his father's parents] on holidays every now and then. We sometimes eat at their house on Shabbat. I really like the way Grandma cooks. I love them very much; they're nice, gentle people. But they are not as warm as my mother's parents. They do a lot for us. She's the grandma I call after tests. I mean, I need to call. I enjoy it as well – I know that it makes them feel very good when I phone. I also call her when I'm on a trip, so she won't worry. When I went to Germany, of course I called Grandma and Grandpa. It helped them a lot."

"Did they mind that you went?"

"I don't think they minded. They got used to the idea. They simply separate it. It's not that they forget. They remember every now and then and then they talk about it. They talk about it with a lot of agitation and really live it. But they separate going to Germany today and buying things there, things like that. They don't try to even the score and . . . "

"Did you have a problem with it?"

"I had a problem and still do. I went with a handball team to a training camp in Germany. We were in northern Germany and German families hosted us in their homes. Well, my [host] family was very nice and they had a nice old grandfather. But you always think, 'nice' . . . what was he doing forty years ago? That is, you need to give everybody a chance. When I met those people, that family, I liked them a lot. Yes, and I appreciated their hospitality. They were very good hosts. But I sensed a sort of feeling that they needed to atone for something. It sounds like a big deal, but they went out of their way to be hospitable. The way they took us in seemed as if they were trying to be overly nice.

"Of course the Holocaust didn't come up. There may have been moments, but I don't remember details. It was when I was in eighth grade and I only remember that I recoiled from Germans. Let's say I don't like them. Perhaps it's unconscious. I see those Germans and I don't say 'Nazis,' 'disgusting people,' or 'murderers,' but I'm afraid of them. It is somehow connected to my unconscious [thought] of what once happened. I don't feel this way about other Europeans, do you understand? It must be something unconscious that causes you to feel dislike for someone, that you have something against him. I have something against the Germans. I won't boycott them; I may buy their products. But I feel I recoil from them. I'm just not crazy about them."

"Let's go back to your grandparents."

"I'm getting into the psychology of other people. Grandma has to do things for her whole family. That is more important than anything else. Do you understand? I also think that the family is important, but she gets carried away sometimes. For example, my cousin and I – I was very busy with my matriculation exams and I wasn't in touch with her. I didn't talk to her on the phone. When I see her, I feel open and I think we get along quite well. And Grandma, it is very important to her . . . 'Did you talk to Na'ama today?' My cousin's name is Na'ama. 'And please call Na'ama, she loves you so much, and it's so important to me that the two of you talk to each other.' And that is one of her principles. Grandma is a calm person, but this is something that can drive her crazy. And when you think about the big things that didn't drive her crazy . . . and this little thing [and], I didn't answer her with disrespect. I said: 'Okay, Grandma, I have a test. We'll see about it later on.' I didn't really promise and that made her furious. She's not obsessive, she's indirectly obsessive.

"She won't tell you 'Do this or that,' but she is capable [of coercing you], of getting you to do things because you love her and don't want her to get angry. And that gives me an unpleasant feeling because I don't keep in touch with my cousin only in order to fulfill my obligations to my grandmother. She thinks it's terrible, that family is above everything, it is very important to her and it agitates her a lot. That's it . . . I got carried away again [laughter] I've just never had the opportunity to talk about my family in this way, to analyze them.

"During the past few years, my mother's sister has started coming to the [Passover] Seder; they spend one year with us and the other with the other side [of the family]. They are very happy and it's very nice having the Seder with them. It extends the Seder. It's nice when there are more people, good food, a nice atmosphere, yes. It's not that I look forward to it, but it's nice going to the Seder. Every now and then my father's brother comes too. They usually go to the other side of the family. I love my father's brother very much. I enjoy it when they celebrate the Seder with us. There is more atmosphere, a lot of humor, and then Grandpa tries to read seriously, and that's funny, because he does it humorously. He goes into a trance all of a sudden and begins to read seriously. And he skips words and . . . we don't laugh at him, but he's the type that is sometimes serious and sometimes not."

Yoav is beaming and I try to imagine Ze'ev reading "humorously."

"Mother always tries to get us to sing. She really loves that. Everyone tries to get the others to do what they want, Father with his jokes, and my sister and I sit there and enjoy it all. I think we get along very well. I don't want it to change. I love my sisters. I also love my parents, but it's just a relationship. My sisters and I have gone through so many things together, the little experiences, the stories and children's games. Razia is much younger than I am but nonetheless I feel very good with her. And Shani, my middle sister, is my friend. She tells me things; we think alike, we think the same things are funny. It's enough for the two of us to look at one another at one of those meals for us to laugh and understand one another. I know she's good at keeping secrets. Not that I have a lot of family secrets, but if I need her to do something for me, she will. She has no problem covering for me. I don't use it a lot, but I know I always have someone I can depend on. Friends come and go, but the family remains. Even though some friends are just like family. My relationship with my sister is a little more [serious]."

YOAV'S MONOLITHIC CONSTRUCTION REPLACES THAT OF GRANDFATHER ZE'EV

To an extent, Yoav's story reveals the role of his mother, Hannah. Although she feels uncomfortable with the story of her life and even refrains from describing her role in raising her children, the interview with her son leaves no room for doubt about her part in raising him, including the optimism that he radiates. Perhaps she made him aware of the oppression of the past that she spoke of in her interview, and perhaps it is this sensibility and ability to express it that allows her son to be able to express his feelings in such an open way. And, as mentioned before, styles of building life stories can also be attributed to the gender roles in this family.

Yoav describes a typical teenage boy's world: girls, school, and sport. But within the flow of speech is also a mature worldview:

> What do you live for, after all? I look at life differently from other people, and not only in relation to the army. In general, I don't think that I make a big deal out of life. I mean, I don't want to die or anything like that; I love life a lot. But I don't think that life is the time you are alive, but rather what you do with it. Because you can live for thirty years and be a nobody.

The emphasis on a love of life and action is reminiscent of Ze'ev's life story.

For Yoav, as for Ze'ev, the family constitutes "absolute good" – the anchor in the face of a stormy, unpredictable world. Yoav expresses this almost poetically: "Friends go, the family remains." Even when he criticizes his grandmother, one feels his warmth for her: the grandma who is "indirectly obsessive." Here Yoav unwittingly coins a new concept in psychology with regard to the Holocaust. The interview is nonetheless primarily a stream of experiences pertaining to the monolithic self, formed from a young age by means of continuous activities and self-imposed tests. However, Yoav's story has no mention of any explicit Other. Presumably, in his life there is no longer any need for coping with the kind of Other his grandfather Ze'ev knew all too well and described with such difficulty. He sees no value in learning Arabic. On the other hand, Yoav has an unremitting need to prove himself at sport, school, and especially, as he describes it, his army orientation. He seems to have internalized standards against which he must be tested. Whose standards were these and how do they apply to the existence of a hidden Other that directs and hurries Yoav's steps?

It seems that for Yoav, the military test was a peak experience of monolithic self, countering hidden past and present enemies in his story. The army constitutes an appropriate answer to the latter. He describes his dehydration during the orientation as the height of the test, the nearest thing in his experience to his grandfather's experiences with the partisans. An earlier expression of Yoav's need to compare his achievements with those of someone else in the family, appears in the description of his successful participation in the national handball playoff: "For me, it was a highlight because we got into the national play-offs and then . . . that was also a highlight,

I think, in comparison to what you will find in this family." How do we know that Ze'ev is the anchor to which Yoav compares himself? Because, ultimately, he belittles his story in comparison with his grandfather's stories: *"I was a pretty mischievous child and I was curious and did all kinds of stuff, but as yet nothing big has ever happened to me."* What are these "big" things Yoav is referring to? There is a hidden, subtle expectation here that this might happen during military service; that he, too, might come home with heroic stories like his grandfather Ze'ev, whom Yoav clearly adores.

Only when Bosmat asks him about his relationship with his grandparents does he deal with "it": the Holocaust. He does this through telling of his visit to Germany with the handball team:

> So my [host] family was very nice and they had a nice old grandfather. But you always think, 'nice' – what was he doing forty years ago? That is, you need to give everybody a chance. When I met those people, that family, I liked them a lot. Yes, and I appreciated their hospitality. They were very good hosts. But I sensed a sort of feeling that they needed to atone for something. It sounds like a big deal, but they went out of their way to be hospitable. They way they took us in seemed as if they were trying to be overly nice.

Ze'ev's monolithic Other flashes up in Yoav's words. But if in Ze'ev's personal experience, the Germans were "absolute evil," what remained for Yoav was mainly the fear, lack of love, and an unconscious recoiling:

> Let's say, I don't like them. Perhaps it's unconscious. I see those Germans – I don't say "Nazis," "disgusting people," or "murderers," but I'm afraid of them. It is somehow connected to my unconscious with regard to what once happened.

Nonetheless, Yoav does not impose this generalization on all *"goyim"* as does Ze'ev. Yoav specifically says he does not feel this about other Europeans.

In conclusion, as they weave their life stories Ze'ev and Yoav illustrate the construction of the monolithic Other and self in Israel. The essentially external Other threatened and annihilated family members during the Holocaust and, to this day, must be regarded with suspicion. In contrast, a physically strong, active self forms who can protect himself with heroic acts in the face of past dangers and those that await us in the future. The family constitutes an internal anchor around which the self is built. This is a family that was almost entirely destroyed during the Holocaust and which miraculously returned to build itself within the Israeli reality. No criticism is leveled at the family members who live in Canada or the United States, for they too are building renewed selves set apart from the murderous Other of the past. But Ze'ev and Yoav choose to locate themselves within the Israeli self, not so much out of ideological belief but as a reality of life. Ze'ev specifically says so: "I came here, this is where I want to be. . . . That's it." In Yoav's story, it is taken for granted; there is no need to illustrate it in words. He is bent on enlisting, an Israeli experience that is central to constructing the monolithic self.

TWO The Present I: Disintegration of the Monolithic Construction

Although monolithic construction is generally associated with unity and simplicity – a black-and-white viewpoint – the monolithic construction of the Zionist-Israeli self has been difficult to manage. This has been particularly true as it developed in opposition to at least three[1] Others, with whom relationships were always complex: the Jewish Other of the Diaspora, the ethnic Jewish Other who emigrated from Afro-Asian countries (usually Arab countries) to reach Israel, and the alien Other who threatened the Jewish-Israeli society from the outside. According to the psychodynamic approach, each one represented an aspect of the collective self that was suppressed (Shapiro, 1965) and thus projected onto these Others. The preservation of the monolithic construction of the self in Zionist-Israeli identity therefore necessitated a rather complex process. The use of Hebrew language in songs, theatre, and dance and cultural rituals and festivals reinvented from ancient Jewish tradition served the monolithic construction of the new Zionist Jew (Almog, 1997). Those representations of the Other relevant to the time and situation received continuous emphasis. At the

---

[1] In addition, one could consider the "gender Other" (Izraeli, 1997; Lomsky-Feder, 1994), the "peripheral Other" (often geographical distance from the center led to social exclusion as well), and the "impoverished Other" (Yiftachel, 1998). I address here only the three Others I have hitherto discussed because the debate is complex as it is. I am not taking a stand with regard to the relative significance of the Others in contemporary Israeli society but with regard to their centrality in the present discussion, in which I describe the historical development.

same time, incompatibilities and contradictions, which slowly manifested
among them, were repressed and undermined.[2]

Perhaps the monolithic construction in collective Israeli identity began
to disintegrate primarily because at the same time that it developed, the
various Others existed and were "activated" as well. Though the normative
and hegemonic artificial unity of the society suppressed this activation, it
was only a matter of time until internal contradictions would emerge to
erode the monolithic construction from within. It may also be that that
the disintegration process could not evolve when unity was an existential
need during the early years of statehood. Instead, the process manifested
itself when the state of the collective and its external environment was more
relaxed. Thus, once the peace process with Egypt was under way, these
contradictions could slowly surface and be discussed openly. However, the
potential for internal contradictions in collective identity construction may
nonetheless have existed from the very early years of statehood.

The previous chapter described briefly the appearance of the three
Others in a certain chronological order when Zionist-Israeli identity was
developing: Zionist history began with the Jewish Diaspora Other, later
joined by the ethnic Other in the early 1950s, along with the alien Other
in the form of the external enemy. Nevertheless, arguably, the three Others
existed within the collective self throughout its development, even if only
one Other at a time could dominate collective memory. It would appear
that at a later stage of Jewish-Israeli society's development, a more complex
picture formed: For different components of the population, or in different
contexts, different "Others" were evoked, either in parallel or in succession.
For example, when secular Israeli Jews clashed with the religious minority,
their accusations ("you don't serve in the army!") served to distance them
from the passive image of the Diaspora Other. Many Orthodox citizens
do not join the military, a constant source of tension between them and

---

[2] Some claim that the religious Other was never clearly distinguishable from the self in
Zionist Israeli identity, and it was this that later created the need for the remaining
Others and destroyed the Zionist self from within (Shenhav, 2003). Other scholars,
however, view the hatred of the Orthodox Jew in Israel as a remnant of the scorn
directed toward the Diaspora Jew during the early constructions of Zionist self (Segev,
1992).

secular society. When tensions arose in connection with Shas (a political party that appeared in the 1990s composed mainly of Sephardic religious Jews), the "ethnic demon" was released from the bottle (and even the use of this metaphor is not fortuitous), and when there was a terrorist attack, or when anti-Semitic slogans were heard in Europe, attention naturally focused on the threat of annihilation from the alien Other. For each of these attacks on the hegemonic monolithic self, there was a ready Other to refer to. As seen earlier, different strategies were employed to cope with the Others: distancing in the case of the Jewish Others, "looking through" the Palestinians as if they were not present, and when that became impossible, demonization, as with the Nazis.

Although social consensus prevailed during the monolithic construction period and public attention was primarily directed to a single dominant Other (namely, on the eve of the 1967 war, the neighboring Arab countries), the monolithic construction of the "self" could be managed in a rather stable fashion. But when situations arose – especially during the 1990s – that brought different Others to prominence for one part of the population or another, then the management of the monolithic construction of the "self" in Israeli identity became much more difficult and complicated. In this sense, Yitzhak Rabin's murder by Yigal Amir in 1995, which fused the three dominant Others in an unprecedented manner, made the continuation of the monolithic self almost impossible. This murder brought to the surface antagonism toward the Diaspora Other (Amir was a religious extremist, and the secular majority identifies religiosity with the Diaspora), the ethnic Other (Amir was Yemenite in origin), and the alien Other – the Palestinian (Amir's "cause" was to prevent Rabin from compromising with the Palestinians by "giving away" parts of Israel, which for certain national-religious Jews is unforgivable). The destructive effect on the collective Jewish-Israeli self of the combined, simultaneous appearance of all three "Others" accelerated the disintegration of the monolithic construction within Israeli-Jewish identity. It was particularly difficult for those who had perceived themselves as representing the collective self, who still believed in the possibility of perpetuating the monolithic construction and did not understand that the writing on the wall spelled disintegration. Amir's three bullets symbolized the end of the "childhood" of the Zionist monolithic self.

There was another reason that the disintegration accelerated: the growing discrepancy between the monolithic system of interpretation and the social reality that this system was meant to clarify (Lanir, 1990). The monolithic construction's black-and-white perspective failed to account for increasingly large parts of what was happening in Israeli reality, including the political empowerment of "ethnic" Jews and the beginning of a peace process with Arab countries. For some, this discrepancy caused massive processes of denial and distortion of the changing social reality (Garber & Seligman, 1980). For others, particularly among the younger generation, a growing discrepancy between Zionist ideological discourse and their social reality became too burdensome. They saw this discourse as no more than a thin cover of personal or group political interests that allowed one hegemonic group to control the others (Ram, 1993).

No one could promise that the disintegration process would be characterized by an immediate recognition of the internal contradictions existing in the collective "self." Rather, it was a gradual process of much suffering and pain, engendering a sense of loss, grieving, and helplessness (Wiztum, Malkinson, & Rubin, 1993). Some researchers maintained that within the collective, identity contradictions have *always* existed, and that in fact the process of disintegration meant the self's becoming aware of them, which could begin to stimulate an open internal dialogue. Others emphasized the *process* that slowly evoked these contradictions in identity, as a result of local and global dynamics that have come into play especially since the fall of the Communist bloc (Ram, 1993).

According to the contention (psychodynamic in nature) that the contradictions were always there, we project onto the Other those parts of the self we cannot deal with in the early stage of forming our collective identity. Examples in the case of Zionist-Israeli identity are internal characteristics deemed negative and pinned onto the Jewish ethnic Other (with labels such as "primitive," "Oriental," and "irrational"). Similarly, characteristics such as femininity and weakness are projected onto the Jewish Diaspora Other. Ultra-Orthodox Jews, with their distinct modes of dress, appear grotesque to the secular majority, perhaps reflecting the internalization of anti-Semitic aggression.

The notion that tensions within the self are the fruit of changes in the external environment is supported by transformations taking place in the collective "self" as a younger generation takes over in Israel. Other examples are seen in external events such as the 1973 Yom Kippur War, the peace process with the Egyptians, or the fall of the Communist bloc in 1989. These political changes created pressures and tensions in various directions. Heroism was redefined as a result of the Yom Kippur War, when not only fighting but also surviving came to be viewed as heroic, and as a result of the change in the balance of local and world power following the fall of the Communist bloc in Eastern Europe. Each external change introduced pressure on the construction of the monolithic self, requiring its reinterpretation and thereby creating internal contradictions within the self.

The monolithic Zionists had an idealized scenario for how collective Israeli-Jewish identity would develop: When no external threat remained, the monolithic construction of identity would disintegrate as part of its own maturation process, as a snake sheds its skin. Then a new identity construction would be established with new physical, social, and psychological meanings. This change would enable a gradual relinquishing of the repressive process that involved rejecting aspects of the self, projecting them onto the Other. However, optimal processes such as this are unusual. Outside of fairy tales, the disintegration begins before existential and psychological security is established. Thus the dissonance that can develop between a reliable representation of reality (the collective self's multicultural voices) and the monolithic, traditional representation, with further dissonance about the "right" timing for the process. It is difficult to bear the monolithic construction's disintegration before our sense of internal and external security has been established, which leads to the neo-monolithic backlash that will be described later.

Several examples based on recent research illustrate the process of disintegration in the monolithic construction of identity. As in the first chapter, these are examples on a micro level, representing macro processes that I describe in the social arena. Because I demonstrated the monolithic construction in the context of the Holocaust, I begin by presenting the cracking of that construction in the same context. Through the interviews with Ze'ev and Yoav, I attempted to illustrate the interweaving of the alien Other with the Jewish Diaspora Other and how "Israeliness" constituted an adequate answer to the perceived threat, whether domestic or external.

Using extracts from an interview with Alon, the son of a Holocaust survivor, I now attempt to show how this "Israeliness" is beginning to crack. The interviewee – son of an Israeli army officer – attempts to tell his life story as part of a heroic *sabra* legend. The Holocaust appears in his narrative as an alien and dissonant experience; the fact that his father was a child-survivor appears to have been suppressed in the family story. Though apparently not recognized as a meaningful part of the process of building their collective self, this chapter of the family biography could not be completely denied. Descriptions of the Holocaust broke through Alon's story at the least appropriate stage and in a way that bordered on pathological discourse.

This example shows a connection between the crack in the monolithic construction of Israeli identity and an inability to recognize aspects of the masculine self that incorporate weakness and vulnerability. The memory of the Holocaust represents one such aspect and the memory of shell shock in the early Israeli wars represents another. Therefore, I present the second crack in the monolithic construction of collective Israeli identity through research attempting to discover what happened to people who suffered from shell shock in the 1948 war.[3] Wiztum and Levy (1989) have already established that there were shell-shocked soldiers in that war, a fact long ignored by Israeli society. Although the expertise to diagnose and treat combat reactions existed in 1948, the knowledge was not formally implemented. The monolithic construction of collective identity during that period legitimized only heroic stories, while suppressing stories of what was perceived as weakness and helplessness. This prevented recognition and treatment of shell shock both then and later on. The people who suffered from it in 1948 were labeled "degenerates" or "cowards," or if they fled the scene of battle, they were called "the disappeared" – as if the earth had swallowed them up. Some of the people we interviewed in 1996 still insisted that in 1948 no one in the army suffered from shell shock. We found this interesting. The popular claim was that "there was no shell shock in the Palmach. Perhaps some of the Gahal soldiers were 'like that.'" (The elite

---

[3] Supervised research with Eldad Rom and Lital Bar, Department of Behavioral Sciences, Ben-Gurion University (1996–97).

Israeli-Jewish military units of the Palmach, strongly associated with the kibbutz movement, trained secretly under the British Mandate and were later the backbone of the Israeli army during the 1948 war. Soldiers in the Gahal unit were Holocaust survivors.)

Because coming to terms with shell shock in 1948 leads to cracks in the monolithic construction of Israeli-Jewish identity, as does understanding the "passivity" of Holocaust survivors, it is interesting to compare the two cases. By the mid-1990s it was already permissible to relate to the experiences of Holocaust survivors, even the less heroic aspects of these stories (Langer, 1992). But a taboo with regard to shell-shocked soldiers of 1948 endures. Perhaps this indicates the hold of masculine heroism on the *sabra* monolithic construction to this day. It is interesting to note the process of change in the legitimization of shell shock in Israel from war to war, however. The first formal legitimization was given in 1973, following the Yom Kippur War, when the numbers of shell-shocked soldiers could no longer be ignored or suppressed. As a result of lessons learned in that war, a military-medical-psychological procedure was developed. It was first implemented in the 1982 Lebanon war to rehabilitate, treat, and document the shell shocked in that war. Sufferers of this syndrome were indeed found and treated, in even larger numbers than in 1973, although objectively, since the battlefield was less fierce and the losses fewer, one could claim that the 1982 war provided far less external justification for these phenomena.

In terms of our debate, the interesting point is that with the first *Intifada* (1987–92) the legitimization of shell shock "vanished" again. Formally, according to the Israeli army, there was no shell shock or combat reaction during the years of the *Intifada*, but for different reasons than in 1948 or 1956. In the early years, the powerful monolithic construction with regard to heroism prevented recognition of "weakness" among fighters. The *Intifada* saw a new political and moral meaning. Both psychologists and soldiers now perceived it not only as part of the crack in the monolithic construction of identity, but also as taking a stand in the national debate over recognition of the Palestinian cause. Thus, in terms of our debate, shell shock in 1948 represented unwelcome evidence of the Diaspora Other in the Israeli self. Shell shock during the *Intifada* indicated the power of the alien Other to undermine the moral superiority of the Israeli self. It sounds absurd that to this day the *Intifada* has not been clearly recognized as a war. Recognition of this would indirectly have led to breakdown of Palestinian invisibility and to recognition of Palestinians' "voices" and claims. An aspect of this ambiguity is that we do not yet know what happened to those suffering from phenomena of shell shock during the *Intifada*. Neither do we know what scars were left on the psyche of those who suffered a moral and spiritual crisis during the course of their military activity. This consideration is also relevant to the *Al-Aqsa Intifada* that began in 2000, though at that stage the neo-monolithic construction became dominant, and we perceived ourselves as if again at war for our existence.

For some of the soldiers involved in its suppression, the *Intifada* created moral problems. That is, it presented not only an inherent, physical threat, but also a psychological threat to the Israeli-Jewish monolithic self. In our interview with Shimon, a reserve officer who told of being exposed to "possible imminent massacre" in Gaza, he reported the danger of "psychic death" being worse than physical death. His experience indicates the inner cracks in the monolithic construction of his Israeli identity, as a result of his military activity.

My last example of fissure in the monolithic construction of Israeli identity draws on analysis of my interviews with the children of Nazis in Germany. Through presenting interviews with this group of people – whose parents Israeli-Jewish society still sees as belonging to the most alien and totally evil Other (Hadar, 1991) – I attempt to humanize them. Seven moral arguments identified in the interviews with these descendants demonstrate the various ways in which they try to approach or distance themselves from the ethical implications of this chapter in their family biography. Hints of human complexity emerge that researchers did not anticipate or that Israelis have refused to include in the construction of the cruelest enemy ever known to the Jewish/Zionist/Israeli self. If this demonic alien Other of half a century ago is not a monolithic entity, is there also a chance that the alien Other facing us today – the Palestinian – can be perceived in a less monolithic and stereotyped fashion? This is a test still opening up before us, and one that I shall address in the last chapter.

PERSONAL WINDOW 2

The idea of "pseudo-sabraness," which is central to the next section, reminds me of a process I went through during adolescence. Though I was in fact a *sabra*, having been born in Israel, I grew up in the home of German refugees, and on *Shabbat*, the Sabbath, we played chamber music in our home and listened to the 10:00 A.M. music quiz on the radio with the kind of reverence and constancy displayed by others who went to synagogue. The heavy mahogany bookshelves were filled with the prose and poetry of Thomas Mann, Goethe, and Schiller. Our food was European, and German was the reigning language in conversation with friends, relatives, and acquaintances. Outside this beautiful European environment, in the street, the inherently different Israeli *sabra* culture was in the making. There were years when I enjoyed both worlds, but as I grew into adolescence the tension between them became unbearable for me. I remember one particular conversation with a young neighbor who attended my high school. He said bluntly, "If you continue coming to scout meetings in those pants, do you think any girl will look at you?" It became abundantly clear to me that there was some sort mysterious code and I was not a part of it.

My response was not long in coming. At the age of sixteen, I left home, changed my name from Bruno to Bar-On (without my father's consent), and went away to Kadoorie (an agricultural boarding school attended by heroes such as late Prime Minister Yitzhak Rabin twenty years earlier). In short, I took on the markers of a "real" *sabra*, an identity that did not feel like mine in my home environment. To tell the truth, I didn't succeed too badly. I learned to dress untidily but in conformance to the sabra norm; I traveled around the Galilee on weekends; my classmates and I organized ourselves into a group to settle on Kibbutz Revivim; I learned to sing Palmach songs and bang rhythmically on the table. I also learned how to be a farmer – to herd sheep, and grow fruit trees. While I did not become the complete farmer – this seemed to be a boundary I was unable to cross – I was undoubtedly happy then and felt part of something that was big and good.

The counterreaction came many years later, in 1967, when I returned from the Six-Day War. Perhaps it was the death of a good friend in that war, someone who had managed the orchards with me on Revivim. Perhaps it was the shock of what I saw during the war itself that overcame the *sabra* trumpet of intoxicating victory. Somehow, I began to sense the cracks in my *sabra* identity, a shell underneath which were other processes that I tried earlier to ignore and deny. But it took a few more years, and it was only after I returned from the 1973 Yom Kippur War that the chinks became a chasm. It then became clear to me my "pseudo-sabraness" was not the whole truth for me anymore. I had already begun to wonder who among the "real" sabras living around me had an exterior persona hiding layers that were unfamiliar and unknown even to them. For while the sabra fruit's prickly skin conceals a soft, tasty interior, my faux sabra exterior masked increasing inner turbulence and discord.

Years after I had left the kibbutz, and become an "academic" (here too one could apply the terms "pseudo" or "ostensible," but this is not a part of the present debate), I began to interview three generations of refugee families who had survived the Holocaust. It so happened that as part of the research, one of my students interviewed a family she knew on Kibbutz Revivim. When I read the interviews I was amazed. I had known this family for twenty-five years and had never thought of them as a family of Holocaust survivors. Over and above my own blindness, I wondered how much energy they had invested in not being identified as part of this social category. I am almost certain that, to this day, they would refuse to define themselves this way.

2.1 BEING A "SABRA" IN THE SHADOW OF THE HOLOCAUST[4]

In contrast to Ze'ev, the partisan-fighter, many Holocaust survivors who came to Israel during the forties had to deal not only with a new language, climate, and culture, but also with painful social judgment: "Why did you go like sheep to the slaughter?" The Israeli, monolithic self, then fighting for the establishment of an independent state, could not cope with the perceived passivity of the Diaspora. As Witztum, Malkinson, and Rubin (1993: 253) maintain:

> The Zionist idea . . . serves as a wide field for stories of heroism that are an antithesis to stories of the Diaspora and the Holocaust. An image of an Israeli native was created, a good-hearted, sociable, strong person who was

[4] The interview was conducted by Yael Mor as part of her master's thesis for the Department of Behavioral Sciences at Ben-Gurion University of the Negev (Bar-On & Mor, 1996).

good looking, with rough edges but a sweet interior like the fruit of the Sabra, a hero who never cries ... A son of Israel, he symbolizes Israel's sons and daughters in a nation that is being renewed. He gives his life for his country. ... and Israel commemorates his memory forever as part of the cultural memory that is created over the years.

Tom Segev adds, "the willingness of the survivors and their ability to change, to identify with the stereotype of the Sabra and be like him, were demanded as a 'declaration of loyalty,' as an 'entrance exam,' like a ritual demanded of those entering a tribe" (1992: 164). He quotes Yehudit Handel (163–64):

> In Israel there were almost two races. One race was god-like; they had the privilege and the right to be born in Degania (the first kibbutz) or in the Borochov neighborhood in Givatayim ... of the others it was definitely possible to say out loud – an inferior race. People ... with some sort of defect, some sort of hump, and these were the people who came after the war.

The survivors who wished to integrate into this monolithic culture had to adopt the norms of Israeli "sabraness." To a large extent, they had to deny what they had experienced in the Diaspora in general and the Holocaust in particular – all that was not in accord with this concept of becoming an Israeli. Since changes in these heroic, monolithic concepts took place only after so many years, initially as a result of the Yom Kippur War, until that time, and even beyond it, unresolved inner conflicts about the monolithic construction of identity were transmitted to the next generation.

Alon grew up with a father who was an officer in the Israeli army. He sensed how significant this heroic identity was for his father and how incompatible it was as part of his own identity as a survivor's son. His father had immigrated to Israel from Galicia at the age of sixteen, immediately after the Second World War. Most of his family had died in the Holocaust. I describe what happened in the father-son relationship as the creating of a "double wall" (1995): The father tries to separate the Israeli experience from his past by creating an emotional wall. The child growing up beside the father senses this wall and builds one of his own. Through the two walls, a message is transmitted from father to son that certain subjects must not be addressed. Even if the father later tries to open a window in his own wall, he is likely to meet with the wall of his son, and if his son were to make such an attempt, he too might encounter a wall.

Alon himself was a *sabra*, raised among other *sabra*s, the son of a moshav-born[5] mother who herself was born in Israel, a daughter of the founding generation. He seemed to have every reason to feel good about the monolithic construction of his Israeli identity, as did Yoav in the previous chapter. He could in fact have told the story of his life in the context of his mother being a *sabra*, emotionally distancing himself from the subtle conflict inherent in his father's life story. But this is not what Alon chose to do. He tried to continue his father's army tradition and, at the age of 14, on his own initiative, he went to a military school in Haifa to begin a military career. But he left shortly afterward, ostensibly for "ideological reasons," and similar oscillations continued during his army service and his time on the police force, until he found his niche as a lawyer.

Alon's narrative is full of failed attempts to adopt the ethic of the Israeli fighter. He seems to be struggling with a norm of heroism that is difficult for him to adopt. Perhaps this is why he begins his main narration (which continued for only ten minutes) with a negative statement: "Ah, I will not tell my story in the context of the Holocaust . . . but the Holocaust will probably pop up here and there . . . " From this, one could assume that Alon guessed the interviewer's intention. But he states his complex attitude to the subject of identity with this opening sentence. It can already be surmised that he won't choose to tell his life story in the context of his mother being a *sabra*. And this is borne out in the following sentence: "I was born in Hadera [a town half way between Haifa and Tel Aviv]; my father was then in the permanent military forces. He emigrated after the Holocaust when he was quite young . . . " Here three elements appear that form the rest of his life story and his identity: he was born in Israel, his father was part of the Israeli fighter ethic, and the Holocaust was (a hidden) part of his past. But there is no open conflict between these elements. In the following sentences, he does

---

[5] The modern Hebrew *mosb*, dwelling, derives from *ysab*, to sit or dwell. A cooperative agricultural settlement consisting of small separate farms, the moshav differs from the kibbutz, which is communal.

in fact mention his mother and her "pure" Israeli affiliation, but she then disappears from the story (he maintains he does not remember her), and he concentrates on descriptions of his father: "My father served in one of the Golani [combat infantry] units . . . so I had direct contact with the army and with my father . . . " He describes an evening with his father's unit when he sang Israeli songs with all his father's soldiers. He also describes the move to kibbutz and his brother's birth there as a "very Israeli experience . . . very Israeli."

According to Aulagnier (1994), to be able to express and feel emotions, one needs to accept a historical version of one's life as a reason for living. We need to know how to answer the question: Where do I come from? When surrounded by silence instead of answers, a difficult and basic dilemma arises. It is at this stage – after Alon manages to establish his being a *sabra* and an Israeli, as well as establishing the military and Israeli character of his father – that his verbal narrative breaks down with an outburst of laughter and a story about his maternal grandmother, who came to Israel before the Holocaust. The story's implications are vague and its meanings unconscious:

Now this grandmother was an intellectual type and she had a book that she loved very much [Alon begins to laugh], a small black book with pictures of horrors from the Holocaust. [He laughs.] Now, how did I learn about the Holocaust, you may ask. She would take me into bed with her, sometimes with one of my cousins, boys and girls, and she would open the book and turn the pages and cries of "*oy oy*" would escape from her throat [a loud laugh], and now, ah, my father was a counselor in the army officers' course then [he laughs and I join in]; I don't know if all the officers in his military base would wear peaked caps and the Germans [he laughs loudly] the SS and the Wermacht also had peaked caps [he can't get the words out because he is laughing so hard] and I didn't [speaking slowly] understand it [laughter] – that is, what I am trying to say is that the matter [speaking quickly] of the army was also quite important for me, for my father; when I saw him in his uniform and I saw the black-and-white photographs, I didn't quite understand – my grandmother was lamenting the actions of the [German] soldiers and these soldiers appeared positive to me, and I am not a psychologist, but I imagine that this made me look at the Holocaust in a special way, and I must add that I liked that book very much.

Here the slightly romantic monolithic picture that Alon tried to paint of his Israeli identity in the previous paragraph all at once disintegrates. But this disintegration is still subconscious and distressing for Alon. With laughter he tries to overcome the alarm, confusion, and helplessness. The fantasy about his father's army cap in relation to SS officers' caps, and the explanation that they seemed "positive" because they wore the same caps, suggest what psychoanalysts call "subconscious internalization of the aggressor." Alon is confused about "Where do I come from and where am I going?" The Israeli fighter father is momentarily perceived as a perpetrator, similar to the Nazi soldiers. It might be more important to Alon that his father was active and a fighter, and he is thus not obliged to relate to the fact that his father, seen from childhood as an Israeli hero, was during the Holocaust a weak and helpless victim of those SS officers. He later admits: "I couldn't picture him among the many kinds of victims there . . . because of his self-confidence, for instance . . . the look in his eyes . . . details of clothing . . . and the fact that he had a revolver or a rifle . . . I could not identify him with the victims."

The more he avoids presenting his life story in relation to the Holocaust, the more trapped he becomes in this confusion. In the second part of the interview he tells about dead Holocaust victims showing up in his dreams – "people's black hair" . . . "someone following me . . . looking at me from a distance." He tells about later when his grandmother died, but immediately, in the same breath, he adds: "She of course did not die in the Holocaust, but her entire family died . . . and my grandfather had a cousin . . . the survivor of a family that was murdered in Romania." Alon has another uncle who survived the Holocaust and had a severe emotional crisis at the age of sixty. It seems easier for Alon to characterize the Other emerging from the Holocaust through his uncles (the one characterized as a "pathological liar"). Afraid of this Other, he tries to eradicate it from his own biography.

Alon completed his story thus: "That's it, that's what I can tell you about myself." And what else could he tell? Alongside the enormous desire to preserve the mask of the *sabra*, the image of the father as an active fighter, Alon is hounded by figures and fantasies from his father's past. He went through a process that was still subconscious, his monolithic construction disintegrating while he spoke. It would appear that Alon no longer owned his monolithic biography construction, but he was unable to cope consciously and contain the varied content which constituted it. He vacillated, sometimes hanging onto the Holocaust-Diaspora Other and sometimes onto the Israeli self, and he had not yet found a way to create an open dialogue between these two parts.

PERSONAL WINDOW 3

To me as a child, the generation of 1948 was one of giants. It began with the fact that even my late brother Michael, who was six years older than I, did not belong to this generation. I remember the two of us during a rare moment of togetherness in our youth, sitting and singing "Bat Sheva" and "Bab El Wad," poignant songs of patriotism, struggle, and loss, and feeling his longing, perhaps even stronger than my own, to be a part of this great experience. Later on, when I attended the Kadoorie agricultural school, there, looking down at me from the walls, were photographs of the first classes, with Yigal Allon, Chaim Guri, and Yitzhak Rabin – almost hallowed figures – among the pupils. Our wonderful headmaster, the late Ya'akov Piat, could share his personal memories of these legendary days. We were the twentieth class and they were from the first to the fifth classes. When I joined Kibbutz Revivim, affiliated with the Kibbutz Hameuchad movement, this journey of admiration continued. It was gratifying to rub shoulders with people who were protagonists in S. Yizhar's influential book, *Hirbet Hizàh*.[6]

But in any natural maturation process, the time comes when idols are deconstructed. For me, this stage began after the Six-Day War when, together with my military commander, I confronted Golda Meir [Israel's prime minister at that time] on the Palestinian issue. In the early seventies I even dared to write an article in the Kibbutz Hameuchad weekly about the need for a Palestinian state. A week later one of the leaders of the movement (Israel Galilee, at that time a major minister in the government, arrived at Revivim to participate in the general meeting and he spoke about the need to pull out "bad weeds" at the roots. At this time we established a branch of the left-wing political movement "Sheli" in Revivim, the largest branch in the Kibbutz Hameuchad movement – much to the mortification of

---

[6] One of the best novels written by an author of that generation, *Hirbet Hizàh* describes a Palmach unit trying to conquer a post from the Egyptian army and the inner and external struggles of the soldiers in that Negev desert campaign in the 1948 war.

Golda Meir, who considered Revivim "her" kibbutz. As far as she was concerned, the Palestinians were not a people, and they were, quite simply, "nonexistent."

During this time, I began to perceive the "absolute good" I had once admired as the "absolute evil" to be resisted. It was only in the 1990s, when I began to interview the generation of 1948 on the subject of unreported shell shock, that I truly grew up. Now, for the first time I could feel their helplessness and pain. Only now could I relate to them as people, mortals, and acknowledge the pain they had held in, with no legitimate outlet. How long it has taken me to mature with regard to the issues of identity! Does this stem from my own limitations of idealization or from the slowness of the social process taking place around me – or perhaps both of them together?

2.2 THE SOCIAL ROLE IN AVOIDING ACKNOWLEDGMENT OF BATTLE SHOCK[7]

Assessing the impact of shell shock during the 1948 war on the later disintegration of the monolithic construction is difficult, even more difficult perhaps than with regard to the silence or silencing of Holocaust survivors. The course and outcome of the 1948 War of Independence has to a great extent formed the state's image, its boundaries, and the power patterns of the entire area. The war, initially a violent struggle between Jews and Arabs within the boundaries of Mandatory Palestine, became a struggle beyond those boundaries with the declaration of the establishment of the State of Israel and the invasion of Arab armies (Horowitz & Lissak, 1989). The Jewish settlement in Israel paid a heavy price: about six thousand people were killed (1 percent of the Jewish population at that time) and a much greater number wounded. In the spring of 1949, the war ended with the signing of cease-fire agreements between Israel and several Arab states.

[7] This section is based on research carried out with Eldad Rom and Lital Bar during 1996–97. Seventy-three 1948 combatants were interviewed. Twenty-three refused to cooperate or claimed there was no phenomenon of shell shock in 1948. Seventeen had a vague partial memory of combatants' battle reactions. Eighteen could remember cases of battle reactions in detail; four of them reported their own. The interview presented here is one of these four.

A romanticism and yearning for a simpler time has developed around that war, wrought especially by those known as the generation of 1948, a group that wholeheartedly adopted the monolithic ethos of the "fighter." This ethos is still strongly rooted in the personal and collective consciousness of Israeli society. The essential naiveté inherent in the Zionist revolution and the collective memory of the Jewish nation gave this ethos its unique significance. The "new" Jew; the myth of the *sabra* was forged in reaction to Diaspora by a society that came to see itself as besieged, long before the trauma of the Holocaust reinforced the ethos. Lomsky-Feder (1994) defined the basic codes of the ethos as determination, initiative and resourcefulness, friendship, daring, danger, sacrifice, the "purity" of weapons, and professionalism. She maintained that this ethos originated during the struggle for the existence of the state and its Jewish settlements and the state. The war of 1948 constituted a foundation and a heroic reference point in the course of collective memory. It is therefore easy to understand the words of Dr. Wolman, a chief physician in the early army, about the Hebrew youth in 1948:

> The Hebrew soldier has the highest standard of ethics and ideology. Hebrew youth is imbued with love for the homeland and his heart's desire is to serve his nation and his country faithfully. Every young man in Israel is always prepared to report for the duty of protection. From childhood they are educated in an atmosphere of pioneering nationalism and when they reach maturity, their hearts are burning with the elevated ideals of the nation. (Quoted by Wiztum & Levy, 1989)

The phenomenon of shell shock in the 1948 war in any form was denied in recent interviews with members of that generation, even as they indicated that there were in fact such reactions. For instance, C.R claimed, "I know of no case of shell shock . . . there were no such cases. Absolutely not . . . I do know of shirkers; cowards who simply ran away from the fighting . . . That's all. No shell shock." Declarations of this kind consistently arose in conversations with members of this generation. However, in the light of what we know today about battle reactions and their frequency among combatants exposed to difficult experiences during the war, their relative rarity among

1948 combatants seems surprising and doubtful. It is more probable that society played a role in silencing the phenomenon of shell shock in 1948. It helped pre-state Israel or Jewish settlements in Palestine preserve the monolithic aspect of the "fighter" ethos. Thus the phenomenon of shell shock was turned by the military hegemony then into a conscious or unconscious wish to shirk army service.

Battle reaction is not a new phenomenon. Since the first world war it has been recognized that those wounded emotionally, or "shell shocked" to varying degrees, are an inevitable part of war (Noy, 1991). Solomon (1993) sees participation in battle as a situation of extreme stress requiring massive coping resources to overcome external and internal pressures. When a soldier is confronted by extreme demands and feels he cannot implement an effective coping mechanism, then "battle reaction," also known as "shell shock," will occur. It sometimes seems that in such extreme conditions of pressure as war, the "normal" response to such an "abnormal" situation would be to escape from "external madness" to "internal madness" (Guri, 1995).

Any attempt, however, to attribute vulnerability to the *sabra* combatants of 1948 (by recognizing emotional battle reactions as a normal response to the pressure of battle) – were doomed in advance. Nonetheless, total repression of the phenomenon became impossible, if only because of its many expressions. A solution was found: projecting the phenomenon onto an opportune Other, the new immigrants recruited to the Gahal army units.[8] The figure of the immigrant from the "Diaspora" stood in sharp contrast to the "fighter" and the brave *sabra* ethos. Wiztum & Levy (1989) maintained that all national-social discourse indicated a contrast between the volunteer who was native-born and imbued with heroic spirit and those who joined later on in the general recruitment, particularly those immigrants who came after the Holocaust and were regarded as "cowards" and unfit for fighting.

---

[8] Gahal was a military unit of Holocaust survivors. Many of its young soldiers were recruited upon arrival from Europe, in the midst of the fighting, with very little training. As a result, a large number died in a very difficult battle against the siege of Jerusalem that took place around Latrun in the spring of 1948.

This kind of prejudice made it almost obligatory to attribute battle reactions in 1948 solely to Gahal soldiers. And indeed, some of our interviewees put sole blame for any such cases on these recruits. An echo of this appears in the words of Professor Halperin, a neurologist and psychiatrist who was, for a time, well-known as the editor of the Hebrew *Medical Weekly*:

> We were surprised by the relative scarcity of emotional problems among our soldiers ... in our youth beat a strong, fearless heart ... the psychotic cases increased as the entire army increased ... the storm of the war swept away the fainthearted as well ... the cases among new immigrants still not released from the emotional blows of their tragic past ... and who are unable to withstand the mirror of the shock of what happened in the war. (Wiztum & Levy, 1989)

We found no empirical evidence for this claim. The opposite claim is made in the testimony by C.R. which follows.

It is hardly surprising that Wiztum and Levy's historical survey of the sources referring to treatment of battle reactions (1989) indicated that despite the large number of casualties, virtually no emotional wounds were observed in the war of 1948. However, the state of affairs in Israel during that period makes this difficult to accept. Today, as documented in the same study, we know that battle reactions occurred on all fronts and in all units, including the elite Palmach and Givati units. Nonetheless, in the scanty early medical literature it was difficult to find any indication of the phenomena at all. The shell shocked were often described as "cowards, hypochondriacs, shirkers psychopaths, those who couldn't take it, those who lacked the spirit of willingness for military activity," and so on (Wiztum & Levy, 1989).

Wiztum and Levy claimed that there were many emotional casualties in the 1948 war; some severe casualties, some mass battle reactions. It seems that we must look for psychosocial explanations for the absence of battle reaction testimonies and reports from this war. The labeling inflicted on those shell shocked reflected moral judgment. Social condemnation was so severe that when fifteen of the "degenerates" in the Harel unit hid under a house in Kiryat Anavim (after being bombed by Arab forces), their "healthy" friends took malicious pleasure in the fact that they ended up being wounded due to their "cowardice."

The power of these mechanisms is indicated by the fact that even today, more than half a century after the war, many 1948 combatants continue to firmly deny both the existence of the phenomenon in their midst and the issue it raises. The condemnation and denial of the phenomenon are so rooted that we had difficulty exposing the full extent of it even in interviews we carried out during 1997. The bond of silence is still maintained, and preoccupation with the subject is akin to putting salt on open wounds. Ignoring them, so it seems, is preferred to attempting to acknowledge and heal them.

What happened, then, to people who did suffer from battle shock in 1948, when this was "forbidden" by the predominant social code? How did these people cope with it without receiving treatment at the time? How have they coped with the social labeling all these years since, while living and raising their children and grandchildren within Israeli society? An extract from an interview conducted with C.R. in 1996 tells the story of the shell shock he suffered in 1948 and only recognized years later.

"I am 65 and I was 17 then. The age difference between us is so great – he hides inside me, but he is only a small part of me. . . . Can I give you an example? . . . I am not typical of that period, but this event is typical. I had a friend, he was older than I . . . I'd prefer not to give his name, but he was a veteran member of the Palmach unit; he was a hulk of a man, like those *Palmachniks* who later became truck drivers or worked in construction or things like that. He was a real man; I mean, I was a young kid and to us he seemed a real man. During the battle at the Kastel,[9] we were on top and . . . it was a tough battle and suddenly the guy was terrified. He ran the whole way from the Kastel to Kiryat Anavim and . . . hid somewhere . . . I remember him screaming, the guy screamed 'mama, mama,' or something like that. It didn't, I couldn't even grasp it. How a strong, healthy man like that . . . afterward I didn't see him again, I mean . . . the man with shell shock was so ashamed, and all the others were so ashamed, that they transferred him and the whole matter was forgotten, and I don't know if there are five men today who would admit, 'He had shell shock.' They'd say 'he ran to

[9] Most of the places mentioned in this interview are on the main road to Jerusalem.

get help,' or they'd say . . . I don't know what . . . but . . . and there were lots of cowards among the heroes.

"In the battle when I got shell shock, my commander . . . he ran away from that battle – what can I say? He denies it, others defend him. Everyone who was there knows he ran away from the battle. Now, to this very day he can't accept it, he can't accept that he ran away from the battle, he abandoned us because he was overwhelmed with terrible fear. Now, the connection between fear and shell shock wasn't understood then, because in fact the fear wasn't rational, not exactly – everyone was afraid, but you get over the fear; you're young, you're a fighter. I was frightened all the time, but I fought. Everyone was frightened and they all fought, except for Raful[10] maybe, who was always enthusiastic. But . . . people got over it, and what is today called shell shock was misunderstood then. It was understood then as someone's attempt to say about someone else that he was afraid. They transmitted this in all sorts of ways.

"As I see it, a lot of things happened as a result of this. For instance, someone else had shell shock in the war. He wasn't frightened of the battle itself but of the responsibility of the battle, so in his case the process was simply to fall asleep and he missed the battle. So I don't really know where the boundary lies, what exactly to call it. Because it wasn't shell shock, it was fear of responsibility. Maybe for my commander it was fear of the situation he faced as commander . . . when he was ambushed. With me it was simpler. With me it was really like classic shell shock. It was on the way to Jerusalem. I was in other battles but I didn't get shell shock.

"The big mistake was – I'm beginning at the end – if it had happened in a modern war, someone would have noticed me and spoken to me, or would have . . . done something with me; my entire life would have been different. I wouldn't have hidden it away inside myself for so many years; it wouldn't have bothered me so much, it wouldn't have become a nightmare I've had almost every week since '48, and it's been many years now. I mean, somehow, I'm not . . . I'm not much in favor of psychiatric treatment. I

[10] Rafael Eiton, later chief of staff during the Lebanon war of 1982 and then a member of Knesset (parliament).

mean I don't have anything for or against it. But, there's a place, when something happens, if someone opens you up or you express what you are feeling, you can talk about it ... there was no one to talk to then ... The main problem that I vaguely remember about all the people around me was that ... it was forbidden to be afraid, it was forbidden to cry. Ah, you can't take children of 17, 18, and turn them into robots without even, let's say, appropriate preparation. In America, for instance, they take them for a year's training in the desert with iron discipline – what did we know in the Palmach? There was no discipline, nothing. I mean, there was no military-school background like the parachutists [have] today. For instance, they go through backbreaking training and in the end they get through proud and prepared. They took us from our homes, put us through a little mini-course, and sent us to war. Our commanders hadn't fought a single battle before they took command of us, and then four hundred people were killed in our unit, a third of the battalion [silence].

"So I think that this subject ... is not researched today, but ... it's still taboo. Because ... we still can't talk about the commanders who got shell shock, and there are a lot of them. My own story was very simple. I ... we went out there, three or four armored vehicles, most of us were demolition experts, and we had to sort of cover for the other side in a battle where the main line failed and ... we were ambushed and ... there was a tough battle and ... the commander turned the vehicle around – the only one who managed to turn the vehicle – and fled, said he was going to get help, and he knew there was no help to be brought; it was just an excuse, and we were left there without command and ... without going into details, about twenty or twenty-two men were left there in the end. The other armored vehicles went over mines. The only operable vehicle was the commander's. The driver was excellent and ... when he gave evidence, he said that he took the commander and they went to get help. If you think about it for a moment, the commander – why didn't he send me to get help? Why did he send himself? It wasn't the driver – the driver was carrying out an order. I suddenly remember they refused to take some of the wounded because they were in a hurry and ... but we were left, and this ... and we were left there, surrounded, and ... the Arabs in the ambush were afraid and waited for the Jordanian legion to arrive.

"So we were left, each one in his own corner, most of us pretended to be dead, it's hard to know what the others did, I pretended to be dead [quietly]; I don't know about the others, I only know that . . . the Arabs were sitting round us a few dozens of meters away. They were sitting on hills and . . . there's a small wadi there and . . . we had a lot of wounded. They were slowly dying. Now, the Arabs around us had time and they were making coffee, we saw them . . . the smoke and the smell and . . . they didn't have anything to do so they shot at the dead; at who they thought was dead. I, and others beside me, were pretending to be dead, and they kept shooting at the dead and they didn't hit me. For some reason – all it took – it took an hour or two, hundreds of bullets were fired and . . . my friend was lying next to me, I could feel him trembling, his blood draining onto me, and how he died. And they kept on shooting, shooting and laughing; I mean, they didn't think they were shooting at us, it was just to get rid of tension, and . . . at some point, I don't know when, maybe 'round about 4:30 or 5 o'clock, a cloud or shadow came down against the far mountain, and it got dark . . . and . . . suddenly, I got up, at the same time two other men got up, and we started running [silence] it was as if . . . without deciding together. We were the only ones who survived. I don't know how many died there, I don't know. How many died before, how many died afterward, I don't know, but three of us remained alive – one was killed later on and two of us were left. The other guy wanted to take revenge on the commander for years afterward, then, that very night they took the commander in . . . an airplane to . . . the Negev. And there, he, he was promoted and transferred from our unit.

"We ran to Kiryat Anavim or Ma'aleh HaHamisha, I don't remember which; we ran to where there were people, then I lost a day and a half, to this day I don't know what happened – [quietly] that time is lost. What came back later was the day . . . I didn't remember it all. I . . . I remembered that something had happened and I kept telling a different story. When I got to the top, and I remembered, and I knew that something terrible had happened. I didn't know what had happened. It's hard to explain, but I didn't know exactly what had happened. And immediately after that they took me to the frontline, to fight. They gave me a day to rest, and no one behaved as if something unusual had happened."

"Did anyone talk to you at all?" I asked him.

"No one! I don't remember anyone asking anything, I mean, it was all...out of twenty, three people returned, one of whom was [now] dead; they didn't even ask what we'd done...I don't remember anything and I was sent off to fight immediately after that. I mean, I fought for two months in harder battles. And...there was someone, I don't remember if he was with us or not, in any case, he knows the whole story of that battle, and he always talked about me and I didn't remember that it was me, he would talk about me and I didn't remember a thing. And then...about twenty years later this memory suddenly came back. I remember being near Caesarea or Herzilyia and suddenly the story came back to me. And I was in shock, for a few weeks, I couldn't move, and then I wrote it down. I mean, I haven't gotten over the nightmare. Once or twice I tried going to a psychologist, but it didn't help, and then this discovery came too late...It came as a story – it wasn't me anymore. I am already 65 and I was 17 then...the gap between us is so big; that 17-year-old is hiding inside me, but today he is only a small part of myself [silence].

"Now I think that it was typical, that the commander of that battle was shell-shocked, I was shell-shocked, and others were also shell-shocked; all of us were, each one in a different way, and nothing was investigated, nothing...no one drew conclusions. Did a certain commander fall asleep or was he tired? Was he really so tired that he couldn't get up for a battle he had planned and that later failed? That battle was meant to be the largest in that area during that time. A battle that was meant to open up the way to Jerusalem at the hardest point, when the Kastel was already in our hands – that place remained in Jordanian hands until '67. Then they were very afraid of it, so that...many people were left with a scar. People were killed there...a whole generation of commanders brought to take care of us was killed there. But I was half a kid...I joined up when I was 17. I was maybe the youngest there. And...I was extremely sensitive and afraid, and I fought rather well to overcome it, and maybe I fought a bit too much, I mean, someone even told me once: What do you want, do you want to be a hero? When I was wounded, I even sought that challenge, but...now, I know it was a kind of shell shock."

"How did you get through the fighting after that?" I asked him.

"I only know I was there because there were witnesses, but I hardly remember a thing. I was like a robot. I think I got through that whole period, from that day to the day I was wounded during the attack on the Old City and we were taken to hospital. There, part of my memory slowly came back to me. But in the middle of the battles, I no longer remember the order, but I participated in at least ... let's say five or six large, hard battles. I hardly remember a thing. Now, people remember me wandering around the catacombs [in the Jerusalem battle field], but I don't remember anything. That moment ... when we were lying there pretending to be dead, I remember every detail – going there, how many we were, who was in the armored cars, and how we were suddenly ambushed, and ... how the mines ... and how they fired at us and how we got out of the armored cars, and how the commander's armored car turned around ... I remember lying there. I didn't remember it all immediately, but after twenty years when I remembered ... I remember lying there in a ... a kind of execution ... I mean, I can only translate it in terms of – putting me up against a wall, covering my eyes, because I could hardly see through half-closed eyes, twenty soldiers firing at me – each one firing and no one hitting me. I don't know, the feeling of being shot at – at least once a week I wake up from a nightmare of them still shooting. I see them shooting me and ... I want to scream.

"I'm really sorry that there were no ... no more precise investigations then. If you try and research the War of Independence today, I will tell you one thing, someone else will tell you something else; there is no history – each one writes his own history from his own point of view. What is left of the War of Independence is not only inaccurate, it is ... each one has his own version. There is no one truth. All I know is that there is not one single version of the truth. How can they know? No one can, there were no photographers, no reporters; a reporter came once or twice, but nothing else was documented. After all, there are no photographs – all the photographs we see were taken afterward; none were taken at the time.

"My nightmares began in Israel and I had them overseas too. I began to be depressed – people were afraid. For instance, there was a party six months after the war and ... everyone who had been together in the youth movement came. I got up on a chair and made the sort of speech that made everyone run away. I was good-looking, but I would go out with a girl and she would run away after half an hour. I brought death with me. It stayed with me, I wore black. And I was left with a sort of depression, till now; I mean, I can get into a depression for a week, and I have tried all sorts of medication, decided it wouldn't help. But the nightmares began after I was already depressed. I got it out in all sorts of ways. I went back to the war and couldn't get over it.

"I fell – the first thing that happened, I fell – and then they put me on board ship to fetch immigrants, Holocaust refugees, and bring them to Israel; people whose suffering was a thousand times greater than my own. As for me, my identification with them was so deep that I was able not to think – it was the first and best therapy I had. When I got to the ship I met survivors, all of them from Auschwitz and camps like that. We traveled by train to fetch them. There were three thousand people on the journey, packed in like sardines. And they still talked then – told me the story once or twice a day. Some of them talked and I talked with some of them, I felt as if what I had gone through was dwarfed because I could not remember the true story. I suddenly thought – about the Kastel – we fired, they fired at us, it . . . there . . . they had no weapons . . . I remember the story of someone who searched Jews' rectums, found diamonds and sold them . . . stories, stories they still told then, before they also stopped talking, before they learned to be silent and before they again learned to talk about it later on. When people came and talked. [Silence] and . . . my identification with them was an escape . . . from what I had gone through. Because . . . if someone went through the Holocaust, it was like overcoming something much more difficult than what I went through, for instance. That was my way."

"Maybe they didn't want to listen when you would talk about it," I suggested.

"No, no one wanted to listen and I didn't want them to. The truth is that, until five years ago, I don't remember ever having talked about what happened there. I talked about it in general and they related as if it was a wonderful war. And why was I giving this kind of testimony, and what about the Palmach spirit, where was the heroism . . . look, I didn't have a satisfactory explanation for seeing things differently. Maybe I didn't remember stealing chickens and how – how we sat around on the grass . . . and how we screwed some gorgeous kibbutz girl, or something like that. I only really remember that fear – the dead, the wounded. I mean, if an evening were arranged today, with twenty people from my generation, and I were to say what I have said to you – they'd kill me."

"Still?"

"I mean, they wouldn't kill me, they know me, they'd say 'poor guy, he had shell shock' and 'he's crazy, unbalanced,' but, no, it wouldn't be something to take to heart. I'm still a macabre sort of joke."

"Has someone ever approached you over the years and said, 'Listen, something similar happened to me,' and told you a story that he felt you were open to hearing?"

"No one has approached me. The first time I saw shell shock victims was in Nes Tziona during the seventies. There were a few more who were hospitalized from the Six-Day War – then they hid in trenches . . . look, I think that my story has elements of a great many problems . . . the problems of veteran Israeli society and its effects . . . and maybe in a certain sense, it has an effect to this day. Because, after a year or two the new immigrants stopped talking, and after a few years the entire generation is unaware of it, and today there is already a young generation that says "I'm afraid." At that time, being different was impossible. In my children's generation, being different is far more acceptable. At first I wasn't different; I was a good fighter, and I was one of them, and I joined the Palmach at only 17 – I was among the builders of this country, this cannot be denied. All these things – it all began from the fact that no one told the truth. No one investigated, no one was questioned, no one gave an account. Maybe too much is accounted for today, maybe too much is done . . . but what happened was that I had shell shock and I am not ashamed of it, I don't have a problem with it. But, to say at this stage, 'Well, he had shell shock' – how can this lead to real research? How can it?

"Look, after the war we would all sit around, we all had a period when we were – mentally ill – it's impossible to describe . . . we came . . . before I went on board the ship, I don't remember much before that time, during that year when we returned from the war, and there was a place in Tel Aviv called "Institute for Determining the Condition of Soldiers Who Left the Army

Through No Fault of Their Own," and there were wounded Palmach people there. We would walk about at night. During the day we would sit around at Kasit Cafe and go to a matinee and go and eat at Geula's, and we would sit in Cafe Nussbaum, and I remember, we had a need, we had a need to be together ... and we didn't talk about ... we talked about all sorts of things, looking for things, and there were new immigrants selling watches and guys, a few guys from the Palmach, who brought gold teeth from an Arab, it was a ... when I think about it today, [taking teeth from a corpse] makes me shudder, but then, I suppose I was, I was restless and didn't know what was happening to me, and no one came and asked, what's making you ... and I, rather hung around all the guys during that time ... And to this day they sit around, sit around the whole day, for two to three hours, and talk. They say – 'D'you remember eating ... ' 'It cost two pennies for a kilo in Or Yehuda, and then I went there,' 'But it wasn't in Or Yehuda, it was in Ramat Gan,' "No, it wasn't, it wasn't in Ramat Gan, it was ... ' Sitting around for hours and they remember the names, And there is always someone who says, 'Listen, what was the name of that girl who slept around?' And that's what they have talked about all day for all these years; they come and they talk. They've moved somewhere else now, but it isn't the same anymore. They only remember up to '48, after that, nothing! Thirty years have passed in Solel Boneh construction company, thirty years in Ma'atz road construction company; they've made money, raised children, they've got grandchildren, today they come from America for this! They come from ... some come and sit, I tell you they live in America today, I don't know how long they've been there, they come for one or two months, they sit, and they talk the whole time. It starts off with, let's say, 'Maccabi Tel Aviv lost,' 'Ah. Yes.' 'D'you remember ... Halevi when he was the goal keeper?' 'He got three goals then from Patz.' 'Not from Patz.' 'Patz was in Beitar Tel Aviv then,' and it starts like that and it always gets back to the same things – not the difficult things, though; not the fears, God forbid.

"I sat there listening to them for a whole year. They didn't mention a word about the hardships I told you about before, and nonetheless, they're people who have participated in a lot of battles, a lot of wars. Not all of them are guys who say they were in the Palmach, and in Etzel, and in Lehi [the 1946–48 underground movements] – so they had to be in all the places . . . to this day, I, when I think back over the years – I mean, I met a few guys from America who were in the Palmach with me. One of them was a porter, another worked in a shoe shop . . . brilliant guys, I mean – something happened to them. After the war they were never the same again. One of them, he's been stuck in America for fifty years already and no one has seen or heard from him, no one . . . and I'm sure that what you are dealing with [he addresses me], is much wider than what someone like myself is willing to tell."

I ask more questions. "During those first years, did anyone ever say to you, 'Listen, something's happened to you,' did anyone manage to sense something of all this?"

"No. None of those guys. You can talk about it in Sweden, but not here. Who can you talk to about it – the young guys? It won't mean anything to them. I have, let's say, if I think about it, ten people I'm close to, and, except for one . . . not one of them really knows the story. Who knows? What it did to me doesn't interest them either. A few months ago some American published a book about depression and it was translated into Hebrew. And this book did something good in Israel, for the first time it legitimized the depression of men. Because when I used to say 'I'm not coming . . . ' 'Why, are you in a bad mood? Got a fever?' Up till six months ago, the people of my generation and a little younger did not accept the word 'depression' unless it related to people who fitted the theoretical profile of psychologists and psychiatrists. But, in my group . . . serious people, I don't know, that word 'depression,' they didn't understand it. There were periods when I would just sit around without moving, something like that. Who could I explain that to? To my wife, or to a couple of younger people, but I couldn't explain it to my friends. And then this book did something very important for us. A person, a man, someone born in this country and so on, can get depressed! It is suffering that – cannot be measured, not by fever and not in a laboratory. I think this whole generation is messed up. I keep my distance today. [Silence.] But, sometimes one feels something, you know."

"Among the doctors then, or people in the medical profession, wasn't there anyone who tried to relate to it?"

"Look, firstly, from '51 I went overseas to get away from myself. Not so much from Israel. And then I was able to be in a different reality. And there, no one knew the difference between catacombs and valleys [in Jerusalem] . . . I painted and did all sorts of things and traveled around. I lived a rather American-style life – in the sense of . . . an America that no longer exists, that of Charlie Parker . . . but there, stories of battles and wars were offensive, and they didn't know that I had been through hard things. There was a psychiatrist, a great one, studied with Freud, and . . . he was a family friend. I was sent to him and he tried to help me, but he always looked for the connection between my stories and what had happened to me in my childhood with my parents. Though this too was problematic. But every time I'd relate to the war in any way – I still didn't remember, but I would relate to fears, nightmares – I didn't know where they came from, I knew something had happened – but I said to him, 'I lost two days during the war.' And he always tried to connect this with things that happened to me when I was three and four . . . so it didn't help me. Later on, when I came back, there wasn't anyone who asked.

"I worked on myself for years, and some of the nightmares have disappeared. I have overcome a lot of the fears I used to have. I was afraid to go out, I was afraid to be with people, afraid of closed places, of elevators . . . I was afraid of sitting in the middle of a row. There wasn't anything I wasn't afraid of . . . no phobia that didn't attach itself to me, almost all of them, I overcame them. I mean, it's still hard for me to be with a lot of people, still hard, I dream at night, I wake up. There were also times in New York when I . . . really broke down emotionally. There was no one there to share it with. I would get to the root of it, of the age of 17, and suddenly, a hell you never got out of. So today it's finished, but that hell was inside me, and I softened it through [association with] Holocaust survivors, but it isn't my story. Nonetheless, I think that shell shock of the kind I went through, in such hard conditions . . . after all, there was no army and no rear. It was – we were besieged. There was no food, no water. So it was something that . . . never, one can't . . . and who knows, how many people there are in this country, and who knows how many mistakes, how many errors, and how many blunders and how many terrible things have happened because they did not know how to relate to emotional things. I don't know, there are people at the head of this state today, people who were soldiers, and they probably haven't resolved their emotional problems from that period or others later on. I don't know how it affects them today, how it affects their decision-making, don't know ... you see it all the time, but you can't put your finger on it, can't place it.

"Maybe it doesn't matter today, but, to sit in some room, for an entire night, with three to four other people: let's share what we went through. How we hid it, how ashamed we were ... because I assume I was ashamed, otherwise how could I have forgotten it like that? If you take a young guy today, put him through shell shock, put him in ... pretend to be dead ... look, I am really alive ... then they'll bring him to hospital – the psychiatrist will talk with him, there will be people he can talk to. Whereas two days afterward, I was already fighting again.

"Now, there was no shell shock in Gahal. They were the bravest combatants, the ones I fought with, and they outdid everyone. One of them was killed next to me, someone who had arrived by boat from Cyprus maybe two weeks before, maybe before they closed the route. What a fighter! But we didn't know how to talk to him, we forgot to ask him for his name, and he died, and when I went to the commander and I told him, 'Do me a favor. There's an unknown partisan here,' and he thought about it, said 'Okay.' And I didn't know who he was, didn't know what ... and ... just a moment, they're all [called] 'weaklings' ... And the only time in my life, the only time – apart from once when I hit some Arab during a battle, when he tried to kill me with a knife – the only time I hit someone was when he called a new immigrant a 'weakling.' It sounded terrible to me, but then when I worked on the boat and I saw them and when they came to Israel ... "

The deconstruction of the monolithic 1948 sabra fighter myth

C.R. was willing to tell about his own case of shell shock in 1948. Through reflecting on that period he was also able to identify others who suffered battle reaction (the soldier who ran from the Kastel), battle exhaustion (the commander who fell asleep), and shell shock (the commander who went with the armored car, ostensibly to bring help, although he knew he couldn't do a thing for his soldiers who were scattered about in the area). He gives us a detailed description of shock and paralysis during battle; the resulting robot-like action; the total, immediate, and ongoing amnesia; the difficult depression accompanying the amnesia; the never-ending nightmares (to this very day); and the memory that overwhelmed him twenty years later. C.R. describes how the encounter with Holocaust survivors on the boat to Israel provided him a sense of perspective for his own distress ("the first and best therapy I had"). He denies the popular notion that it was the Gahal recruits who tended to shell shock. He describes the limited ability of his friends to talk about the difficult things then and now and how this difficulty made brilliant people wretched. His description of the less heroic aspect of the battles, deconstructing the monolithic nature of the myth of the tough fighter, is painful.

Talking to someone who was willing to listen, willing to contain the difficult things he experienced, might have helped a younger C.R. Today C.R. is past sixty-five. He may be willing to reconstruct the horror felt by the seventeen-year-old who experienced these things, but that youngster is already a small part of the whole personality formed in the meantime and of the biography written and rewritten many times during his life. Thus a heavy sense of loss attended the interview, which, to an extent, aided continued suppression of his impressions – if it had hitherto been impossible to release the burden, would it be worthwhile now? I sensed a regret for missed opportunities – for my being late on the scene, as if he was asking, "Where have you been all this time?" Particularly among people like C.R. who have spoken out, yet still feel the loneliness inherent in having suffered shell shock without being able to discuss it, the silencing remains to this very day an incalculable burden. This is particularly difficult in the light of other silences that have since been broken in Israeli society. For example, those shell shocked during recent Israeli wars are better acknowledged and accepted, and greater legitimization is now given to Holocaust survivors to tell their stories, including the less heroic chapters. It is the shell shock of 1948 that is still totally silenced. Is it the last shred of the monolithic construction in Israeli collective identity?

Some Palmach veterans from the war of 1948 still feel that this legitimization has not been granted them, or they feel they are unworthy of it. They are still required to serve as a collective symbol – or, perhaps, they are unable to escape this image of themselves. Even when cases of shell shock are talked about, they are often accompanied by the sharp self-criticism of that time; by lack of forgiveness, lack of acceptance of fear and weakness as human reactions – an echo of the distress of those times, as if this denial is still being enforced. An example of this is the testimony of N.G., another veteran. Having told us about cases of shell shock, in the end he still felt impelled to repeat the initial principle: "Look, serious people didn't get shell shock or anything like it."

In a sense, these people still live with a feeling of siege – on one hand, it is as if someone is still firing at them at close range, and on the other hand, they bear the burden of responsibility for the existence of the entire collective and of themselves as a part of it. Nonetheless, they feel the pain of loss, the absence of tenderness – of acceptance of weakness – that they have so badly needed. In this sense, one can only wonder at the ability of individuals such as C.R. to find a personal, private way – in the face of the collective silence – to discover for themselves what happened and cope with the heavy burden, perhaps in the process overcoming, even if only partially, its negative effects.

It is better at this stage to present their words as spoken, including what is incomplete and rough, or formulated as half sentences and contradictions. There are many ways to interpret such interviews. Among the testimonies collected, responses ranged from absolute denial and the charge that we, the psychologists, invented the phenomenon, to lack of cooperation because we are traitors and denigrators, to the decisive, affirmative statement: Of course there were such phenomena, maybe everybody had shell shock, it was only human that these things happened during and after the 1948 war. This range helped us accept the fact that the same person can go from one extreme of total denial to the opposite extreme of telling us about his ongoing nightmares and how he and his friends are unable to talk about these aspects during their frequent encounters.

I noted the details of the phenomena, from battle exhaustion and stress to suicide, as well as other examples, both before and after battle. It is significant that, as in the case of C.R., when someone opened up and responded to our questions by telling about his own case of battle reaction or that of others, memories returned. The examples were different and varied, but they were all still accompanied by a feeling of guilt or a sense of loneliness and reticence. C.R.'s statement stood out here: When he asked for help, the psychiatrist in New York preferred the familiar, psychoanalytic interpretation

(C.R. had problems with his father) to the possibility of post-traumatic syndrome. Perhaps it was unfamiliar to him at that time (the 1970s). Female combatants (or aides) whom we spoke to did not entertain the possibility of shell shock any more openly than the men in our small sample.

It seems that psychologists such as Witzum and Levy and I have opened up a Pandora's box, and it is by no means clear what still lies concealed there. As a psychologist, perhaps I should have gathered the subjects who were able to tell about themselves in a group setting and helped them develop a voice that would encourage others to discover the long-term effects of the events on themselves and their children. But there are new questions about shell shock now that had not been identified or investigated during the *Intifada* years. And who, at the beginning of the millennium, had time to deal with unrecognized stress from fifty years ago, when our agenda was burdened with new unresolved events; with new questions concerning our future? We have not yet begun to investigate how the silencing and suppression of shell shock in 1948 affected following generations. Could some of those shell shocked in 1973 or 1982 be the children of untreated shell shock victims from 1948 or 1956? Could our present disquiet be affected in a more general way by our inability to contain those events, ingrained in the psyche of those 1948 combatants, as well as many others who were marked by wordless havoc though they were not on the front lines? Could these very factors that aided in the preservation of the monolithic construction in the past (heroism, silence, ignoring feelings and identity conflicts), also have been instrumental in its disintegration from within in our time?

2.3 DECONSTRUCTION OF THE MONOLITHIC MYTH IN THE FIRST *INTIFADA*: SHIMON'S TESTIMONY

If the silence surrounding the battle stress of 1948 had a unifying function (preservation of the collective identity's monolithic construction of heroism, the silence surrounding battle stress during the *Intifada* was inherently different. The political consensus of the first years of statehood had long since been replaced by a deep chasm between the political right and left, particularly with regard to recognizing the "legitimate rights of the Palestinians." If, at the beginning of the 1970s, Golda Meir could still claim that there was no Palestinian nation (meaning that we did not even see them as a legitimate Other), the Camp David agreement (1977), and the 1982 Lebanon war against the Palestine Liberation Organization made it clear that there can be no political solution in our region without taking these rights into account. The alien Arab Other has now become the Palestinian Other. Nonetheless, when the *Intifada* broke out, in December 1987, the Palestinians' determination and persistence surprised the military and political leadership. But the warning signs were there long before. Those who read David Grossman's *The Yellow Wind* (1987) attentively and were aware of the level of despair in the Palestinian street, were not surprised. The conceit of the "enlightened oppressor" was replaced by impromptu policy of "breaking arms and legs" and "preserving public order."

In this atmosphere of growing political and social schism, the army attempted to preserve a monolithic front and remove itself as best it could from the political debate. It avoided characterizing the *Intifada* as a war in favor of terming it "low intensity conflict" – in which there was no reason for battle stress (Bar-On, 1993). Of course, there can be no battle stress if there is no war. Those who claimed such phenomena often took part in the political debate over whether or not the *Intifada* was harmful to Israeli society. It is particularly interesting that the reasoning that denied *Intifada*-induced battle stress was internalized not only by senior officers, but also by psychologists (who cooperated with the system by not diagnosing or treating the phenomena), as well as by regular soldiers. The latter preferred to keep their experiences to themselves and deny any psychological effects of "operations" that required pursuit and capture of stone-throwing children or entering homes in the middle of the night to look for suspects. In situations involving low-intensity violence on the part of the army, without the use of live ammunition, or comprehensive violence on the Palestinian side (Gal, 1990), the definition of the enemy blurred. In fact, in the eyes of certain military officers, the whole population became a potential enemy, as "every child could throw stones, and a wanted terrorist could be standing behind every woman" (Gal, 1990). Though the physical danger to soldiers was less than in known battle situations, the emotional and moral risks became significantly greater when the military had to suppress civilian protests.

Silencing the moral dilemmas and the question of the soldiers' emotional stress allowed the army, and perhaps not only the army, to preserve a monolithic perspective. Yet this was not an entirely sound or systematic solution. According to Spence (1982), there is no hermetic silence: there is always some kind of leak leading to topics that are considered "undiscussable" (Bar-On, 1999). According to his description, this constitutes the paradoxical basis of denial: one is partially aware of what cannot be mentioned, because to deny something, one must know what one can discuss freely without unwittingly penetrating the "denied area."

The question is how the silence surrounding the dilemmas and stress of the *Intifada* also helped to preserve remnants of the monolithic identity construction. The monolithic construction of collective Israeli identity might have been thought to no longer exist by the time of the *Intifada*, given the political and social polarization since 1982. But the very need for the army to preserve a national front in the atmosphere of social and political polarization indicates – as does the silencing of the phenomenon of battle stress – some sort of monolithic concept of identity within the system, at least in relation to the alien Palestinian Other. If, for example, the army became a volunteer force as part of the political and social polarization, then one might assume that when operations were carried out, only those who supported such activity would volunteer (for example, settlers or the national religious right wing). Presumably, either the phenomena of battle stress would then hardly exist (their frequency nonetheless rising in situations of disorientation and perceived threat), or there would be no need to deny them, once the societal consensus that they once threatened ceased to exist. The ongoing silencing of these phenomena bears witness to an indirect need to preserve monolithic remnants of identity construction, despite the difficulty of doing so in an atmosphere of political polarization.

But as we have seen in the discussion of shell shock during the War of Independence, silence does not stop the disintegration of the monolithic construction; it only pushes the process forward in time. Thus the question arises: what has happened to those young men in action during the *Intifada*? Will they, like C.R., tell us fifty years later how they had to suffer for years from phenomena that Israeli society did not wish to recognize, with no help? I will demonstrate, with the help of extracts from an interview, how Shimon coped with the monolithic construction of his Israeli identity, during activity as an army officer in the 1987–93 *Intifada*.[11]

Shimon: "The death of the soul is worse than the death of the body"

Shimon, married and the father of an infant, describes his reactions to a situation in Gaza in 1990 when he and a unit of his soldiers first started serving in the reserves. While on reconnaissance in a refugee camp, they were trapped in an enraged crowd that was returning from the funeral of a Palestinian killed by Israel Defense Forces (IDF) soldiers the day before. Shimon and his soldiers tried to retreat, but they found themselves surrounded, the furious crowd advancing on them from all sides and throwing stones, pieces of iron, and other objects. Shimon placed his soldiers in a circle and radioed for help while firing into the air. It was clear to Shimon that if the crowd continued to advance he would have to shoot into it to save himself and his soldiers. This "pre-massacre" situation continued for about forty minutes until a rescue force of border guards arrived and enabled them to get out with relatively few wounded on both sides.

"We waited a long time," Shimon recounts. "To us it seemed endless. My life wasn't in danger as it was during the Lebanon War, but here my soul was in danger... Everything I believe in. I wanted to scream, and I hated those who had put me in this impossible, crazy situation. I'd already experienced these overwhelming feelings inside, but now I couldn't stop them. The death of the soul is harder for me than the death of the body... I had participated in the Lebanon War and moved through areas of booby traps and land mines. My commander was killed by a booby trap in a car and one of my soldiers and a few others were wounded when they went over a mine... When you understand the necessity of a task, you are prepared to sacrifice, even your life. But when you feel as if someone is moving you about like a pawn on a chess board... then I cried and didn't understand why my parents might have to look at my headstone, another statistic... But the whole situation of Lebanon was easier to bear than the one in the refugee camp.

---

[11] Shimon gave his testimony in 1992 (Bar-On, 1993).

"I tried to imagine what would have happened if I had had to protect myself and my soldiers by firing into the crowd – women, children, and old people... How could I live with this afterward? Maybe I could have excused what happened because I had no other choice, but inside myself I would have known. My mother was born in Egypt and I have heard Arabic from childhood. Arabs are human beings too. I neither hate nor have a need to kill them. How could I have continued to live knowing that I had participated in the massacre of these people? I would have wanted to bring members of the Knesset to that square and let them press the trigger and turn women and little children to paste.

"I was raised to love people and revere life. I am still so young. I have already seen so much death... What right does anyone have to deny me laughter and the pleasure of sunsets over the sea or the love of my child's smile? Isn't there a drop of sanity left in this country? That evening I spoke with a veteran soldier in the unit, an exemplary soldier, who throughout the years always visited the families of fallen soldiers from our unit... He told me he couldn't bear it any longer... from then on he intended to be a 'bastard' and avoid going out on operations... I envied him... I too didn't want to have the blood of a five- or eight-year-old on my hands... I wanted to yell: This war is intolerable, it's tearing me apart! I can't go on like this, but I can't abandon my soldiers in this situation... I feel so helpless... This whole thing is so depressing... I can't discuss it with my wife because I don't have any more words, but for weeks now I haven't stopped thinking about this situation... It would take a thousand loving eyes to even partially close this wound... There are probably some who would say I am cowardly and emotional and a few other expressions of weakness. To those people I want to say that they already neither see nor hear nor feel anything so there is no point in arguing with them. The truth is that strength is the capacity to stand before the truth even when it is almost unbearable. We have already forgotten this, but we don't have much time left... the way we are going we will lose our humanity... and I am not talking about money for dentists or even about a change in the voting method, all right... but I simply want to stay alive and stay human – tell me, is this asking too much?"

Shimon's story is not like C.R.'s difficult description. He focuses on the fear of the "death of his soul" as the result of firing into a crowd (which, in the end, he was spared). One could claim that Shimon did not suffer from battle stress as a result of the *Intifada*, or, at most, suffered from battle stress as a result of the war in Lebanon that manifested itself only in the incident during the *Intifada*. However, he poignantly expresses his searing doubts about being caught between his commitment to his soldiers and his appreciation of Arabs and the sacredness of their lives. Over and above this, there is no one he can talk to about his doubts, not even with his wife, as he doesn't have "any more words." He manages to talk only to the exemplary soldier who has already decided to avoid any military activity in the Occupied Territories. In his own way, Shimon asks, "Is staying alive and staying human asking too much?"

What would a psychologist do for Shimon, were he to turn to one? Help him readjust to military activity? Or help him preserve his humanist identity by refusing to carry out orders that from his point of view are inhuman? This dilemma has undoubtedly paralyzed not a few psychologists during the *Intifada*, at a time when the need to adjust is at odds with the need to preserve what Shimon calls "the human image." We are, in fact, witnessing the disintegration of Shimon's monolithic construction of his Israeli identity, as he claims the principles according to which he had been raised, of humanism and preserving the sacredness of life. Like the veteran soldier whom he admires, Shimon too would like to avoid having the blood of a child on his hands. But he is torn between a sense of responsibility, humanism, and his principles, with no further means of containing all these together in the chaotic reality of the *Intifada*.

In the following chapter (Chapter 3), we will see that – in contrast to Shimon's cry, which reflects severe emotional tension, if not repressed battle stress – Adi represents a combination of a monolithic deconstruction that questions fulfilling his military duties and a neo-monolithic construction that does not allow itself emotional expression like Shimon's and perceives the Palestinian Other as untrustworthy. Adi's narrative is more typical of Israeli-Jewish discourse during the later *Al-Aqsa Intifada*.

PERSONAL WINDOW 4

I was in the middle of writing *Legacy of Silence* when the first Intifada broke out in December 1987. The images conjured up by the interviews with Nazis' descendants and the news reports of Israeli soldiers running after children in the alleys of Gaza and Hebron gave me no peace. With the appearance of the first photographs of what was then called "the breaking of norms" (and bones...), it was impossible to remain silent – though at the time I was chief psychologist of the southern region in the army reserves. Professional norms dictated that my role as consultant to an organization was to help it function better, particularly in a state of emergency. On the other hand, there was also the human norm to consider, and the possibility of crossing "red lines." Like many others then, I asked myself whether statesmen had the right to order soldiers to break arms and legs, as then-Minister of Defense Yitzhak Rabin had. Was this what the name Israel Defense Forces meant? Or was the purpose of this violence to break the spirit of Palestinian civilians in revolt against an endless oppression, so that they would continue to work for Israel and accept their fate with resignation, as they had done for decades? Did statesmen have the right to make soldiers carry out any role they demanded, even when it seemed clear that this would imprint another generation of youngsters (Israelis and Palestinians) with the violent conflict? Would all hope of living together be lost; would such a generation subscribe only to the belief in "living by the sword forever"? A military survey that I carried out, together with Professor Charlie Greenbaum from the Hebrew University, sharpened my sense that from a purely military point of view, breaking the norms of today will create the norms of tomorrow. In this new, nonconventional war situation, the army needed, in a sense, to be saved from itself and the negative long-term effects of forceful suppression of rebellion. Interviewed by journalist Ronit Matalon, we predicted, "The exception will become the norm" (*Haaretz*, February 8, 1988). Regrettably, all our grim forecasts materialized. The IDF today cannot be compared with what it was before the two *Intifadas*, as witnessed in the second Lebanon war in the summer of 2006. It has become a more violent, less truthful army, and it is politically split, threatened by soldiers' refusal to carry out orders and the shirking of duty at both political extremes. Moreover, *Intifada* has penetrated our civilian lives, as seen in increased violence and in patterns of conversation: the need to create an "*Intifada*" to discuss every contentious subject, lest no one listen otherwise. The late Yeshayahu Leibovitz observed after the 1967 war that the conquerors lose their humanity at (at least) the same pace at which the conquered lose property and lives.

2.4 THE LOGIC OF MORAL ARGUMENTATIONS: DESCENDANTS OF NAZI PERPETRATORS IN GERMANY

In this final part of the discussion on the disintegration of the monolithic aspect of collective Israeli identity, I enter even deeper waters: the Nazi component in the definition of the alien Other. If anything still unites the Israeli collective, even at the beginning of the new millennium, it is the total exclusion from humanity of the Nazis who perpetrated the *Shoah* – the extermination of European Jewry during the 1930s and 1940s. Their demonization allows the Israeli collective to define itself in terms of "absolute good" as opposed to "absolute evil" (Hadar, 1991). The evil manifested itself in the murder of women, men, and children, young and old, whose only mistake lay in their being Jews, as defined by Nazi racial laws.

In a personal attempt to move beyond this stark dichotomy, I went to Germany several times during the mid-1980s in the course of my research. There I found and interviewed some ninety of my contemporaries, about half of whom were sons or daughters of Nazi perpetrators (Bar-On, 1989). The fathers of my interviewees were doctors who had participated in the "Euthanasia" program, a man who had killed a Jew in his town on Kristallnacht, *Einsatzgruppen* officers who had carried out killings in the Ukraine, an SS general who had been responsible for the extermination of the Jews in the whole of northern Russia, commanders and perpetrators in extermination and labor camps, Gestapo officers, and Nazi government officials. The parents of the other half of my interviewees also lived in Germany during the war. Some were enthusiastic members of the Nazi Party while others were not. What made them different from Nazi perpetrators was, in my opinion, the fact that while they may have known or heard about the extermination, either directly or indirectly, I could confidently conclude that that they did not actively participate in any part of this process. Thus, I considered them a "control group" for purposes of comparison to the Nazi perpetrators.

One question that interested me was: How did the descendants live and deal with this part of their family biography and what were their characteristic reactions? During the 1980s, the concept of "descendants of Nazi perpetrators" did not yet exist in German society, neither in professional literature nor in the media – literature, newspapers, or television.[12] I was already aware of the concept "intergenerational transference," as it was termed in the literature, with regard to families of Holocaust survivors, and I wondered to what extent there was any kind of transference of trauma among the families from the "other side."

To reach my interviewees, I had to cross quite a few barriers of denial. I remember one instance when I was the guest of a German engineer, in charge of an Israel friendship association in his town. During a casual conversation, I asked him what his father had done during the war. "He also worked on the railroad," he answered, "but he only drove ammunition trains."

I was surprised by the curious addition to the sentence and asked him if he knew where his father was stationed at the time.

"Yes, it was in the region of Bialistok."

"When?"

"Around '43."

"Aha . . . there were a lot of trains going to the death camps then. And how do you know that he only drove ammunition trains?"

"Because he told me so," he answered with great naiveté.

"You're a train driver; tell me how they organized it then. Did some drive ammunition trains while others drove trains taking Jews to their deaths?"

My companion shifted uncomfortably in his seat. "If you like, I could ask him again. I'll be seeing him at the end of this week."

We met again a week later. He came to take me from the hotel to a lecture before a group of Friends of Israel. When I sat down in the car, he at once returned enthusiastically to our previous conversation: "I asked my father again and he reconfirmed that he only drove ammunition trains during the war."

I got angry. "And did he also tell you that he didn't even know about the death trains? Tell me, train drivers used to sit and talk over a tankard of beer in the evenings. Did he never hear anything from anyone?"

---

[12] The concept was discussed for the first time in *Die Zeit* in 1987, by a German journalist, Dorte von-Westerhagen, the daughter of a Nazi perpetrator whom I had interviewed. Her article appeared shortly after the publication in German of Peter Sichrovsky's *Born Guilty* (which appeared in English in 1988).

Again I had made my companion feel uncomfortable. "Generally speaking, he didn't know. Just once someone told him something and made him swear not to tell anyone else."

I despaired of this dialogue and then, just as we were getting out of the car, he suddenly added, "This time, for the first time, he told me that toward the end of the war, he witnessed the execution of a group of Russian prisoners at a station they stopped at. The soldiers took them off the train and shot them there in the station."

I was amazed. "That's a terrible story. Is this the first time he has told you about it?"

My companion nodded slightly. I was rather stunned by the story, but we didn't have an opportunity to continue talking. I noticed that my companion continued to behave completely naturally that entire evening, with no sign of distress, while I was agitated by his father's last story. About a year later I decided to edit some video-recorded interviews. I asked this train driver if he would come to the studio and he willingly agreed. We conducted a lengthy interview concerning his childhood and adolescence, but I noticed that he did not repeat his father's story. Toward the end of the interview, I asked him if there was anything else he would like to tell me. When he did not respond, I asked him if he remembered our last discussion; if he remembered what his father had told him for the first time about his experience toward the end of the war. My partner searched his memory but nothing came up. He had simply forgotten his father's story.

In retrospect, I had to acknowledge the effect of the question my companion had passed on from me to his father. It had caused the father to open up a chink in his wall of silence and pass on to his son a "little" story from the days of the war that apparently still weighed on him. The son had passed his father's story on to me without internalizing it. It is likely that it so threatened the monolithic construction of his identity that he did not open up a chink in his own wall of silence. And, therefore during the interview at the recording studio a year later, it appeared that he had totally "forgotten" the father's story. This incident showed me the enduring power of the walls of silence and denial among many of my interviewees in Germany. To what extent could minimal information about their fathers' participation in the extermination process completely deconstruct their concepts of "ideal self," crumbling the identities they had painstakingly constructed after the war?

I deliberated for a long time over what to do with the interviews I had recorded, written up, and translated into English. At first, I tried a conservative research approach, attempting to characterize the interviewees according to various research variables. Who came from a large city and who from a small village? How many siblings were there in the family? Were they practicing Catholics or secular Protestants? Had the father already died? Was he prosecuted; had he committed suicide or been executed? How and when did the mother appear in the story? Did the son or daughter know about their father's actions during the war? And which of my interviewees' reactions could be attributed to this chapter in their family biography?

With all the defining and quantifying of these variables, the only significant result to emerge was that perpetrators' children were less likely to marry or have children than those in the control group (Bar-On, 1989). None of the other variables yielded any clear findings. I did, however, discover that I had taken this approach to analyzing the stories for my own particular reason: It was my way of maintaining a distance from the material evoked by the interviews. My need to try to preserve the monolithic construction of my own identity was threatened by the complex information they contained.

Having understood my motive, I again listened to and read the interviews. Then I began to analyze them in terms of content. Together with Professor Israel Charny (Bar-On & Charny, 1992), I attempted to find the logic of the moral argumentation used by my interviewees to construct identity despite problems that stemmed from their parents being part of the Nazi regime. Altogether, we defined seven types of moral argumentation, some before analyzing the interviews, on the basis of what we discovered in the literature and newspapers. Others were defined only during an initial analysis of the interviews. We hypothesized that most of the interviews would be structured around one, perhaps two central arguments. We also hypothesized that the analysis of the interviews would reveal concealed argumentation that might be uncomfortable for the interviewee to express openly to a Jewish Israeli interviewer. These were the various approaches:

1. *"The Holocaust did not happen"* or *"The Holocaust was justified."*
   Although, from our point of view, these two arguments are very
   different, they offer a similar exemption from moral deliberation. If
   the Holocaust did not take place or was justified, a son or daughter
   has no moral dilemma concerning the father's participation in the
   Nazi regime. Although we were familiar with both claims from the
   literature and newspapers, not a single interview was found to contain
   one of them, even in a disguised form. It may well be that some of
   the people who made such claims refused to be interviewed by an
   Israeli-Jewish psychologist.

2. *"The Jews brought it upon themselves."* We were familiar with this
   argumentation from the professional literature. A 1978 analysis of
   children's essays during the seventies found that about three hundred
   children groped with the subject of the persecution of Jews in answering the question, "What do you know about Adolf Hitler?" About a
   quarter of them claimed that "the Jews brought it upon themselves"
   and therefore they (the German children) need not be troubled by
   this subject. This argumentation conforms to the hypothesis of the
   "just world" (Lerner, 1974): If someone falls victim to misfortune, he
   is probably responsible for some aspect of what happened. Among
   my interviewees, only four hinted at this. Again, it could be that
   people who accepted these argumentations did not feel comfortable
   exposing them to a Jewish-Israeli interviewer.

3. *"Things like Auschwitz happened before and after World War II."* This
   argument already admits to certain moral doubts: Germans committed crimes against Jews or other ethnic minorities. But the additional
   claim that other nations have borne a similar burden implies an
   attempt to diminish the weight of the onus. In *Legacy of Silence* (Bar-
   On, 1989, Chapter 1), Peter relied on this type of argumentation for
   almost the entire interview. A limited number of other interviewees
   used the same "line of defense."

4. *"We suffered too."* This is not necessarily moral argumentation. Many
   interviews described the suffering of German families during the war:
   hunger, destruction, fear of the bombs, a father who returns from

Russian captivity, and so on and so forth. These were the events
of that time. But when the interview began and ended with this
claim, it too became a moral defense. It was as if the interviewee was
saying to the interviewer, "With the help of the descriptions of my
suffering and that of my family and nation, I am trying to ignore
or at least diminish the meaning of the suffering caused by my own
people to other people, especially your people." Approximately a
sixth of the sample used this type of argumentation in this way, most
of them not descendants of Nazi perpetrators. It seems that moral
argumentation of this kind did not constitute sufficient protection
for identity construction when someone knew that his father actively
participated in the systematic annihilation of other human beings.
It offered a certain refuge for those whose parents lived through
that time but did not actively participate in extermination process
themselves.

5. *"Atrocities were carried out by the Germans. But none of my relatives
were involved in this, or they were forced to do things against their will."*
This argumentation shows significant moral deliberation. Germans
undoubtedly perpetrated the Holocaust against European Jewry and
other minorities. Yet this person tries to distinguish between the phenomenon of evil in Nazi-era German society and his own "good" family. This boundary perhaps protects the monolithic construction of
the interviewee's collective and personal identity. Again, understand-
ably, this argument was more prevalent among children of wartime
whose parents did not take active part in the process of extermination.
However, some of the perpetrators' descendants were also found to
use it.

6. *"Atrocities were carried out by Germans. My father/parents participated in these actions."* In this argument, the "line of evil" comes one
step closer to the interviewees. They accuse their parents, especially
their fathers, charging them with active participation in the process of extermination. But by means of this accusation, they seek to
cleanse themselves of evil. They are ostensibly saying, "If I acknowledge my father's responsibility for atrocities, I am a good person who
is incapable of carrying out similar actions." The moral and mental

health aspects of this argument are at odds: it is good for a person to acknowledge perpetrators' responsibility for their actions, but it is not so good for a person who is past adolescence to continue to see his parents through a mirror that is so "black and white" (Erickson, 1968). Naturally, most interviewees who espoused this argument belonged to the sample of Nazi perpetrators' descendants.

7. *"Atrocities were carried out by the Germans. My father/parents participated in these actions. I am not sure that if I had been in that situation, I would have acted any differently."* This admission eliminates any protective distinction between the interviewee and the evil. Exposed to the criminal acts of the father during the Holocaust, the son or daughter has no defense, escape, or any other means of protection from these acts. Very few perpetrators' descendants were found to employ this moral argumentation, and it was evident that those who did suffered their daily distress over this part of their family biography.

In a second content analysis, I tried to discover different stages of "working through" in the various interviews, looking at how the interviewees located their identity in relation to their fathers being Holocaust perpetrators. I found some five different stages:

1. Psychological processing would begin with the discovery of new facts concerning the Holocaust period and the father's role.

2. When these facts became known, the interviewee had to understand their historical, moral, political, psychological, or religious meaning. This involved creating a "picture" in which the facts could be located as parts of a puzzle, though previously the connections between them were obscure. Without this understanding, it was impossible to make any progress.

3. Understanding the meaning usually led to a strong emotional reaction. This could be a very negative one toward a father whose child felt deceived by his hiding from her his role in the extermination process. Or, it could be very positive, as, for example, in the case of "Gerda" in my book (1989), who stood firmly at the side of her father after she learned the facts and understood their meaning.

4. Following this is the fourth stage of the emotional conflict, a counter-reaction to the first emotional response: For instance, after anger at the father, the daughter would remember her love for him (or his for her). Or, protection of the positive image of the father was followed by anger, as in the case of "Renate" in my book.

5. Very few of my interviewees reached the fifth stage by themselves, able to integrate the complexity of knowledge, meaning, first emotional reaction, and the emotional conflict, whereupon they could say to themselves, "Now I am living my life independently of my father's life." In certain cases, as a result of a descendant being exposed to new facts – for instance, that the father was placed in charge of extermination units only after someone else had refused this role and been released unharmed – the entire cycle began again. An interviewee who went through this process successfully once before might again be able to pass through all the stages, but this can by no means be guaranteed.

Those interviewees who progressed in working through the identity conflicts were helped by their spouses and, occasionally, by successful therapy. Their main source of support was their participation in a self-help group of perpetrators' descendants that began in Germany in 1988, following my research. This group continued to meet regularly until 1992. They then began to meet with a group of Holocaust survivors' descendants from the United States and Israel, called TRT (To Reflect and Trust and they continue to meet once a year to 2007; Bar-On, 2004/2006). I will come back to discuss this group in the postscript.

The shades of moral argumentations and the stages of working-through among the descendants of Nazi perpetrators are not a simple matter for many survivors' children to accept, with their monolithic approach to the German alien Other. Not only were the descendants of the Nazi perpetrators in different stages in the process of working through, employing varied moral argumentations for their fathers'/parents' actions, but some of them could describe the same perpetrator-fathers as warm and loving at home, to both their spouses and their children. The narratives sometimes illuminated the close proximity of good and evil in these perpetrators, and that it was the different situations that activated the one or the other in their psyches.

In light of this data, it was difficult to support the idea of personality or identity as one monolithic construction existing in people no matter what the situation. On the basis of this research data, it appears more likely that identity is fragmented, and the fragments emerge and disappear in various situations. But out of our human need for coherent stories, we try to reconstruct identity from fragments, emphasizing those parts of people that suit us and help us to preserve the monolithic construction of our identity in opposition to the alien and evil Other. From this point of view, disintegration of the monolithic construction is part of a maturing process that clarifies these differences. Monolithic construction has been an artificial way of avoiding acknowledgement of the heterogeneity that exists within the German society and the processes of change that has taken place within the German society over the last few decades.

It seems that the spectrum that exists among descendants of the perpetrators, in terms of their working-through processes and moral argumentations, could help deconstruct the Israeli-Jewish image of them as the continuation of total evil. For many Israeli Jews, even sixty years after the *Shoah*, the Germans still represent that unmitigated evil. The results of this research pose a challenge to that attitude, providing a richer and more complex mosaic of intermediate shades between the black-and-white representation that dominates within Israeli society.

THREE The Present II: The Neo-monolithic Construction

As mentioned in the introduction, at present we see both the disintegration of monolithic identity construction and a backlash in the form of neo-monolithic construction. At the backlash stage, the processes of disintegration and neo-monolithic forces work simultaneously. In the whirlwind this creates, orientation becomes extremely difficult.

In the previous chapter, I showed how the disintegration of monolithic Israeli-Jewish identity creates havoc and fear of the unknown, together with anger at the loss of the ostensibly stable construction – an anger that is projected at whoever is identified as the cause for this (Shavit, 1997). The neo-monolithic identity, to a greater degree than the monolithic one, is manipulated by political leadership, making its construction more of a top-down process rather than a bottom-up one. While a top-down process may have been part of the original monolithic construction as well, there was also a broad-based societal need to create a distinct Israeli-Jewish collective. When today's politicians use frightening events (such as the outburst of the second *Intifada* in October 2000 or the attack on New York's World Trade Center in September 2001) to "unite" people in the "war against terror," they are also trying to interfere with the ongoing disintegration process. But if the cracks are already too deep, the disintegration of the original monolithic construction cannot be stopped. What can, however, be aroused and manipulated within Israeli-Jewish society are old, unresolved traumatic events (foremost among them, of course, the Holocaust). Invoking the threatening, alien Other in the present evokes painful memories from the past.

Managing the difficulties of the monolithic construction's disintegration generally requires a degree of external stability. New outbursts of violence and terror only add to the havoc and chaos of disintegration. This brings polarized political debate over the value of the disintegration process itself. Usually politically conservative groups take a negative view of the monolithic construction's disintegration. The rallying cry: "Everything is falling apart – we must unite!" Others view the disintegration in a positive light: "Finally we know what was repressed all along." The important potential outcome of the disintegration process is obscured: development of a more nuanced perspective about oneself and the Other.

The neo-monolithic backlash suggests, among other things, that disintegration, which some parts of society viewed as functional and progressive, is once again considered regressive and dysfunctional. For example, many members of the Israeli-Jewish political center and left wing that supported the Oslo peace process were "disappointed" by the outbreak of the *Al-Aqsa Intifada* in October 2000 and Palestinian support of it. Prime Minister Sharon's rise to power was the clearest representation of the neo-monolithic backlash in Israel.

The *Al-Aqsa Intifada* reinforced the traditional Israeli-Jewish political right, which already maintained that disintegration of monolithic identity construction was regressive and dangerous. Throughout the Oslo years (1993–2000), the right argued that the external threat had not yet been removed and thus conditions were not safe enough to relinquish the monolithic Zionist self. It was too early, they claimed, to expect that Israeli Jews as a collective could cope with this, particularly at such a critical stage of external threat (by the Palestinians and by the Arabs in general) as well as internal threat (economic dependence and the demands of "absorbing" the Russian emigrants).

The terror attacks of September 11, 2001, created a similar trend in the United States, and the proximity of these two events created an alliance of sorts between the neo-conservatives in both countries, reinforcing the neo-monolithic backlash. The polemical response of the traditional political left, negating any reaction to the terror attacks, suppressed the need for a more complex understanding of the current situation and a more sophisticated response to it (Zizek, 1989).

Debate over the disintegration also divided Israeli-Jewish society before October 2000. However, in the pre-*Intifada* stage, it was only certain extreme elements in the religious-nationalist camp who questioned the need for more mature concepts of collective identity or the need for a transition from monolithic to multicultural collective-identity construction. The debate then focused more on the question of timing: Can we permit ourselves to enter the stage of disintegrating monolithic identity construction? Familiar arguments ("After all, we haven't yet reached a real peace process with our Arab neighbors" and "We are still threatened at home and abroad") were heard then, too. Threats to Israel at home and abroad were invoked. But, as suggested earlier, the *Al-Aqsa Intifada* made the question of timing seem irrelevant. Conditions did not seem ripe for change at all.

I would like to emphasize that even before the violent events and the neo-monolithic backlash – even when the dispute was still mainly about the issue of timing – there was no paradigm change: the softening, complexity, and dialogue that might have been expected to enter the political discourse was rare. Instead, parallel to the monolithic Zionist narrative, an alternative, post-Zionist narrative developed that was no less monolithic. Though it addressed basic issues in the Zionist narrative (such as the plight of the Palestinian refugees in 1948 and the impact of Ashkenazi hegemony), its discourse was also characterized by polemic. Although debate helped accelerate the Zionist monolithic construction's disintegration, the polemic tone of the challengers prevented a real dialogue (Bar-On, 1998). In a paradigmatic change, parallel voices will enter into dialogue and be valued – the traditional Zionist voice included.

Arguably, the strength of the hegemonic Zionist monolithic construction meant that only a polemic voice could pose a serious challenge to it. However, the price of this development should not be underestimated: The pendulum-like movement of the debate between the extremes paradoxically served to reinforce the polemic discourse and thereby helped the revival of the neo-monolithic backlash when external events brought that on.

Social psychology usually characterizes people who are able to "contain" conflicts as being more able to cope with ambiguity. They can contain the contradictions and conflicts among values without trying to deny or dismiss them (Tetlock, 1987). According to Moscovici (1976), one may interpret the monolithic construction of the collective self as a process in which one part of society (the "hegemonic") represents the whole, speaking in its name, while ignoring and suppressing other, different voices. Only when the monolithic construction of the self disintegrates does it becomes clear that the hegemonic part suppressed other parts of the collective self. Disintegration enables other voices in the society to achieve independent expression. At this point, the question of a different hegemony or a more pluralistic cultural society can be addressed. The ability to contain different Zionist views, however, was not usually seen as an essential part of the post-Zionist concept.

Part of the problem may stem from the fact that those voicing the post-Zionist line have come largely from Israeli-Jewish society's Ashkenazi elite. They may subconsciously fear the disintegration of the monolithic construction and the resulting multiculturalism no less than their traditional Zionist colleagues. Ashkenazi Jews dominated early Zionist monolithic construction, and its disintegration could result in an end to Ashkenazi hegemony. A different hegemony may or may not develop instead. Hegemony of the Sephardic Afro-Asian groups would reflect their majority status in the Israel-Jewish population. In contrast, a more pluralistic hegemony (less monolithic) could perhaps contain those contradictions and opposites that exist in the collective Israeli self. Some Israelis Jews on the political left, heirs to Ashkenazi hegemony, interpret moving toward pluralism as "regression" from a trend toward liberalism or Westernization that they believe in – "progress" that would enable the continuation of their hegemony. The multilayered and paradoxical nature of these processes increases the difficulty of a simple evaluation of their social-psychological significance.

Ashkenazi Israeli leftists have not appreciated the possibility that Sephardic Afro-Asian leadership may be better suited to contain the Arab "alien" and to integrate into the Arab Middle East (Shenhav, 2003). The Israeli political left reflects Western cultural norms, and many of its own members as well as Arabs perceive it as colonial and paternalistic. These leftists have not taken into account that the monolithic construction's disintegration could adversely affect their political position by bringing about change in the social-cultural hegemony. Their support of disintegration applies only to the breakdown of certain obsolete, political constructions of past events (Maoz & Buzaglo, 1997).

In contrast, though many labeled the political right "regressive" for clinging to the monolithic construction, some right-wing politicians supported the rise of Sephardic political power, thereby helping to advance the dismantling of traditional Ashkenazi hegemony. Yet paradoxically, the neo-monolithic backlash enabled the reascendance of traditional Ashkenazi hegemony, even within the political right, in an attempt to gain stability through unity against the enemy. Neo-conservatives are usually not interested in relinquishing political power to other groups. Part of the complexity inherent in the disintegration process lies in the concept of "privatization" or individualization as a way to bring about the monolithic collective self's deconstruction. Those who favored deconstruction of the monolithic Zionist ethos initially perceived the internalization of Western values as an adequate answer to an overly strong collectivism that dominated Israeli-Jewish society during earlier periods (Ram, 1993). They associated monolithic disintegration with the disintegration of the collective identity. So they viewed American-style individualism as a goal that could be reached on disintegration of the collective identity altogether. However, even in the United States, it became clear that individualism was a reaction to the collectivism of Communism, which was perceived as obsolete.

A multicultural or multivoiced society is inconceivable without an orientation that combines individualism with family, ethnic, or even additional forms of collectivism (Oyserman, 1993). This has been particularly true in diversified societies such as Israel, which has several ethnic groups, different religions, and cultural traditions emanating from varying influences. Therefore, the worship of individualism could not be seen as a paradigm change either because it challenged monolithic collective constructions rather than seeing the possibility of creating a dialogue between the more positive aspects. A paradigm change will take place only with the manifestation of an Israeli-Jewish collective identity that will "contain" contradictions inherent in this society, without merely changing the direction of the projection by 180 degrees from collectivism to individualism or from Zionism to post-Zionism.

It is not surprising that when violence broke out and fear of the Other compounded the pain and fear aroused by the chaotic nature of the disintegration process itself, the absence of a paradigmatic change in the process paved the way for neo-monolithic constructions. Yet, the neo-monolithic backlash not only did not resolve the chaos, it made it worse, for the earlier monolithic construction continued to disintegrate. What I described as the whirlwind between these two opposing dynamics made orientation quite impossible. On one hand, this accounts for the public wish for strong leadership that would provide at least an illusion of strength, security, and continuity. (The ascendance of former Prime Minister Ariel Sharon's party is a clear Israeli example). On the other hand, with security challenged daily and all the other internal economic and social tensions, even such a figure could not provide the public with a political solution. The frustration has led to unilateral acts of despair, such as the security barrier between Israel and the West Bank and unilateral disengagement plans. These proposals suffered from a similar limitation: They did not resolve the phenomena of the whirlwind. Could such developments lead to some form of paradigmatic change? This remains to be seen. What we know in the meantime is that the neo-monolithic backlash has not resolved the problem it was constructed to solve; it did not create stability and relief. It actually became part of the problem rather than its solution.

The combination of a disintegrating earlier monolithic construction of collective identity and a neo-monolithic backlash is not only seen in Israel. I mentioned before that whirlwinds also characterize the United States, especially since the terror attacks of 9/11. Similar processes can be observed in countries that emerged from the monolithic stage of identity construction upon the fall of the Communist bloc. The Communist monolithic construction was exchanged in some of these countries for an alternative monolithic construction in the form of neo-nationalism, neo-religious hegemony, or some combination of the two. In other countries, the disintegration of the monolithic construction of Communist identity threatened the continuation of a common national existence and resulted in neo-monolithic backlashes or total collapse of the society. In Bosnia, for instance, the Serbs attempted in a bloody war to impose continuation of their dominance over the Muslim and Croatian minorities (Ron, 2002). There the disintegration of the monolithic construction was extreme, with no conditions established previously to secure a dialogue between components of the society, except through the barrel of a gun or cannon. Conservative Middle Eastern countries such as Saudi Arabia, caught in struggle between tradition, their social elites, and extreme Islamist monolithic groups (for example, Al-Qaeda), face their own kind of problems.

Comparing disintegration and neo-monolithic backlashes in the collective identity of other countries illuminates a painful, difficult process that can take on catastrophic and destructive dimensions (as seen in Bosnia or Rwanda). One of the instinctive reactions of the monolithic collective self, threatened by the process of disintegration, is a neo-monolithic backlash that manifests itself as strong religious fundamentalism or extreme nationalism bordering on fascism. Positing an alien, life-threatening Other legitimizes the renewal of the monolithic identity as well as political hegemony in the present. Societies without previous experience in creating a complex identity construction, as well as those that became embroiled in violent reactions of the fundamentalist or nationalistic kind, have difficulty facilitating the gradual transition from monolithic construction through disintegration to the stage of recognition, dialogue, and construction of more complex identity forms; those that contains contradictions that the collective self had hitherto been unable to contain.

This is the particular kind of difficulty that exists in Israeli-Jewish society. It may account for the fact that successful disintegration took place only in regard to the monolithic construction of the Jewish Others identified earlier (the Diaspora Jew and the ethnic Jew). The disintegration, together with the renewed violence, created the backlash, strengthening the monolithic construction of the Other, especially after previous peace agreements with Egypt, Jordan, and the Palestinians made "giving up" the enemy" a real possibility. The backlash also showed that this possibility was perhaps too much for people to endure at that time. This backlash could also account for the fact that although the disintegration of the monolithic construction of the Jewish Others had begun after the 1967 war, Israeli-Jewish society became entangled in messianic myths that took hold on both the political and religious right and still had no place for the Palestinian Other. In summary, the maturing process for Israeli-Jewish identity, in the present economic and social reality, following two thousand years in Diaspora, is far more complex and difficult than mixing cement, plowing, and defending the Zionist settlements in the first stages. How can a meaningful dialogue be created between the various components of the Israeli-Jewish identity? How can that help develop a dialogue with the alien Other? And how can such steps be translated into meaningful social, political, and economic settlements? This is the task that lies before us for the next fifty years at least, if not for many more generations to come, as indicated in the fourth chapter.

I present here two examples of the whirlwind of the monolithic pattern's deconstruction and the neo-monolithic backlash. First, I analyze an interview with another Israeli officer who participated in the 1987–92 *Intifada*. As we will see, Adi (pseudonym) has difficulties orienting himself between the opposing dynamics in which he first finds himself. On one hand, he takes a moral stand, reflecting on the danger that experiences in the *Intifada* will lead to a loss of humanity among Israeli officers and soldiers, with the inherent damage to fighting capacity that ensues. The four stories he tells all concern this problem. At the same time, he hardly mentions the wounding of Arabs. In his view, they are not part of his problem. When it comes to the Other, the brief cracking of his monolithic identity construction is soon reconstructed. In this respect, he reflects a rather broad segment of Israeli society: Even as monolithic constructions around internal Others (the "Diaspora" and "ethnic" Jews) start to crack and disintegrate, there is a renewed tendency to apply neo-monolithic constructions to the Palestinian Other, still perceived as a threat to the physical or psychic independent existence of Israel as a Jewish state.

The chapter also tells about my work at PRIME (Peace Research Institute in the Middle East), which started during the hopeful times of the Oslo peace accords. When we suddenly found ourselves caught in the storming whirlwind of renewed violence, my Palestinian colleagues and I had to decide whether to continue our joint projects.

3.1 ADI: BETWEEN MONOLITHIC AND NEO-MONOLITHIC IDENTITY CONSTRUCTION[1]

Adi, age twenty-seven, was an engineering student at Ben-Gurion University of the Negev in 1994. He did his army training in the prestigious Golani unit. A year and a half after joining the army in 1986, he took an officer's

---

[1] Tally Verner and Sharon Amir interviewed Adi in 1994 (Amir, Yitzhaki-Verner, & Bar-On 1996).

course. He returned to the same company as team officer and as division officer of company recruits and was promoted to the rank of company commander of a course for unit commanders. In his four years of service, mainly in Lebanon and the Occupied Territories (Gaza and the West Bank), he was in the reserve army in Gaza only once.

In a brief opening to the interview, Adi uses laconic and military language – never saying the word "I." Then he sums up his army service and one of his periods in Lebanon (distinguishing between service there and in the Territories):

> This is something I only understood at the end of my regular service . . . when you do these things you don't really appreciate the implications of what you are doing. It isn't until someone in your company is wounded or killed that you understand you are playing with very dangerous stuff. You do things as if they were a game and you go out on ambush or out to open up a line – people get hurt in these things. This is something I only understood at the end of my regular service, and, after I was demobilized; I said: Wow, people die in these things and we played . . . somehow – maybe it's an advantage and maybe it's a disadvantage – but when you are engaged in something you are aware of the danger, but you cannot imagine the implications.

When Adi begins to talk about the *Intifada*, his manner of speaking changes ("What was it like? Cool, no big deal.") He laughs, but then continues seriously:

> When you're in Lebanon, you know damn well what you're doing, and why and how . . . I mean, there are different kinds of service in Lebanon. But in the *Intifada* . . . It's terrible, terrible, terrible. There's a lot of violence. Violence with stones and Molotov cocktails . . . a demonstration some place and you're a small force facing crowds, and there's not much you can do because you aren't going to shoot people, and you have to disperse a demonstration, and it gets physical when scores of women shake and scratch at you and you have to keep them away. It's very dirty work, a lot of times when you think – I wouldn't get into this situation, I wouldn't be in this place – and you do unpleasant things, like breaking up a demonstration, like . . . you try and catch stone-throwers. They throw a stone at us – a brick was thrown at one of the soldiers; it's quite dangerous – so we start chasing the guy. I was already an officer then, an officer. So we caught the guy, near

his parents' home, and all the women come out – they live in extended families – the mother, the sister, and the aunt and the sister-in-law, and they grab you. They come to me as the officer, grabbing and shaking. Now, on one hand, you have a purpose and you want to arrest the guy and, on the other hand, they're jostling around you, so you push the mother. To them that's an insult. It all gets out of hand and sometimes something small becomes a big incident. It's no fun at all running after little kids. They often know the area better than we do, all the alleyways and so on. So at some point you stop running after stone-throwers because it's a waste of time. You can't stop this phenomenon, and . . . I've lost my train of thought . . . it's no fun because those places smell, you have to go inside, inside the houses. It's hard work because there's a lot to do, reconnaissance during the day and arrests at night, and it's winter and raining and there's a lot of work, and on the other hand, even though it's a mess, you're trying to educate soldiers. After all, being an officer means educating younger soldiers, trying give them values, so you don't lose control. I don't believe in losing control, but you teach them values on the base. And when we get into the street, it's different. There you meet the reality and you don't always behave the way you expect to.

In this extract, there are swift transitions from "you" to "we"; between three levels of language – from military *Intifada* language to a description of specific incidents, to a more personal tone. In contrast to the monolithic self of the previous extract, here it is hard for Adi to define himself within the unpleasant situation in Lebanon, a situation that from a military point of view is less clear. What seems particularly hard for him is the jostling, the blurred physical boundaries: "They come to me as the officer, grabbing and shaking." This kind of description is confused and uncommitted, personal, and repeated in other interviews with soldiers who served during the *Intifada*. It seems that they have developed general codes around these situations, one that is comprehensible mainly to soldiers who were there, but it is difficult for them to use a more personal language that includes a defined "self." Perhaps in the military confusion of the *Intifada*, and the accompanying confusion of values, there was no possibility of examining who this self was. Perhaps this was the stage when the monolithic construction of the self disintegrated.

Adi uses several specific descriptions that indicate his feeling helpless in the face of violence – a war against women and children. He also describes his own internal conflicts. Among the descriptions there is a slightly more personal description of the "period when I was already an officer," an attempt of sorts to begin a story, but Adi is not yet ready for this exposure and retreats to an ordinary, general description of "chasing small children."

Adi proceeds to tell the first of only four stories during the entire interview.[2]

> For instance, we were on reconnaissance in Nablus once, and I had a new sergeant, a rather disturbed character; he wasn't with me very long, but in this instance we were chasing someone – it was in the casbah in Nablus – and he ran into a house. We went inside the house and this guy broke the door in with his head, sent it flying. The guys were fresh out of basic training and still very naive . . . they stood there, their mouths open, in shock. The sergeant was still going a bit wild inside the house, so I told him to "get out of there" . . . Really, these young guys arrive, high school kids, very naive, they don't know what it's about, and when they come up against this sort of violent action, it's disturbing.

Here, Adi takes a personal moral stand ("I told him to get out of there"). He is distressed by the negative behavior of the sergeant (distinguished from the others as a "rather disturbed character") when he views the situation through the eyes of the naive young soldiers. What emerges here is that Adi believes that the education and image of the young Israeli soldier should fit the monolithic Israeli identity construction as it existed before the *Intifada*. He is less interested in the fate of the Palestinians and the results of the violence perpetrated against them. This is expressed in such common truisms as "it's unacceptable" and "one shouldn't behave like that." Adi also tries to conform to military norms. This is borne out in other words of his:

> So we claim that our advantage, as opposed to other armies, lies in the human material, so this is where we can find it – in our attitudes to each other and how the commander talks to a soldier; how I talk to a citizen.

---

[2] A number of characteristics distinguish the story from a description or an argument. It has a chronological beginning, middle, and end; it deals with a specific situation, the tension rising and developing toward a climax; and the narrator expresses more personal feelings (Rosenthal, 1998).

Not this incident, no, but I think that serving during the *Intifada* has changed my opinions. When I was in high school, my opinions were rather right-wing, and after serving in the army, everything I went through in the *Intifada* – not that I started liking Palestinians, not at all, but I became more moderate. I became more moderate because you can see that their living conditions are harsh and, all in all, they are under our rule and are our responsibility. So it's not that we have to do everything, but they live in very harsh conditions, many in one room and without sewage, and the sewage flows in the streets. It's not pity, but coming to terms with the fact that it cannot go on like this and under these conditions. Other children will throw stones, grow up to be terrorists, and this process won't end if we don't do something. So I've become more moderate in this direction; I can't say it is because of any particular incident, but all in all, serving during the *Intifada* has made me more moderate in this direction.

Adi maintains that his perception of the Arabs has not changed because his army service, but serving during the *Intifada* has made him reach clusions regarding desirable Israeli behavior and this is because of the plications of the *Intifada* for Israelis, for the army, and for the nation. His cern is the possible harm to us and not particularly the harm done to Palestinians. "It's not pity, but coming to terms . . . other children will throw stones." His worldview as an officer is that whoever is under Israeli ority deserves elementary concern and that Palestinians living under li rule in poor conditions harms Israel-Jewish society.

rving there doesn't do the army any good, because in principle the army humane, as much as it can be, and there are no orders to abuse the population . . . but every now and again there are always those "hotshots" who go wild. The longer we are there, the more this phenomenon will read because there are a thousand and one incidents of abuse by soldiers officers who have repressed things that they are now letting out. I'm not re that they don't behave violently at home . . . it's asking for trouble.

this impersonal argument, Adi reiterates his concern for a humane . His yearning for the monolithic Israeli-Jewish identity construction is His attitude to "hotshots" reveals a contradiction in which he locates lf – on one hand, the army is an ethical one; on the other hand, Adi ness to abuse. His intuitive explanation is that "a few hotshots" cause

Adi believes in the principle of Israeli superiority ar
that threaten this. He moves on to the second story, v
encounter with a Jewish settler nearby the Palestinian t(

> For instance, we were on reconnaissance in Kalkilya, and
> pass through Kalkilya because it is close to the center [of I:
> through with Israeli flags on their cars as a provocation, ;
> from one of the Border Police commanders in the area t(
> tell them to remove the flags. So we stopped a car, in the 1
> and we asked him to remove the flag, so the guy goes w
> officer, you're behaving like a Nazi, why are you gettin
> getting the Arabs?" And he started yelling and cursin;
> confrontation; you have to be polite, you aren't about
> something like that, so it was a difficult encounter.

In contrast to the first story, Adi here transfers from
"you" when his response is required in the light of the
attack. Adi doesn't tell us his response, only what it
his restraint, the words "so there's a confrontation . . . :
ently express personal conflict over how to manage to
manner. Further on, Adi describes his feeling durir
returns to the use of first person. He expresses his 1
and anger:

> I felt bad, I felt like shit. There I am, breaking my back,
> has to do, guarding him, and him – not even minim;
> him to cooperate with me, he doesn't cooperate. The
> says I'm betraying the country and things like that.
> something I remember clearly, it's an incident that
> feel – why am I doing it? My parents are in Beer-Shev
> Sheva, I don't live in any of those settlements, all I'm (
> people, and that's how they respond. So it's a bad fe

Adi was insulted by what he took as the settler
(the epithet "Nazi"). It seems that Adi is still seek
does not exist in the field; a monolithic middle p(
relate to all sides in the controversy humanely an
Similarly, in his response to the next question, "I
for you – opinions, feelings?"

this, but this does not explain the increase in abuse. Therefore, Adi seeks a solution by accusing the situation of being an invitation to trouble.

"Do you have any examples?"

> There are many examples. We'd arrest guys in Gaza and they were locked up in tin huts until the Civil Authority or the police came to get them. At that time there was a guy there who would go in and just beat them for nothing; he wasn't supposed to do it. He would beat them with a stick on the palms of their hands, and you don't do this. You just don't do this . . . and they'd come out with swollen, black hands. Or I saw Border Police – I don't know if they were interrogating a group they'd caught, or asking questions – they lifted up the hood of an engine, the guy would put his hand there, and they'd slam it down on his hand, they'd break his hands. Then there are those rubber bullets they put in rifles; they're very dangerous at close range because they fly out powerfully. I saw guys firing into someone's stomach from a range of a few meters away. That's a serious wound to the stomach; it's a crime, after all; once they do this they're criminals, but they aren't guys who, before the *Intifada*, I'd have said were potential criminals. Absolutely normal people, that maybe the situation and everything going on.

Here Adi tells us about some of the harder things he witnessed during the *Intifada*. He judges the acts by defining them as criminal. Under normal circumstances, a criminal is punished for his crimes, but Adi's reference to the actions is external to the situation, and in this way, it indirectly absolves soldiers of their guilt: It isn't them, it is the situation. Similarly, he absolves himself of his responsibility as a commander to prevent soldiers from committing such acts. Indeed, here too he resolves his own cognitive dissonance: I belong to a humane army; the soldiers are ordinary people who became criminals. The conclusion: The situation is to blame. There is no reflection on Adi's part about who is responsible for the situation. Through the description, Adi gets to the third story, describing how he twice got carried away:

> I myself got into situations – I don't know if it's loss of control, but I didn't act according to my beliefs. We had returned from some incident in the center (of Israel) and were driving back by bus to the Territories. There is a directive not to sleep in the Territories because, if something happens, a guy who is sleeping doesn't respond well, so you make sure that they stay awake. You make sure that they're not sleeping. It was evening, it was already dark,

and the guys were always sleeping. Soldiers sleep on the bus; you can't do anything about it. So you get them on their feet and all kinds of nonsense to keep them awake; we were two buses, and they [Palestinians] threw a Molotov cocktail. It passed through and exploded between the buses and caught fire on the road. So we stopped and the commanders got off and there was a point when we didn't see who threw it, but we saw from which direction it came and soldiers got off, soldiers – I was one of them – we got off the bus and we got our weapons ready and we shot in the direction of the thicket there. Luckily, we didn't hit anybody because if we had hit someone it wouldn't have ended well, because you don't shoot without identifying an enemy. The instruction is to perform the arrest procedure for a suspect – unless you see him in the act of throwing, when he is endangering your life. But life-threatening danger had already passed, so we were not supposed to shoot, we were supposed to search, to search thoroughly and arrest, but not kill. That's one thing, and the other thing was, when we got back to the bus, it was, of all of them, a great guy, my best soldier, so I put him up against the bus and I shouted at him, "Do you understand now why you don't sleep, do you understand?" Now we are speaking quietly, but then it was with yelling and I didn't exactly put him up against the bus gently. So that's one time when I felt – here I lost control of myself a bit, and it's not right, but, perhaps, under the circumstances, it was appropriate. But the first part where we got off and shot, you don't do that, no matter how upset you are – you don't do that, not only according to our norms here, but according to the norms of the army . . . all in all, these are things that stay with you. I don't remember another incident like that, that you regret afterward.

Adi takes responsibility and includes himself in the events: "people – I was one of them." He has a capacity for critical observation of his failures as an officer in the field, and he examines the events on the basis of con-temporary principles and perhaps even those of the period in which the events took place. In this sense, he is an example of an officer who "works on" the monolithic construction of his identity and does not flinch from the implications thereof. Yet it is the background of his concern for the army and his soldiers and his severe self-criticism as an officer that makes his indifference to the Palestinians stand out. In this regard, one questions whether these were his only failures as an officer, or whether these were the failures he "permitted" himself to remember, forgetting the others (a phenomenon discussed in "The Hypothesis of Paradoxical Morality;" Bar-On & Charny, 1992).

In the next sequence (in response to our question), Adi for the first time expresses his view of the Palestinians as part of what shapes the way in which he understands his world: the "victim-perpetrator" dichotomy. "I thought that they hate us, that they don't want us," he says, "and I still don't think that they are crazy about us." He defines his perception in the past, and he emphasizes that it did not change even in the light of present-day reality. When asked whether they are different, he answers by saying that *we as Jews are different from everybody else* and he compares this "us" to all of the Arabs; the Palestinians are similar to them and different from us. In this way, he establishes Jews as exceptional, and he avoids making a direct or equal comparison between Palestinians and Israeli Jews. Continuing from this juxtaposition of "us" as opposed to "them," he goes into some detail, giving three short examples:

> They tell you to arrest a person, so you do the job although you see their life is down the drain. So perhaps it clashes with smaller things. They tell you to impose a curfew and a couple is walking along the street and the woman is pregnant and she tells you: I need to go to the hospital. So here, perhaps, it clashes and you need to use your judgment as commander about what works and what doesn't work, so here it clashes.

"How would you resolve such a case?"

> Ah . . . I often think that I would send them back home because it has to be clear to them that the army doesn't relent or retreat. Maybe because this is our only advantage over them, because they know that we are organized and that when the army imposes something it is carried out. I once had an instance like that when I sent the couple back home and there was another instance when some old man was going by and he didn't feel well and I let him pass. So maybe it really depends on the mood. Listen – if someone really has doubts, there is no problem about referring to a higher level so that they can resolve it but, in principle, if it's an extreme case you don't need to give in, you need to stick to the primary task because that's where our strength [lies] in the situation of the *Intifada*. It has to be clear to them that there is unity here and that it is impossible to do a sloppy job.

It is difficult for Adi to suddenly deal with the day-to-day dilemmas of a military occupation of civilians. When he is asked a specific question, he answers in the present tense, and he reverts to army language, though his army service during the *Intifada* is over. Perhaps this helps him deal with the dilemma. Adi is systematic and strict about putting conflicting feelings and emotions aside in order to perform his job well. He states that the clash appears in smaller, humane issues about which he needs to use his judgment as a commander. Orders give him cover and aid him in distancing himself emotionally from the situation. When he has no specific order, he must become involved and this is difficult for him, even though he terms the situations "smaller issues."

In the case of the couple on their way to the hospital, he needs to exercise judgment to decide whether to let the pregnant woman pass. He retreats to the central motto that constantly directs him: the superiority of the army. This time, however, organization appears instead of morality. He raises the argumentation to justify the act that perhaps, deep within himself, he is not altogether at peace with: *"the army doesn't relent . . . when the army imposes something, it is carried out."* In the third instance, he lets the old man pass despite the curfew, and he feels that he must find an explanation for the fact that this is not in keeping with the army policy that had previously directed him. He uses his mood as an excuse, and perhaps he also feels the need for an example of when he behaved in a more "humane" manner, tempering the severity of the previous example. Adi closes the sequence by returning to the argumentation that almost sounds as if he has been brainwashed: sticking to the task, the force of the situation, the uniform policy, the impossibility of doing a sloppy job. This may indicate that he feels the need to return to a safe shore of law and order, an attempt to hold on to the military way of understanding the world that protects him from insoluble human dilemmas.

Quite unexpectedly, a kind of "confession" or reflection appears that breaks the sequence of the "responsible" commander's argumentation. Adi asks rhetorically, do we succeed in showing that there is a uniform policy?

In principle, I think so. But it still doesn't solve the problem. There was a stage, after a certain period, when I stopped believing in things I do as commander, as a soldier, because I felt that the army doesn't intend to resolve these things either. I felt bad about the things I was doing. I said – I want to finish my army service quietly. I don't want these problems – let's say, just any situation of rioting, or arrest of a suspect – and I might shoot and someone would be killed or wounded, and then there'd be investigation committees and trials. I don't want all of these things. So perhaps I shirked my responsibility here . . . because at some point you understand that you can run after kids who throw [stones] for a million years and in isolated cases even catch a kid who throws a stone, but he usually knows the place and you can't compete with him. And in these tasks – we'll call them police tasks – well, perhaps I was sloppy, because . . . I didn't see the point; I didn't want to get into too much trouble. I don't know how many people this happened to. Personally, that's what I felt. That was only in the later stages, after enough time in the place, that's how I felt.

Adi's understanding of his role as commander, which colored his service (and the interview up to this point), changes toward the end of his service to a more detached viewpoint. He stops believing in things that he does as commander because "the army doesn't intend to resolve these things either." This is Adi's *only attempt* to move out of monolithic interpretation based on his motto of responsibility as a commander. The language he uses is in the first person, very open, a small confession that does not appear by chance. Perhaps it is an exception that proves the rule, or perhaps it is a first sign of the ambivalence that characterizes disintegration of the monolithic construction. Perhaps a conceptual crisis occurred earlier and emerges retrospectively as a confession.

In the next sequence of the interview, Adi is asked how he perceives the Palestinians as people. He shifts from relating impersonally to specific mention of a child who saw him as a soldier and thus as a threat. Instead of answering the question, Adi's reply reflects how *they perceive us*. Perhaps it is an argumentation that can explain his absence of his feeling – it is impossible to love people who feel such a deep-rooted hatred toward you (the Hebrew root of the word "hate" reappears six times). In his opinion, peace can lessen the burden, but it is threatening in that it lets "them" progress. Adi, it seems, is frightened of such a possibility.

Adi's conflicting feeling almost develops into a story, but ultimately he pulls away from it by using impersonal language: "I remember times when

you go in . . . to houses at night . . . and a little child looks at you and begins
crying, terrified." Here he details a certain instance of fear from the viewpoint of the little boy who sees him only as a threat – something that shocks
him and leaves him with unpleasant feelings "because I know who I am,
but to him I am just some soldier who is walking around with a weapon."
Adi cannot bridge the distance between his self-perception as a humane
and moral commander and the child's perception. This is a sensitive point
for him. The innocent Arab child who looked at him with terror during a
night search is the only one who momentarily touches Adi – a moment of
softness, a short hesitation. However, quite quickly the role of commander
overcomes this personal contact that might have demanded a much more
stringent internal confrontation.

Adi is asked about the future:

> I wish I knew. In my opinion, the acts of terrorism will continue and the
> army will only have a harder time dealing (with them). Because when you
> are in the area, you can take care of things, and when you have no right
> to act within their areas, it will be very hard for the army to deal with it.
> And we will be dependent on their security forces, who won't necessarily
> meet us halfway. That is to say, perhaps they will have an interest in meeting
> us halfway and . . . I think that there is a need to do something, but I am
> very much afraid that perhaps we're going too far without security. If the
> business [of withdrawal] fails, or explodes, we will be in serious trouble
> because the territory is no longer under military control. The security
> forces will have a big problem taking action. I mean, if the whole thing
> blows up, and terrorist attacks start happening all the time, and (terrorist)
> squads infiltrate the country and kill and murder, I am quite sure that this
> phenomenon of extremist factions will only continue. That is to say, on
> one hand I don't really hope so, but I am also afraid because even if the
> politicians don't explain to the public exactly what is settled and how it
> is settled, a lot is not known and this not knowing is usually frightening.
> That's what I think will be: Hope with fear.

Here Adi moves into neo-monolithic backlash. After the two more personal previous sequences that showed some softening, the new sequence
suggests that Adi cannot manage his feelings toward the Other. His vision
of the future is pessimistic. One might assume (based on the slight "mod-
eration" in Adi's opinions and the apprehension about the effects of army

service) that he would regard the withdrawal of Israel's army from the Occupied Territories as positive. Yet, he is troubled by the possibility of losing control to the Palestinians because he does not trust them. He feels that he needs many security measures (for the country, for the nation, for the citizens). Even though he defines this as "hope with fear," it seems that there is more fright than hope in his words. Adi this time expresses his pessimism in terms of ongoing fear of the Palestinians. Interestingly, peace may create a certain threat to our own identity as a distinct collective:

> I know that I am personally not interested in coexistence. I want to live my life here. I don't want to go buy something in Gaza or have him come here to buy from me. I have no problem continuing this way, he in his corner, with his work. If it is possible for the workers from the Territories to stop working in Israel, then they shouldn't come to work here. They should have enough jobs there. In my opinion, the less interaction with them, the better. Personally, that's what I think. I have no desire for anyone from Gaza to open up a grocery store. I have no problem with it continuing the way it is today. I would prefer not to rub shoulders with them because . . . again, it's a matter of building up trust; there is always the chance that someone with whom you are in daily contact will stab you. And it's a matter of building up trust that will take a lot more time before these gaps are bridged . . . I have no desire to live in coexistence. From my point of view, they should live their lives in Gaza, in what they are allotted in Judah and Samaria. They should enter Israel as little as possible.

"Is it only a matter of a lack of trust, which can be solved one day?"

> I don't know. I am not interested in some rich Palestinian buying a villa nearby. If we go to great extremes, let's go as far as is possible, with mixed marriages between Jews and Palestinians, and Palestinian people living here, so the borders become blurred and, if we go further, in many more years, in the best way possible, we will lose our identity as a people and . . . I don't know if that's good, I mean, maybe, maybe not.

How capable Adi was, in March 1994, of prophesying the path of the following decade. Here, in effect, it is possible to identify early signs of the idea of dissociation and separation, which later, because of continued terrorist suicide attacks, became a motto in Israeli discourse. However, Adi adds a new argument that has not yet appeared in our manifest collective discourse: the explicit fear of losing a distinct Jewish identity as a result of assimilation into the Arab culture. "Maybe it's good" is said more by way of rhetoric. Adi is afraid that nothing unifying will remain once "they" cease being the "enemy." Later on, Adi spells out his prejudices against the Palestinians, explaining that he sees no difference between Israeli Arabs and Arabs from the Territories. Thus, in a way, he clarifies his uneasiness at having to live in the Middle East and his sense of cultural superiority.

> The mentality is different, even the smell is different. When you stand in the home of a Palestinian family – it stinks – there's nothing you can do about it. The house stinks and me, I come from Israeli society, I had a hard time with the smell of their food . . . when the woman there cleans, she empties the bucket outside her door, into the street, and we don't act that way – you spoke about the Belgians; well, our mentality is closer to the European mentality than to theirs as Arab people – I don't know.

"Aren't we both Semitic people?"

> That's true. But I think that our mentality is closer to the European mentality than to the Arab people. It doesn't matter where it comes from – the mentality is different. And to change a mentality – it's not as if I could now put them into some fancy neighborhood and they would immediately act differently. It would take a good number of years, I don't know, scores of years in order for things to change.

"Is this connected only to external factors or also to internal ones?"

> It's connected, it's connected to how people dress, for no reason, an attitude toward women. Ah, a woman, like in every Muslim culture, who doesn't have much significance and she is silent beside the men, and all kinds of . . . I don't see myself being quiet around men like that . . . it's different. And dress, that's the way it is, it's dress. And what else? Well that's it . . . maybe it's a result of conditions where everybody sleeps together, where they grow up as extended families and when a couple marries, they build another room and they live together. Their religion is also different and that has an effect; that is, a lot of their mentality is a result of their religion. The Islamic religion is a lot stricter than our religion. Let's imagine them moving into the best living conditions there are, until the mentality changes – in my opinion, it would take an entire generation for it to pass. Perhaps in the generation after us it will be a lot easier to agree to cooperative living or things like

that, but I am not so hot about living cooperatively with them. That is to say, for me, to live separately is good enough. What's so bad now, what do I need to run after? Things are good enough as they are. That is, I don't think that anyone would like – that is, if we go to extremes – a son or daughter to marry a Muslim, a Palestinian. I believe that most people, even the most left-wing, wouldn't like that.

The language in which Adi summarizes his thoughts is theoretical, impersonal. Throughout the entire sequence, he presents a neo-monolithic construction of cultural superiority, emphasizing the differences between "them" and "us." He begins from external signs – smell, cleanliness, dress – moving on to more ambiguous internal values – the attitude toward women, the way of life – and he finds the root of their "mentality" hidden in their "stricter" religion. Adi's entire description is clouded by value judgments without any self-criticism or moral restrictions. He assumes that to be able to live together (and he emphasizes that he has no desire to do so), "they" need to change and "grow," to reach "our" cultural level. Once again Adi imagines a threatening loss of identity through intermarriage, which he believes even the "leftists" would not like. The gaps may be closed within one generation, but still, *"I wouldn't want to live with them."*

This chapter brings us to the present stage of the stress characterizing the whirlwind: disintegration of the monolithic construction on one hand and neo-monolithic backlash on the other hand (Bar-On, 2004/2006). The words of Adi, like those of Shimon in the previous chapter, indicate a complexity of conflicting emotions and deliberations on a micro level – that of the individual commander – which is representative of some of the dilemmas on the macro level. One can sense the heavy burden of the Israeli officer serving during the *Intifada*. Not every soldier was as open, courageous, and conscious of moral dilemma as Shimon and Adi, but their viewpoint reveals something of the distress they felt at the time of their army service and following it. The honesty and force of their words makes the silence and stammering of political leaders or professionals even more salient (Bar-On, 2001). When did we last hear an Israeli leader discussing the dilemmas raised by Adi and Shimon with courage and clarity? This might be the reason for Shimon's alienation and Adi's attempt to find a source of blame for the situations that he and his soldiers faced. We do not know when there will be a thorough public debate over these questions, but I imagine that when it happens, it will be also a debate concerning the monolithic and neo-monolithic constructions of Israeli-Jewish identity, and it will not be by chance that the process will involve a challenge to the military aspect of these identity constructions.

PERSONAL WINDOW 5

During the first weeks of the *Al-Aqsa Intifada*, in October 2000, I felt quite paralyzed. I could not believe that all that had been invested in the peace process in the last few years was going down the drain. I tried to behave as if this was only a temporary aberration. I continued to go to Talitha Kumi school near the town of Beit Jala to meet with Professor Sami Adwan, as I had been doing since 1998 when he and I started PRIME (Peace Research Institute in the Middle East). I felt committed to the course upon which we had embarked and, as he could not come to meet me in Israel, I went to see him at our office even though it was sometimes dangerous because of the shootings. We tried to focus on our study at that time: an attempt to characterize and evaluate Israeli and Palestinian environmental NGOs. It soon became impossible to focus on this. When people are being killed, the problems of sewage and waste and even water shortage seem unimportant. The assumption when we designed our study was that we were in the midst of a forward-moving peace process. But now the context had gone backward. The violent outbreak was destroying such assumptions and precious hope, in addition to the destruction of lives.

As an Israeli Jew, I had to recognize our own inability to let go our monolithic construction. I felt that Israel was to blame for allowing Ariel Sharon to make his provocative, power-oriented visit to the *Al-Aqsa* Mosque in September 2000. I also thought that President Clinton and Prime Minister Barak were unwise in their handling of the Camp David encounter with Chairman Arafat, which led to its failure in July 2000. I felt that many of the Palestinians' complaints about the ongoing Israeli occupation and settlement-building in the Occupied Territories were justified. But I also could understand the fear of the Israeli Jews, attacked by suicide bombers and witnessing the depth of Palestinian hatred. I admired Sami for his persistence and willingness to continue our work and identified with his pain when there was gunfire around his house, while I could live more or less safely in mine.

The number of Palestinians killed every day was devastating. It became clear that Israel was using excessive force to suppress the Palestinian uprising. At the same time, I was afraid that the violent struggle might make things worse. At some point, the same issues that had been on the negotiation table in 2000 would have to be addressed – but more people were going to join the cycle of hatred as a result of the current events.

Alongside the technical difficulties of continuing our joint projects, a deeper understanding slowly emerged, especially after the Israeli elections in February 2001. I had to admit that neither side was ripe for a political solution and much working-through will have to take place to establish such a ripeness. I still felt that our mutual commitment to PRIME was an important anchor in such a process. But the possibility of a political solution became much more distant than it had seemed a few months before.

3.2 WHY DID THE *AL-AQSA INTIFADA* BACKLASH OVERTAKE THE GAINS OF THE OSLO ACCORD?

The outbreak of violence between Palestinians and Israelis in October 2000 has many different and complex causes. In a way, it signaled the end of the Oslo process. The 1993 Oslo Accord was a top-down process that created an illusion of mutual ripeness for a historical compromise between the Palestine Liberation Organization, as the legitimate representative of the Palestinian people, and Israel. The two nations seemed to be ready to let go their ethnocentric and monolithic dreams and to share the land between the sea and the Jordan River in two separate states: one Jewish and one Palestinian. Politicians on the two sides were not yet ready in 1993 to agree on the difficult issues, such as political rights for both sides in Jerusalem, the fate of Israeli settlements in the West Bank and Gaza, and the right of Palestinians to return to areas within the boundaries of the State of Israel. Still, the assumption behind the Oslo Accord was that in the subsequent years the process would yield enough mutual gains and trust that both sides would eventually be able to reach an agreement on these more difficult issues.

In reality, the level of mutual mistrust has become even higher. The murder of Prime Minister Rabin, the vicious Palestinian terror attacks, and continuous Israeli building in the settlements showed how deep and extensive was the drive to prevent a solution, rather than enhance it. The extremists on both sides actually reinforced each other instead of the more moderate parts of the society reinforcing one another, as the architects of Oslo assumed would happen. Palestinian leaders, pressed to promise the Israelis a sense of personal security, lost credibility in the eyes of their own public. At the same time, the Israeli leadership was too weak to struggle with right-wing extremism, especially that of settlers in the West Bank and Gaza. From my perspective, neither side was ripe for the dialogical stage of collective identity construction. Readiness for the complexity of this stage would be a necessary condition for making the pragmatic political concessions required on both sides.

In some respects, the Jewish-Israeli population made remarkable progress following 1993. If in 1993 one could not talk openly in Israel about the possibility of a Palestinian state, by 2001 it was Sharon himself, the right-wing leader, who accepted such a possibility. If the vision of an "eternal," "united" Jewish-Israeli Jerusalem was long a cornerstone for all leaders on both sides of the Israeli political map, in 2000, Barak made it quite clear that Jerusalem will in the end serve as the capital of the Palestinian state as well. Even though public opinion swept overwhelmingly to the right after the violent outbreak of October 2000, the majority of the Jewish population still wanted the negotiations with the Palestinians to continue until a settlement could be reached. In 2003–4, Prime Minister Sharon proposed the unilateral removal of settlements from the Gaza Strip and carried it out in the summer of 2005.

But the limits of the Israeli flexibility were also evident. The violence brought about a backlash among a Jewish public suspicious about the "real intentions" of the Palestinians and their readiness to accept a permanent Jewish state, rather than Oslo being only a stage in a long-term plan to make Israeli territory part of a larger Palestinian state. There was no Jewish-Israeli leader who could accept the Palestinian interpretation of the "right of return": that all Palestinian refugees who wished should be allowed to return to their homes and property in Israel. According to Jewish-Israeli consensus, Israel must remain a state with a clear Jewish majority. Very few Israeli Jews are willing to compromise on this matter; the vast majority insists that the resettlement of Palestinian refugees must be achieved mainly outside the state of Israel. This issue became the major obstacle in negotiations (even in the Geneva initiative of 2003), along with certain symbolic arguments related to the Jewish holy places in Jerusalem. Fear actually re-created the perceived need among the Jewish-Israeli majority for a neo-monolithic construction.

Among the Palestinians, the dragging out of the implementation of the Oslo process raised old-new fears about Israel's willingness to make concessions. Over the past decade, Israel has enabled one million Jews, mostly from the former Soviet Union and Ethiopia, to immigrate to Israel under the Law of Return. Israel continued to build new settlements in the West Bank and Gaza and new houses in the established settlements, regardless of which party was in power. Israeli Jews spoke about peace in negative terms (no more violence); unwilling to share resources such as land and water; they also demanded predominant military control. Palestinians, looking for a *just* peace (Shasha-Beiton, 2002), increasingly came to feel that Israel perceived the Palestinian National Authority's role as safeguarding Israelis from Palestinian extremists (Hamas and Islamic Jihad), rather than establishing an independent state. Neither side was thinking in terms of positive peace: what both sides could gain from a peace process. Palestinians continued to work in Israel as a manual labor force, with almost total fiscal dependency on Israel's economy. The Palestinians needed a monolithic collective identity construction of their own, to replace the "dependent" and "occupied" Palestinian identity. The years after Oslo did not help create the momentum to move beyond this old, insecure identity, which stemmed from previous oppressive regimes – those of the Ottomans, British, Egyptians, and Jordanians.

October 2000 brought to the forefront another, more specific agenda that earlier was dismissed or seen as less important: the status of the Palestinian-Israeli (Arab-Israeli) minority[3] (Kimmerling, 2001). Israeli

[3] These names reflect part of the dispute and the definition of the agenda: Are they part of the Palestinian nation and emerging state or are they part of Israel, an Arab minority in a Jewish state? My use of terms such as "Palestinian-Israeli minority" is intended to avoid making a political statement. This term is wide enough to enable the members of this community to define themselves as Palestinians, as Israelis, or as both.

Jews were surprised when this minority played an active role in the uprising. The devastating result was that the police shot and killed thirteen youngsters during the first ten days of the uprising. Never had public demonstration in Israel been suppressed so aggressively. This turn of events put a special highlight on the Palestinian-Israeli agenda. Should the Palestinian residents of Israel be seen only as part of the Israeli-Palestinian conflict or should their needs and demands be regarded separately? These Israelis had undergone their own collective identity crisis after Oslo. If before they had perceived themselves as the go-betweens, especially when Israeli Jews and Palestinians denounced each other, now they found themselves betrayed by both sides. They were not even invited to Oslo.

The detrimental outcome of the October 2000 protests became one of the major reasons the Palestinian-Israeli population decided to boycott the 2001 elections – paradoxically helping Ariel Sharon defeat Ehud Barak by a margin of 23 percent – the widest margin ever in an Israeli election. In the 1999 elections, more than 90 percent of the Israeli-Arab minority had voted for Barak. Now they felt that he had betrayed them. Unlike Yitzhak Rabin before him, Barak did not try to address and work on solving their long-neglected problems. He did not even acknowledge their warning that he must not let Sharon enter the *Al-Aqsa* Mosque. Perhaps Barak's logic was that their issues should be addressed only after an Israeli-Palestinian solution was attained and he did not want to be accused, as Rabin had been, of leaning too heavily on this sector's vote. But a result, he lost the sympathy of the Palestinian Israelis and could not make any progress on either of the two Palestinian agendas.

The special problems of the Arab minority in Israel have been handled very poorly since Israeli became a state over fifty years ago (Kimmerling, 2001). First they were suspected of being among the Arab enemy. After the 1967 war, though the acute feeling of danger diminished, the Jewish Israelis, committed to their monolithic identity construction, saw the Palestinian Israelis more as a burden than as an asset linking them to the Arab world. The political approach of the Israeli leadership was that the country needed to focus on the more immediate, macro military and political Palestinian-Israeli problems because the Arab minority in Israel was in any case part of the hostile Arab world. There was, at that time, no distinguishing of this minority as part of, yet separated from, the Palestinian issue. As noted, at any time of relative quiet, the tendency to "look through" them prevailed.

This created a very complex and difficult situation for the Palestinian Israelis. Because they could not "win" with either the Israeli Jews or with the Palestinians, they tried to find a way to "walk between the drops" (Al-Haj, 1995; Kimmerling, 2001; Peled, 1993; Smooha, 1992).

The Palestinian-Israeli minority is a small remnant of a wider population in Palestine before the establishment of the State of Israel in 1948. Many people were forced to leave or they fled, as a result of the violence that followed the 1947 United Nations vote in favor of the partition plan, or as a result of the 1948 war. Many relatives of the Palestinian-Israeli minority still live in refugee camps in Jordan, Lebanon, Syria, and the Palestinian National Authority. During and after the 1948 war, Israel initiated an evacuation of part of the Arab population (Morris, 1999). Those who remained had to live under a military regime until 1966, suspected of collaboration with the enemies in the Arab countries still at a state of war with Israel. With their mobility restricted, it was easy for most Israelis to ignore not only their problems but their existence. Even after the military regime was lifted, many of their rights were neglected, in terms of schooling, housing, occupational choice, and other civic entitlements. For example, those who wanted to become teachers had to go through a special investigation by the Israeli secret services. Others were refused jobs because they had not served in the army.

In later years after Oslo, a change became apparent in the way the Palestinian-Israeli leadership set a separate agenda. In a way, they were now constructing their own monolithic collective identity, separate from both the Palestinian and the Jewish-Israeli ones. They emphasize the inequality from which they suffer in Israel, but they also emphasize that they do not want to become part of the Palestinian state. Aspects of their inequality within Israeli society are framed as part of a current dispute over Israel's being a civic democratic society versus a Jewish state. For example, many Arabs complain that they can wait for years to get certain political, economic, and cultural rights that a new immigrant from Russia receives automatically. This inequality becomes even more apparent when we contrast the "right of return" granted Jews who have never before lived in Israel with the negation of the same right for Palestinian-Israelis' family members who are still in refugee camps in Lebanon or Syria.[4]

From the current discussion, we can learn that a deeper level of the unresolved conflict has to do with the lack of readiness on the part of both the Palestinians and Israeli Jews to truly move forward with the new political arrangement. They have been incapable of accepting each other's "otherness." My focus here is Jewish-Israeli apprehension of the Arab Other, our ambivalence regarding our internalized aggression, and our fear of the end of the conflict.

Our *apprehension* is related to our deep mistrust of the sincerity of the Palestinians' intentions. We are afraid that when "they" speak of peace, it is actually part of a long-term plan to annihilate us. This was evident in Adi's narrative. Our *ambivalent approach* toward the use of force and aggression is a remnant of the monolithic identity construction that causes us to feel both very strong and powerful and very weak and vulnerable. This ambivalence reinforces our self-perception as eternal victims of the Holocaust. It causes us to feel acutely the harm the other side inflicts on us, while we are insensitive to what we are inflicting on them. Our *fear of the end of the conflict* derives from the fact that many Israeli Jews have constructed their identities around the conflict, and an end to it will necessitate a fearful reconstruction. In other words, if our existence is not to be determined by our negation of the Other and the hatred of others have for us (Bar-On, 1999), we will have to redefine who are we.

In this process of collective identity reconstruction, the Palestinian Israelis could become an asset rather than a burden. Throughout the years that they have lived among us, they have gotten to know us, sometimes better than we know ourselves. This group has had to develop a social representation of themselves apart from the way they saw us (Moscovici, 1976). Their own collective identity formation often required a complex and diversified internal representation of themselves in relation to at least two Others: the

[4] Interviewed by the author in February 2001, Sami Michael (a well-known Israeli author who was a member of the joint Jewish-Arab Communist party in the fifties) claimed that too many Jews and Arabs populate Israel today, creating vast environmental problems. Therefore, he thinks that rights of return should now be denied to both (Bar-On, 2004/2006).

dominant Israeli Jew as well as the Palestinians in the Occupied Territories and in the Palestinian refugee Diaspora. Once we Jewish Israelis are able to move out the monolithic identity construction based on negation of the Others who, we are sure, "hate and want to annihilate us" (Bar-On, 1999), and past the neo-monolithic backlash, into a more complex and dialogical stage, the Palestinian Israelis could be helpful in showing us the way. Some of them will be willing to share with us the Others with whom they have been in an open dialogue.

Why are Israeli Jews more fearful of the Palestinians today than in 1993? The apprehension has two components: fear of deconstructing their personal monolithic identities and fear of the Other's destructive intentions. If, in 1993, Israeli Jews were more subject to the first dynamic, since October 2000 the second has become more acute. These two fears reinforce each other in a vicious cycle that is very difficult to break through. Both are probably anchored in our long history in the Diaspora, in our insecurity as an autonomous civil society, and in our hesitancy over the prospect of integrating as a small alien Jewish minority into the culture of the Middle Eastern region. Right now, we are also a despised minority because of our strength and the way we handle the Palestinian problem. It should be recognized that Palestinian violence has not helped us cope better with these fears.

In this complex situation, it could be expected that our leadership find ways to desensitize us to the apprehension and help us resolve our ambivalence about our own aggressiveness and vulnerability. Yet, if we analyze the deeds of our leaders since the Oslo Accord (and special note must be made of the period following the second Lebanon war in the summer of 2006), they actually intensified our anxieties, rather than desensitized us to them. This is true of Netanyahu, Barak, Sharon, Peretz, Olmert, and many others. They have shown little understanding of long-term social processes and in fact learned how to manipulate the weakness of the society as part of their political power games. The murder of Rabin in 1995 created a kind of panic, making us worry about whether we are capable of maintaining a just and democratic civil society. The lesson that different social factions drew from the electoral victory of the right wing after his murder was that the use of force pays, and the more it is used, the more resources gained.

This became the name of the game, instead of decision making based on mutual concessions for the benefit of the whole society. The use of force intensified the fear: You have to beware not only of those who face you but also of those behind you. Analysis of our leaders' failure should focus less on personality and more on the undemocratic school of socialization that educated them. We should also focus on ourselves and ask: How did the whirlwind make us let such people control our lives and actually intensify our anxieties instead of reducing them?

The situation has been steadily worsening since I began writing this book. The only positive change in terms of my analysis since completing the initial version in 2004 is that the two societies no longer project all that is evil onto the Other. Both now have to recognize and deal with iniquity from within. In Israeli society, this is reflected in the current lack of trust in the political leadership. Palestinian society is faced with the violent power struggle between Fatah and Hamas. Perhaps recognition of the communal self as both good and evil is an essential step before being able to see the positive side of the Other.

Yet today, Israel and Palestine seem like a giant laboratory in which green and blue mice are raised. Now, as there are too many mice, the experimenters have decided to reduce the oxygen in the lab and torture the mice by starving them. The researchers ask, when will the mice start to eat each other? Will they eat more of their own kind or more of the other? And those who survive – will they develop a more peaceful and democratic relationship or will they continue to eat each other forever? Unlike in the laboratory, in the Middle East, the reality is that we are both the mice and the experimenters. The oxygen is the hope for a peaceful future that is fading away from day to day and the torture of hunger is a reality for Palestinians today, while for Jewish Israelis the torture is the experience of wiping the blood off the streets, the cars, the buses.

FOUR The Future: A Dialogue between Disintegrated Aspects of Identity

As long as monolithic construction is part of a collective identity; as long as the image of the collective self as "absolute good" depends on the Other being "absolute evil," the nature of their discourse is consistent and pre-determined (Bakhtin, 1981). The Other is consistently identified as being different in essence from the self, thereby justifying the continuity of the monolithic construction. Any verbal exchange between the sides is accompanied by suspicion and reserve that hinders consideration of the other side's claims or emotions. Any settlement between two monolithic parties (for example, between East and West during the cold war) is based on force and interests, but it is not accompanied by a social psychological process or by an attempt to break down the monolithic construction and acknowledge complexity. Each side considers ways of defeating the other and thereby proving the justice of its way. The balance of horror alone has prevented total confrontation between world powers.

It is only when the monolithic construction within the collective identity disintegrates that a new opportunity for a significant dialogue is created. Part of this dialogue continues to be internal, but its quality changes. I no longer identify as the "victim" within myself, seek to vindicate it, and manufacture complaints about the evil Other as "perpetrator." I am now willing to identify the "perpetrator" within myself, too, and to try to draw the "victim" and the "perpetrator" into a dialogue. This inner dialogue allows me to acknowledge that perhaps the Other is not a perpetrator to the exclusion of all else but may also have been victimized in ways that I had hitherto refused to recognize. As a result of this representation, I can, perhaps for the first time, consider the possibility of giving up this stark dichotomy between victim and perpetrator around which my identity has hitherto been formed. And now – who am I, if I am no longer only a victim, and the other is no longer only a perpetrator, trying to annihilate me? With this question, a completely new chapter is likely to begin. My personal and collective identity can develop in new directions once they are no longer based on dichotomous and monolithic definitions.

The problem is that knowledge and experience of the monolithic construction can only partially help to prepare us for the process of redefinition of self through dialogue. It is easier to write about this process than to manifest it in a reality that is still filled with monolithic and neo-monolithic images. It seems that human beings find it very difficult to separate from these constructions that formed their identity. Defining the Other as totally evil solves many problems in an economical, almost effortless way. It also leaves the monolithic self flawless. Under certain conditions, this process engenders a lot of energy. A formerly calm person roused to anger against an Other is suddenly filled with hitherto unrecognized energy. Hatred and jealousy can activate and manufacture forces of which one is unaware. It is much harder and more complicated to start an internal and external dialogue between parts that are challenging to reconcile. It obviously requires a great deal of effort and immediate gain is neither clear nor promised in advance. Perhaps this is why we find movement in the neo-monolithic direction during the process of the monolithic construction's disintegration.

Even those who feel the need to free themselves from the neo-monolithic construction, because it no longer is helping them understand themselves or their surroundings, are likely to suffer from the chaotic atmosphere that replaces the monolithic construction. Ambiguity means uncertainty – who am I? Where have I come from and where am I going? And when things are not clear, how can I manage in this world I live in? According to what rules does the world operate, if not according to the clear division between good and evil? Apart from the few, it becomes hard for people to live with these questions for any length of time, not finding definite answers. Who can help with this process? When we enter the river, are we promised a safe shore on the other side? Or will we now have to get used to swimming ad infinitum?

I mentioned before that in ambiguous situations, with the monolithic construction disintegrating, many people have proved unable to endure the lack of clarity for any length of time. Some have sought support in a neo-monolithic backlash into religion. Youngsters join various sects or look for the monolithic support of activity in eccentric frameworks that attack the old "establishment." Others join security forces that support the monolithic construction. For them, the world continues the dichotomous division between the good (us) and the evil (them).

It is more difficult to give up the monolithic construction when there are still indications of internal and external threat that ostensibly justify its continuation. When we looked at the peace process with the Palestinians, for example, we saw that the Oslo Accord did not end the perceived Arab threat to Israeli existence in the Middle East. There were those who claimed that it even increased it, but no one claimed that it suddenly disappeared. When violent events are taking place that ostensibly justify the view of the Palestinian Other as threatening, why should the average Israeli be expected to give up his or her monolithic construction of identity willingly and easily? Another analogy can be suggested, the knight in the Middle Ages who hung up his armor and decided to set out on a peaceful journey, but hurried to take it down and put it on again when he saw mounted knights in armor approaching in the distance. Or from the opposite perspective: How does one manage in a changing world where this armor has become irrelevant?

An interesting question is, Who can aid in the process of coping with the monolithic construction's disintegration, thereby preventing a neo-monolithic backlash? How can one help people to contain conflict and ambiguity as they reconstruct identity? Certain individuals might be willing to accept the fact that their identities are more complex, even if they continue to present themselves coherently as they were before. They could become more aware of the limitations in their presentation of self. However, such people are often seen as being "softer" or "weaker" in a social system that values strength and rigid definition. Their ability to contain conflict is perceived as a "feminine" quality – a disadvantage in dealing with "absolute evil" when the adversary decides to return to the ring. A very supportive and positive environment is required to enable an internal and external dialogue to develop; one that can contain complexity and facilitate awareness and examination of the various aspects of a monolithic identity that has disintegrated. How can this examination be achieved without arousing neo-monolithic backlashes that will make us search for the "armor" that is still "hanging on the wall"?

Giving up a monolithic construction is a gradual process, many times happening before one becomes conscious of it. Yet, the possibility of a dialogue between the parts that disintegrated will usually happen only after one reaches some level of consciousness about it. By way of example is an exercise suggested by facilitators at a cross-cultural workshop at Ben-Gurion University, attended by Israeli-born students and by students who had emigrated from Russia.[1] One classroom wall represented "100-percent Israeliness" and the wall across from it represented "the opposite." The students were asked to position themselves relative to these poles. To everyone's surprise, most of the students from both groups located themselves in the same area, about two-thirds of the way closer to the wall representing 100-percent Israeliness. In the ensuing discussion, the emigrant students asked their Israeli counterparts: "We understand why we are not 100 percent Israeli, but what are you doing here?" Each of the Israelis gave a slightly different version of this answer: "100-percent Israeliness doesn't represent me anymore, because I am critical of 'pure' Israeliness" (of a monolithic identity). Although both groups located themselves at about 70 percent Israeliness, they reached it from opposite directions: one group (immigrants) moving toward monolithic Israeliness, the other group retreating from it. Here the micro level reflects social processes taking place on the macro level. It can be seen as a moment of dialogue between two groups who move in opposite directions.

Two examples in this chapter demonstrate possibilities of dialogue taking place as a result of disintegration. As in the initial chapters, I begin with a dialogue that has a Holocaust background: Yael encourages her father to speak so that, for the first time, she can hear the story of his life during the war years. The dialogue that develops between them is based on mutual

---

[1] The June 1995 workshop was facilitated by Idit Shpitzer and Yelena Karol, themselves Israeli- and Russian-born, respectively, from the Department of Behavioral Science at Ben-Gurion University.

love and deep respect. By means of this dialogue, Yael is able to free herself from her monolithic preconceptions of the Diaspora Jew, in opposition to the Israeli *sabra*. She achieves this change by breaking the threatening silence around her father's experiences during the Holocaust. We not only feel their mutual achievement, as well as the boundaries of the dialogue, but also, perhaps, the dialogue's fragility.

The second dialogue takes place when a group of Palestinian Israeli students confront a group of Jewish-Israeli students. In the dialogue extracted here, two young men, one a Palestinian and the other a Jew, discuss why, with the founding of a Palestinian state, Palestinian Israelis won't automatically move there; why they could prefer to remain in Israel as a minority. It is difficult for the Israeli Jews, who have come from all corners of the earth, to understand. Both dialogues reflect an internal Jewish dialogue as well as dialogue with an alien Other and, at the same time portray, a reexamination of components of Israeli-Jewish identity once the monolithic construction of the Other and the collective "self" are disintegrating.

4.1 YAEL AND HER FATHER

One of my students, whom I will call Yael, brought the text of an interview with her father to a workshop at the university. This class project, which was part of the training for group facilitators, required an interview with a meaningful personality in each student's life. Yael's presentation was three pronged: She read us a passage she had written about her relationship with her father before the interview; she presented most of the interview itself, the text of which included commentary on the interaction of father and daughter at the time; and she shared her impressions of the interview in class. The reason for the interview, she said, was that although her father was a Holocaust survivor, she had never heard the story of his life during that period. A child at the time, the father survived together with his brother and parents, all of whom were now living in Israel. Yael wanted to use the opportunity afforded by the workshop to hear her father tell his life story.

During the presentation in class, a dialogue between Yael and the other students developed that allowed her to reflect further on her relationship with her father. This is my interpretation of what happened between Yael and her father during the interview: His cooperation and his daughter's understanding of his attempts can be understood within the context of a *double wall*. The father had built a monolithic "wall" between painful memories of the Holocaust and the reality in which his daughters grew up. Sensing his wall, Yael had built her own permeable "wall" in response. At different times, each had tried to open a window in his or her own wall but had usually met with the wall of the other. Yael's courageous attempt to make openings in their walls simultaneously, in which her father actively participates, stems from her need to enter into a dialogue in order to separate.

All my knowledge is based on what Yael presented to the class. It might have been advisable to hear directly from her father as well. But even if the opportunity had arisen, it is by no means clear that the father, described as withdrawn and sensitive, would have responded more willingly to a stranger's request than to that of his loving daughter. At a certain stage in the process of analysis, I concluded that the problem lay not in lack of testimony, but in the difficulty of both meeting and separating.

Text I: "My father and I"

I remember the beginning of my awareness of my father. It is winter, night-time, I am crying. Mother quickly takes me out of the linen drawer . . . in which I sleep so that I won't, Heaven forbid, wake up my older sisters, who are sleeping in real beds. She turns on the light in the living room, sits me down, and leaves for a moment. I cry and cry and suddenly hear a voice from behind the door, a very concerned and very calm voice: "Yael, what's wrong? What's wrong, Yaellee?" I don't answer, mother is not in the room, and the voice becomes more worried and less calm. Afterward I remember how on Friday afternoons Father would arrive with a huge package of wafers and chocolates from the army department store. Father was in the army and all of us would wait for him: Mother, my sisters, and I. Father would open up the package and give out equal amounts of the candy. Later on, when I had orthopedic shoes, I remember father putting me to bed and how, together, we would try on the shoes and I wouldn't cry, even though they were very heavy and no one else in the world had shoes like those, and father was very proud of me.

But sometimes it was a bit too much. On one of the first days of the first week of grade one, father came. He came to take me home and he carried my school bag. He was just worried about me: worried I might get lost or get run over, and of course, that I shouldn't carry my bag by myself, because, after all, four hours of school are very tiring, especially for my father's daughter. I wasn't happy about him coming to school. I wanted to be like everyone else, I was big already. I had a uniform like my older sisters, and even though my school bag was very big and I was very (very) small and the house was far away, I wanted to walk home alone, like a big kid, just me and the school bag – but I didn't say anything to father. And that's how I grew up with my father: a father who did not miss one school party, who right up until eleventh grade would come up to my room every morning with a cup of coffee. Indeed, always, from the very beginning, his little girl would drink her cup of hot chocolate covered in "skin" only in the dark. Forbidden to change her habit. Had my teacher not discovered that this was the reason for my tardiness, we would never have been cured of this habit. I can imagine my father rushing eighty miles from Kiryat Ono to Beer-Sheva, every morning, with a cup of coffee. That's what my father is like. And I grew up with my father, for better or for worse. "Where are you going?" "Who are you going with?" "I want to meet him." "When are you coming back?" "Is he going to bring you back?" "Does he have a car?" "What kind of car?" "He must bring you up [to the apartment], he must come up with you in the elevator." "Is there a telephone there?" "Do you have a key?" "Will you call when you get there?" "Take a little more money, you might need it."

Eighth grade. All the kids went on the annual class trip. Not Yael! The route lay through Hebron. Father saw the outbreak of the *Intifada* coming – he was off by a bit, not too much, just seven years. Attempts to convince him didn't work. The hysterics didn't help. And Yael's hysterics were not just hysterics. Yael was not going on the first day of the trip. My father's daughter would not set foot in Hebron. But Yael insisted and my father would do anything for his daughter: We left at night. Father, his brother from kibbutz, his brother's gun, and myself. We drove on a back road (before there were back roads) and we reached the youth hostel. That is how Yael went from her father's care to the care of her first cigarette. Yes, that's what my father is like, and I love my father, and when I tell my father that I love him, his eyes become moist and it is very, very difficult to bear.

Everything is permissible at home. There are no rules and there are no customs and there are no holidays, but on two days a year it is forbidden to leave the house: on Yom Kippur and on Holocaust Day. So, on Yom Kippur everyone meets, plays, laughs, and talks, sort of like a family reunion. It is not that way on Holocaust Day. On Holocaust Day, everyone is home.

Everyone sits in front of the television, the lights are dim and quiet. Every now and then I take my eyes off the television and glance sideways at father. My head does not move because what would happen if he saw me looking at him? What would I say to him? What would he say to me? I see wet cheeks, tearful eyes, and that's all. I immediately escape again to the television. Quiet. On that day it is forbidden to speak. The silence is holy.

What lay hidden behind the silence, I never knew. One night I heard my father cry out in his sleep. Mother soothed him. Then – silence again, as if no one had heard, as if it had never happened. I never asked. I never asked about the war. If the subject had not been required material for the matriculation exams, I would have remained ignorant. I only knew that it was forbidden to talk about it. I only knew that father lived for us, that father works in order to support us. Father breathes so that we will not suffocate. So how can I slip away through his fingers? I need to make it up to him. I owe him the happiness in my life. And often when I think about it, I am afraid of what will happen if it happens, what will happen when it happens. Father deserves to stay longer. Father deserves to rest a bit before he goes.

Yael tells the class about the interview

I won't read all of it; actually, the interview is a bit boring. When I was given the assignment to interview someone meaningful, I thought about interviewing my father. I had never spoken to father before. We have an intense relationship, there is contact, but I have never spoken to him about the wartime period. This time too – I told him: It's not that I want to know, it's for university, I have an assignment to do . . . It was Saturday, I went [home] expressly [for this purpose], but I didn't dare. So I went again another Saturday. I was afraid, I looked for a way out . . . mother knows how to tell things, she also talks to my husband. . . . it's different with my father. I don't know whether I didn't want to know what happened or whether I was afraid that my knowing would mean I would have to remember and not forget, not leave him half empty, but rather let him release this burden through his story. I am afraid that he will go and I won't know; I live with the possibility of my father's death.

Text II: Despite the doubts – An interview with my father!

I know I'm being taped.

We don't play it [in class].

I don't care . . . poor mother; we've left her out.

I am interviewing you and not mother, even though her stories are more interesting; she's like a storyteller. But I know mother's stories and I don't know your stories.

Probably because I'm closed; I don't tell or I don't remember, or I don't want to remember, and I'm sure you won't get it out of me now.

I'm not going to invade your privacy. It might be very interesting for me, but I am not going to force you to tell me. What I do want you to tell me . . .

Oh, the interview has begun . . .

. . . is what happened: childhood, before, after.

Oh . . . it's hard. Flashbacks. Well, okay. So how do I begin?

Where did you live? What was the house like, the kind of life, mother, father, your brother, kindergarten, school, servants; what did you wear?

I remember the house; I remember the street. An apartment building. We were on what was called the *par terre* floor – the first floor. In French, *par terre* means ground floor. But there, ground floors were high up. A few stairs were needed. No, I don't know, I don't remember how many . . . The entrance was through a big gate, and today I wonder if it was really big. I mean, if I saw it today, would it still look as big? But let's say, the trip to Yugoslavia or places like that in Europe, too – when we were together – all kinds of oldish cities or houses – well, that reminds me of some of the area. Actually, you weren't with us in Yugoslavia. Well, there are houses like that. There, the buildings are joined together. There are no separate buildings. The . . . houses are joined along the street from one corner to the next; it's a string of houses, a string of joined houses. There's no distance between them; the courtyards are inside and not between the houses.

So we lived on the ground floor. The entrance was through a gate that looked big; I always think that perhaps I will go back to see, but . . . I don't know; quite big anyway – that is to say, two wings. So, an entrance that's a bit round and paved; you know, paved liked the street. The entrance through to the courtyard is paved with stones; stones, not asphalt, there wasn't asphalt there. There the streets were paved with stones, small ones, close together, or much bigger ones that were called "cats' heads" . . . that look like a cat's head, a round cat's head. So the entrance to the courtyard was like that and inside was a courtyard and a passage to the courtyard. So the back of the second house faces . . . both of the backs face . . . so we are on the right as you come up. You climb up, climb straight up a number of steps, and there's an apartment on the left and an apartment on the right. The one on the right was ours. It had a long corridor called the ante-room. From that corridor, you come in this way: First of all, you turn left to the bathroom. After the bathroom, left to the kitchen; from the kitchen there's an outer door and stairs leading to the courtyard. The upper apartments were also connected behind by communal ramps with metal railings in order to get from one floor to the next and to go outside. I'm drinking coffee [father says this to the tape recorder and continues].

This is the kitchen, straight. Straight ahead there was a long, narrow corridor. I don't know, I think quite a few meters. *Nu* – let's say six or seven meters. And that's the ante-room. *Nu*, to get to the bathroom, to the toilet, in order to get to another room perhaps . . . less. So then straight away you would enter a room called the study. The study is a room like an office, something like that, but it was also a room. There is a desk and a library with encyclopedias, many Gutenberg encyclopedias. He invented printing and they published a large encyclopedia in his honor with thirty-two volumes and I used to look at them a lot. Yes, a lot, out of curiosity. Yes, I'd like to do that today, too. If I retire, perhaps; I've starting looking into it.

Now, there are encyclopedias, Stiematzky publishes a dictionary. They now have a computerized Hebrew dictionary. Okay, let's go back. Thirty-two volumes, with pictures. I used to look at it; it was very interesting. So that was the study. As long as I can remember myself, I slept there. There was a couch there where I slept.

Did you do your homework there?

From there you go straight down the corridor – the bathroom on the left, the kitchen on the left with an exit to the courtyard. Then there's a room with a window facing the same direction as the exit to the courtyard. During [the holiday of] Succoth, they would probably have built a *succah* [booth] under this window. I remember the *succah*. That's where I'd sleep. There was a type of couch, a couch. What's it like? It's a board like those American-type beds; like them, but one side is higher. The higher side is permanent. This higher side is meant for the head. So you need to sleep with your head in that direction, right? Now, if you sleep with your head that way, then when you turn to one side it's next to the wall, because one side turns to the wall, and if you turn to the other side, the head turns outward. I told you that once I slept over at grandmother's, I don't remember why, and there was the same couch but it was the other way round. I said that I couldn't fall asleep; perhaps there were other reasons as well. I said: I can't sleep here because I'm used to sleeping on the right side with my face to the wall, and there it was impossible to sleep [and have] my face to the wall. [I prepare coffee and father says again, as a "simultaneous interpreter" for the listener: "sounds of the kettle, water," etc.]

So I had a sofa there. Did I do my homework there? I don't think so. By the year '39 I had only managed the first grade, and in the first grade, if I remember myself – I do remember myself, I think it was first grade, I think that in another room, the dining room – that's where I'd do my lessons, with mother telling me how to write each letter: "round, round, well up to the line" [father imitates his mother's intonation]. Because the notebook had lines. So: "up to the line, up, connect, don't go past the line."

What was that like for you?

I think it was hard. You can probably see today what it did to me, in every-thing, because I had to be very good, nice handwriting as well. Ahh . . . to this very day, father talks about mother teaching me to write. I'm sure it's because of that that I write so illegibly today. People go crazy when they see my handwriting. That is to say, what came out of mother teaching me to write "round, round, up to the line" – rebellion, perhaps; I don't know – such terrible handwriting. So I remember sitting there, so that was in the dining room. The entrance to the dining room was approximately across from the kitchen, between the entrance to the bathroom on the left and the kitchen. To the right was the entrance to the dining room, in the middle of which stood a round table, a dining table with chairs pushed in. Along the wall was a sideboard; that is, a long buffet just like grandmother's today, perhaps bigger. There were all kinds of . . . no, what was there? I remember well that there were sweets there. Sweets . . . during the afternoon . . . mother would hand them out to everyone after the meal, ration them out. They weren't put on the table, everyone taking as much as they wanted. Everyone got, I don't know, a sort of prize. I remember that the candies were there and only mother was in charge [of them]. I don't remember myself taking things from there. I don't think so. Next to it stood a round table; I think it was round, and on it stood a radio; round like this. A radio shaped like oriental windows – rectangular with an arch on top. Well, it's a radio with a hand that turns. Not a hand that turns lengthwise, but clockwise, and a radio was probably not a common thing then, yes? In front of the radio, in front of the radio, a bit lower down, perhaps, underneath it, I think, stood a vase. A big bowl, a vase, ah, crystal, with slits in it. The crystal was dark blue and the slits, the slits were light. I remember playing with it once, putting my hand inside and twirling it round my hand. I liked it when it spun around. And I think that my father told me not to do it, and I did it and it fell and shattered into pieces. To this day, I know that father did not speak to me for a long time afterward. He didn't speak. I don't know what he did, he certainly didn't speak and it was certainly hard.

Punishment?

Yes, punishment. I am sure that he didn't do it as a punishment. He did it because he was angry, as if I were a grown-up.

Were you really the "grown-up" among the children?

Until the war – afterward, when we were in one of the ghettos, I felt differently toward him [his brother] and I took care of him, but [before] I don't think so. I don't remember the responsibility.

[I try to move beyond the detailed and evasive description of the house.] Do you remember when war broke out?

No. I haven't gotten to the war yet [a sort of warning that I shouldn't press him, a sort of signal "to let me tell it in my own time"]. Yes, I think so. Sometimes it's hard to know exactly what you remember and what stories [are] put into your memory. The source of what is in your memory is not so clear. I remember that one day mother helped us make up. Somehow I remember some type of reconciliation when he agreed to say something to me.

Was your mother good, gentle?

Look, I don't know. It's hard for me to believe that she was gentle; it's difficult for me to believe, because making demands, a lot of demands on a child, I don't think that's good. Demands for rounded letters, to be neat and combed and to sit straight, upright, and to politely say hello to everyone; I don't know [I think that is] a big demand.

And didn't your father educate you? There is a sort of feeling that he wasn't there.

Yes, I think that feeling is correct. I think that feeling is correct, that he wasn't around a lot. Because he was probably busy for a long time before he bought the factory, and today I know that he bought the factory immediately before the war. So I don't know how he could have been the manager, because according to the papers, right at the outbreak of the war he bought it from someone who was bankrupt. Then he sold enamel products and he was a traveling salesman or some kind of salesman, I guess. In spite of the fact that he says, he tells that at the end there was a time when (people would] phone him at home and he would fill out the forms. I mean, he didn't need to run around but he also tells . . .

[It was apparently hard for my father to go on telling: "Should I bring a heater?" "No." "Are you cold?" "No." "You look cold to me." "No." "Should we close (the window] here?" "It's not cold." "We'll close the window, okay?"]

But he also tells how he traveled when he worked, whenever he returned, mother would wait for him at the train station . . . so that's a sign that he traveled, right? Well, I don't remember him being at home a lot. Okay, so there was a radio, some kind of chair, a chair something like the old one at grandpa's, but again, it looked big to me and it had ears on the sides; you could rest your head there, it wasn't just a simple [chair].

Where was the chair? Was it grandfather's?

Possibly near the table with the radio, possibly; I think so. I don't know what else there was in the living room; ah, of course, in every room there was a heater the size of a refrigerator, up to the ceiling, with ceramics on the outside, but one color, with an opening on the bottom where you put in coal, lit it, and it burned as a heater, and that is one of the biggest pleasures in the winter. To stand next to it in the winter and to warm up [father shows me how he used to stand and warm up]. The whole thing was hot, right up to the ceiling. The smoke from it went straight to the chimney. That is to say, there were central chimneys in each house, I think; perhaps not central, perhaps in each apartment. Chimney sweeping was a profession. Black, black poles with a round sort of brush, with a brush at the end and – a sort of rounded steel wire, and they would climb up. They had ladders. They would climb up to the chimneys and they would clean them and it was a profession.

Were you rich?

Were we rich? I think we were bourgeoisie. Now look, I think, first of all, I think that there were stoves like that in all the houses, built in with the houses; it's an integral part of winter heating. Now, of course, it was the maids who would heat and light the stove and put the coal inside and take out the ashes afterward, and all of that.

Did they live with you?

Yes, yes, I remember one, I know from stories that there were two. The servant who lived in [with us], well, she had a folding cot in the kitchen.

Poor thing.

Well, wretchedness is a relative thing. I guess it was worse in her home or wherever she could be. It might have been better for her there, do you understand? She had a home, she had a place to live and eat in, she got a salary, she had a day off once a week. That means that she could leave the house, go out.

"On leave" [an Israeli military term].

Yes, it was what's called "leave" [he uses the army term]. Once a week, a day or half a day, I don't know.

Like [the television show] *"Upstairs Downstairs."*

Yes, I suppose so.

And was it an accepted thing, the bourgeoisie class?

Was it accepted? I don't know, I don't remember [people] coming over, I think that the house was always closed. I don't remember friends coming to visit, even though I hear that mother had a lot of male and female friends before she got married. I don't hear anything from father about his having had male friends or female friends. But from mother I hear, hear all sorts of names and that sort of thing. These acquaintances continued up until after the wedding, but I don't remember these people coming over to our house, for example. Now, I don't remember having a lot of friends then. There was someone, a son of a dentist that I would go to, I don't remember his coming to me, I don't remember exactly.

Now I've told you where I slept, where [I did] homework. My parents had a bedroom, of course, but the entrance wasn't through the anteroom. It had two entrances: one through the dining room and one through the study. That is, there were two doors, yes, and there they brought my brother when he was born. I didn't know what was born but I remember the picture of someone going by in the middle of the night with some sort of screaming bundle, I guess after he was born – the midwife – he was born at home. [People] were born at home and I remember someone like that [like the midwife]; I guess that after mother gave birth to him, they took him out of the bedroom through the dining room to the kitchen. This was probably where the bath was and there they probably washed him and brought him back washed, through the study to mother in the bedroom.

You saw this?

I remember that part.

How old were you, five?

There are five years between us, yes.

See how you remember that part!

But I don't remember the pregnancy or some . . . and who knows what birth and pregnancy were like then, how children came into the world; things like that were taboo. So the bedroom was there, and from the dining room and from the parents' bedroom, windows looked out onto the street, and from the study and from the kitchen the windows looked out onto the courtyard. Later on, I remember where my brother slept and where I [slept]. I remember sleeping in the study.

You remember where he slept all those years?

All of those years, sweetheart – in '39 the war broke out.

When was he born?

In 1936.

He was three years old, a baby.

Yes. This week there was a movie about Wanda's List, about someone who lives here in Israel . . . they would take children out of the ghetto and leave them outside. Ruth [a friend of my parents] is one of those children; they found her in a basket with a letter. She is not one of Wanda's List. She never knew her parents. In the movie, they showed a woman who didn't know anything about her childhood; all she had was a spoon with initials on it.

I didn't want to see it.

You need to see it.

It's very hard for me.

Probably because you're my daughter. Yes, one needs to see things like that, and I don't want to use a word that isn't nice, but I am a *shmuck* [jerk]. I was going to tape it, but I thought that it was enough for me to press [the button], I wanted to, I pressed it, but I guess it was on another station, and I wanted to and I wanted . . .

Holocaust Day will come again and they'll broadcast it again.

No, that's something very unique. Well, that's not our business. Now, [in] the parents' bedroom [were] big beds, windows [facing] the street. There was a silverware closet – a very nice closet, with glass doors; inside there were silver objects, big and expensive dishes. I don't remember what else was in there; I remember myself sleeping there once, perhaps. Once, I guess, when my parents went out. I waited for them to come back and they didn't return, and I guess I was afraid.

What, you were left alone?

No, with the maid. But she was in the kitchen; I don't know, I needed to sleep there. And I remember the tramway, the electric train. Not on our street; on the street parallel to ours. There weren't any houses between the two streets because across from our house there was a garden, a sort of public garden that separated the two streets. I heard the tram. And the tram didn't have bells or whistles; it had a sort of bell. He [the driver] had a kind of pedal on the floor near his foot that he would step on, and that would pound on the rails or on the road and make a sound. I remember hearing it and it was dark and I couldn't fall asleep.

I also remember staying home with the maid once and, for some reason, I ran after her, bumped into her, made trouble for her. And I remember that she closed herself up in the kitchen and the kitchen had a glass door. The window was divided into four, a type of cross, four panes. I came and I knocked with my hand and the window broke. Yes, there is a scar here . . . almost can't see it; wow, it's gone. [He insists on finding the scar.] If you look, here it is, here perhaps, it's this line. You can hardly see it.

A number of years have passed. I broke the window and I cut my hand – why did I run after her, what did I want? I don't know.

Like I would do to Michal [my sister]?

Perhaps. I don't know what you did to her; it's hard being a kid, isn't it?

I don't know why I did that to Michal.

What did you do to her?

I would run after her with the big knife, I don't know why.

My mother's parents lived on the third floor above us. On the floor above us lived nuns, nurses, and they had a big dog – a German Shepherd or a Saint Bernard, I don't know. They called him Orsos and when they [his family] wanted me to eat or to be a good boy or something like that and I wasn't, then they would scare me. They would show me the wires that come out of the electric bulbs: "Look, Orsos is already showing his claws; look, look, Orsos is already showing his claws."

There was ignorance then?

Yes.

They didn't know what to do with a child.

No, no.

He should just behave.

Yes, he should be well brought up, dressed nicely; they used to dress me then. I don't know if you have seen photographs of me, with a tie, clothes out of a magazine, sitting in the park on a stone, legs crossed, a straight back, a nice haircut, with, what do you call it, a wave. Everything is neat, plastered down nicely, with spit. Yes, a good boy, a good boy.

Now, across from the nuns, I remember a family whose name was Alitendorf; Jews. There was one old lady who would walk around, she was so bent over that she was shaped like a *resh* [the Hebrew letter]. [He shows me how she used to walk.] They say or they told me then that she would say – see what a sense of humor people have – that the earth was already pulling her down. And on the floor above lived grandma and grandpa with mother's brother whose name was Maniek – Moshe. And he had a nice German Shepherd –Lourd, they called him – and I guess he was a gay bachelor.

Gay?

Gay. Not a homosexual. I don't know that he wasn't, but that's not what I meant. And grandfather was a tinsmith, but being a tinsmith was a profession that was very . . . impressive, a lot of things were made from tin. There was no plastic. There weren't a lot of things. I remember his workshop. On the same street as the tram. I remember the workshop. Big. Everything was big. And good; they also tell that he was such a craftsman that when they had trouble with the church of Santa Maria in Cracow, one of the most well-known and famous churches – when they had trouble with the tin roof, they contacted him. And despite his being a Jew and not giving work like that in a church to Jews, they gave him the job. The son was also very talented, technically talented, as well as being an athlete, biking and motor-biking and rowing a kayak on the Visla, a river in Poland. Not like other Jews. Not really Jewish. But he was also Jewish. The story was that he would beat up Poles who bothered Jews. He had a brass knuckle in his pocket. Do you know what that is? It's a lead ring that you put on your fingers, connecting them. He would beat up Poles who bothered [Jews]. He would beat them to a pulp. Really strong, I suppose. Yes. Yes. Yes. He also had an air rifle. Full of talent. So they lived there. I remember their apartment. And there was also a buffet and a living room and furniture with glass [that was] nice. Small panes with what is called *shlief*. That is to say, glass with polished mirrors on the side, like our clock. And their apartment was built the same way. In the kitchen there was an oven . . . I don't remember having a telephone at home. At grandma and grandpa's, yes. I remember the smell of laundry. Once a week, laundry day. They'd bring in a washer woman. No, the maid didn't do it. She would come into the kitchen and they would bring a big scrubbing board – I don't know whether it was made from wood or tin – and soap and hot water. She would stand there with [a thing] that you scrub on and launder. I don't know where they would hang the laundry. I think in the courtyard. I hope I'm speaking loud enough.

If you ask me, do I remember the school on the other side of the river – a river cut through the city. One side was called Podgórze and it is underneath the mountain. The other side – Cracow, but both of them were known as Cracow. We lived on the Podgórze side. The school was Jewish. It was called *Hebrew school*.

And I remember going there. I remember the classroom. I remember one teacher. His name was Yerozolimek: Jerusalemite. Later on, during the war, he taught me when there was no longer any school. Then they would give private lessons. [A long silence.]

So I remember school then. I also remember the ice skating rink. They took me skating there. And not too far from there was the respectable part of the city. It was very close to the Wawel palace, the royal palace, as Cracow used to be the capital of Poland. Well, my mother's sister and her husband lived not too far from there and they had a bakery. There you are – I remember myself there too. I also remember myself in the park. There was a park in Cracow; from this city there was a chain of mountains to the south. So the park was high up. You had to climb up to it.

Do I remember the war that broke out . . . look, every year we would travel to Kot to . . . [silence] . . . if I remember how the war broke out . . . I remember the Germans entering Cracow. I remember the army that marched through the streets. And cars. A march. They conquered the city.

And you remember it.

I remember. I wasn't able to understand it. I didn't interpret it as a trauma. I remember it as a picture.

Ah, ah!

Ah. Ah.

[The tape ran out. Father says, "That's it, child. Well, we're finished."]

Wishful thinking. Father. The war broke out and you were with your parents and with Shauli [brother]. Later on, just you and Shauli.

There were two periods like that in the war.

And what do you remember?

[Silence . . .]

That's all that you're interested in. Those periods? Okay. Look, we weren't completely alone. There was a time when they sent us to the ghetto in Cracow. We had aunts and uncles in the ghetto in Cracow. Well, we lived with them. But, of course, we were ourselves and they were themselves. And I don't remember them. I only remember pictures of walking around, drifting 'round this ghetto with Shauli. We walked around the yards and we went to all kinds of places. I remember that I, or we, collected things, collected in the yards; I guess I was the initiator. People would collect bottles in all kinds of places in Cracow and we would go some place and sell them and get money. So, we collected bottles, or I collected bottles. But he [Shauli] was always with me. No, he was attached to me. Of course. I remember having a box of candies, that I wouldn't permit myself to eat. I would give them to him. Sometimes, perhaps yes. But mostly I remember that I would make sure that he got them.

Do you remember being afraid?

I don't remember fear there. But when we were hidden in another place they once sent us to, a village where Hanka's father and Hanka and their family lived – it was far to go and there we lived with them and later on we were there when they built a ghetto, and they had to hide and they also sent us to hide. They sent us to hide in some Pole's [house] in the village and there we had a room where we slept. There, I was very frightened. Every time I heard somebody pass by or go under the window, I would cover myself up in the bed and I would cover up Shauli and I would pray, *Shema Yisrael, Adonai Eloheinu Adonai Echad* [Hear O Israel, the Lord our God, the Lord is One]. I learned this prayer at school. I would pray *Shema Yisrael*. I remember the fear there. We were alone. It was terrible. With strangers. They would give us pieces of dough in milk to eat. I remember that. Milk with pieces of dough. That was something . . .

Father, what do you remember from the war – fear, survival, thoughts, worry?

I tell you, it's strange. Strange. I thought about that, that I don't remember fear except perhaps one time. Well, the time I told you about when we were in the village, sleeping in one bed in some room. [It was] something, a terrible room. I don't even remember where we went to the toilet. They would bring us food. Well, I remember that when there were people walking around, I was very frightened. After that room, I suppose those farmers didn't want to take care of us anymore, so they took us to where Hanka, her father Dolek, and her mother were hiding, and this was in a silo. In the silo, yes. Where they keep hay, very big, big, big stacks of hay. Inside this hay, inside the haystacks, they made a kind of hole and we sat in this hole and we were hidden and we could climb up on a ladder. There were probably a number of bales; when they take out a bale or two, a hole is created. We were hidden inside it. We had to talk in whispers or not at all. So, of course, there was fear. I remember once peeing in my pants there, not only once. But, was it from fear or from something else? You had to talk in whispers or not at all, and I don't remember if they brought us food, and afterward they didn't want to keep us there either, and at night we moved to some other place; to an attic, let's call it. At the top of the house there is something like an attic, under the roof, where they hang laundry; it's under the roof and shingles. There we were hidden and the quality of life was much better because it wasn't inside hay that was square and where it was impossible to move. So, there was more room, but also – there was certainly fear. We were without parents. It wasn't . . . look, I left the ghetto once when my parents sent me some place to bring something, so I went by some villagers to bring food, to buy chocolate. I remember passing by a forest, by a cemetery, and there were shots there. They were shooting and shooting and I knew they were shooting people. I guess they were shooting Jews. But I don't remember the fear. I was more afraid of my parents than of the Germans. It's a terrible thing to say. Because I remember them giving me some money and I suppose I lost it. There was some sort of scene and it was very frightening. I think it was something like that. I did something bad ... you see. Perhaps more fear of that than ... perhaps death wasn't something clear. I remember the place and the shots.

[Silence.]

You see, when we escaped from Poland we would cross the border, the mountains at night, you know, with a guide; I know that there was fear. Fear of dogs barking when we passed by the villages. You pass through fields and mountains and also some village. The barking of dogs. When the dogs heard people passing by. To this day, dogs remind me of that walk.

And you like dogs.

I like dogs.

And trains as well.

And trains as well. But that was frightening. Or during those border crossings, when at night, all of a sudden, in the forest or in the field, mainly in the forest, I would see some light, a little one [light]. In Polish people call everything little, so they say a light, a little light. What does the light mean? That there is somebody there; it means you can be caught. That was frightening. Now, if you're asking about fear, I remember fear before the war; that is, not because of the war. Before the war, in the resort area where we were. I remember waking up at night. All of a sudden, I saw a moon. A low moon before it rises is very dark. To this day I have some ... it was terrible, that light looking into the room. Now – that was fear. Even when they caught us crossing borders and they caught us and told us, "Hands up," and arrested us and put us in jail – I don't remember fear. I don't remember fear. I remember great fear when reaching and crossing a border; we crossed through Poland, through Czechoslovakia, later on, Hungary and we reached Budapest. In Budapest, in Hungary, the Jews were still living well. Okay. But we didn't come there as Jews. We [came] as Poles, we changed our identity and so on. But when we reached Budapest, after all the borders and all the jails on the way and all kinds of things, we were living with a Jewish family in the Jewish Quarter in Budapest. And it was Friday night and there was a Friday night meal and there was fish, stuffed carp, and you cannot believe how tasty it was. Perhaps after all those years in the ghetto too and everything else – there was nothing like that. I get goose bumps from it now. And then there was a knock on the door and the secret police came in and they caught us, and that was very frightening. I don't know. Shauli hid underneath the bed and I begged the police.

Where were your parents?

They were there.

And what did they do?

What could they do? They took us. They took us and locked us up in some jail in Budapest and from there they sent us to some camp. Some kind of labor camp. I don't know what kind of people were there. There were a lot of people. There they separated the men from the women. I was with father. I think that Shauli was with mother. I am not sure. But mother was separate. For sure. And it was a camp. We would go out to work. I don't know if I went out to work, but father would go out to work. There were barracks with beds. With fleas, a lot of fleas there. It was impossible to sleep, and toilets with a hole like there used to be once in the army . . . but if we're talking of fear, then that was really frightening.

So what did you beg them?

To leave us alone. I went down on my knees. I clung to their boots.

You clung to their boots?

Yes. Yes. Yes. Yes. Fear. Fear. Panic.

And didn't they listen to you?

They came to take us.

Did they also take the second family?

I have no idea. I don't think so. We were illegal. We came there illegally. So that was a moment of great fear.

That's terrible. [I am silent.] I have a lot of questions.

I'm here.

Father, today, after the war, you are a happy person, very active, very positive and it's hard for me to understand how that's possible. You came here, you went into the army, you raised a family. Can you think about the implications and how you manage to be happy, as if, in a certain sense, nothing had happened?

In my opinion, the question is too big, too bombastic and general. And here, in fact, Yael's father's story ends. He might have been able to continue telling about the events of those times, but Yael was unable to cope with his descriptions of helplessness. The picture of him as a child hanging onto the boots of the Hungarian police and begging for his family's lives was too difficult for her. As an outcome of the interview, Yael wrote the following poem:

Text III: Even before you go

I will wait for you.
The look in your eyes
Gives me no answer. Will you return?
I am all yours.

And you of course are mine
So don't leave me
Stay. With me.

And if you go . . .
Remember
Never forget.
I will never forget, Father,
*   I swear.*
In my soul, I am all yours,
Even after you are gone.

An attempted dialogue between Yael and her father

Yael shares three different communications. In the first, she returns "simply to being father and daughter again for half an hour." Yael describes the way her father loved her as his little child, his expressions of limitless worry, the feeling of suffocation as well, and her concern: "how can I slip away through his fingers? I need to compensate him. I owe him the happiness in my life." In this way, she provides us with a concrete example of the monolithic guilt and loyalty that prevented her from developing a dialogue with her father through the double wall. Yael expects that the interview with her father, with whom she has never spoken about the period of the war, will open a window that will free her from the guilt and let her continue her life on her own.

In the short monologue that follows, Yael attempts to prepare her classmates – and also herself, perhaps – providing escape routes in case the interview does not interest them and she does not succeed in her attempt to get through the double wall before presenting it to them: "I won't read all of it; actually the interview is a bit boring." In her brief comments, she provides hints to her listeners that propel her toward the next step, reading the interview (the intensity of the connection with her father, the touch, her mother's stories, her fear of asking him, her fear that he will die), while the words undermine the deeper significance that these expressions have for her. Yael does not know if she can trust her classmates or trust herself when she is with them – or when she is by herself. Perhaps she has not yet completely absorbed the full significance of the interview.

Next comes the interview, on which I now focus. After a short introduction in which the two express their hesitations, the father explains his previous silence, especially in contrast to Yael's mother, who is "like a writer": "It's because I am closed, I don't tell or I don't remember or I don't want to remember." He gives Yael these three possibilities in this short sentence, as if inviting her to stop here. Yael wisely gives him the choice (*"I am not invading your privacy"*), but she is determined to know and offers him a way to begin. He still hesitates, but immediately he is swept into a long narrative, a wonderfully detailed sequence with memories that overwhelm him, as if he had never ceased remembering or talking about his childhood home.

Like an architect describing his creation, the father leads his daughter through his childhood home in great detail: He begins with the paved street, up the stairway and through the gate, into the anteroom, and through each one of the rooms, describing each of the entrances and the windows and the directions the rooms face. But Yael's father does not only speak of himself, as if he were entirely present there. He does not forget his daughter's presence: He examines the precision of his description from his present-day viewpoint ("if I were to see it today, would it still look as big?") and he tries to include her, drawing on her memories and noting those that are missing ("places like that in Europe . . . when we were together . . . Actually, you weren't with us in Yugoslavia"). Now, he can for the first time present his Diaspora Jewish self, rather suppressed and not so well integrated into his Israeli-Jewish identity.

At first, the house is described without the people who lived there. Then, very slowly, through the description of the study where he used to sleep, her father, in an almost Fellini-like description, incorporates himself and his own father (around the story of breaking the crystal vase, which led his father to stop talking to him). He includes his mother (who was strict with him about his handwriting and in charge of the candies), and, finally, his memory of the birth of his brother, a "screaming bundle." At first, Yael tries to fit in by asking questions ("Did you do homework?"). This does not interrupt the descriptive sequence (though her father does provide an answer to her question later on). Yael looks for a way to be a participant-listener on equal terms: she responds to hearing of the mother's strictness by asking, "What did that do to you?" and checks whether the term "punishment" applies to the harsh silence of her father's father. Yael is not yet satisfied, though. Is her father trying to distract her from the subject of the war by providing detailed description? Is that information still her main goal or is the resulting process now the important issue? If he is trying to deflect questions concerning the war, she is searching for a way to overcome the long and detailed descriptive sequence that she feels is too slow. Now the father is the adult who tells her no ("I haven't gotten to the war yet"), and Yael understands and comments, when transcribing the interview, that it is "a sort of warning that I shouldn't press him, a signal 'to let me tell it in my own time.'"

Her father goes on with his description. The inner structure of the house still plays a decisive role, framing his capacity for remembering out loud. However, the relationships between the characters in the house gradually become much more central. Now Yael attempts to join in the sequence of awareness that bursts forth from him, either by asking questions ("Was mother gentle?" "Wasn't father around?") or by relating to what he says ("See how you remember that part!" "Like I did to Michal?"). It is as if she were saying, "Look, father, when you talk about yourself as a child, we can be two independent people having a conversation with one another." And the father, perhaps responding, perhaps having difficulty in accepting such a strong change in their relationship, moves between external worries ("Are you cold? "Should I put on the heater?") and answering her questions ("Perhaps. I don't know what you did to her; it's hard being a child, isn't it?"). Within this process, there is a moment that invites progress toward an open dialogue, but the father, who ostensibly created the opening, also controls the pace when he says, "I haven't gotten to the war yet." ("In the movie they showed a woman who didn't know anything about herself except for a spoon." "I didn't want to see it." "You need to see it." "It's very hard for me." "Because you're my daughter, I guess."). Her being his daughter is enough of an explanation for him. He does not examine what is difficult for Yael.

Slowly the descriptive circle extends beyond his immediate childhood home. The memories, though, seem more fragmented. Perhaps it is that the cohesive "glue" of the house walls was lost. We hear of a tram, a schoolyard, grandfather's workplace, the tinsmith, the relations between the Jews and the Christians, and the royal palace in Cracow. Perhaps Yael's father is now moving in circles, reviving his childhood memories before the harsh memories of the wartime that he may have to touch on in a moment. The change in the course of the conversation comes from Yael, who probably understands that she should remain quiet. Finally, her father also falls silent. Then, for the first time, as an echo to the question she posed too early, he says, "Do I remember the war that broke out?" At the end of the tape, he makes one more attempt to escape ("That's it, child . . . we're finished."). And she instinctively answers, "Wishful thinking," but she also stands before him, as if saying, "I listened patiently to you for an entire tape; now go on, I am listening, and I can cope with the description of times when you were in difficult situations."

Her father responds. He is willing to describe moments of fear as a child, moments of prayer underneath the bed; finding a hiding place in the silo where "I once peed in my pants – not only once." A particularly clear memory is of passing by a cemetery while out to buy bread and hearing shots ("I knew they were shooting Jews"), yet being "more afraid of my parents than of the Germans. It's a terrible thing to say now." And he adds that in retrospect, "perhaps death wasn't something clear" – but his parents' anger was. Yael responds by listening quietly, as if saying: "I am with you, go on." He briefly describes the moments of separation and meeting between him and his parents until he reaches an especially distressing scene: In Budapest, living with a Jewish family, they are having a warm Friday night meal and are able to hope that the worries are behind them, when suddenly Hungarian police burst in to the apartment, and he, the child of 9, begs for his life – for their lives.

This humiliating memory is too harsh a test of Yael's restrained listening. She breaks in repeatedly, with a string of questions: *"And where were your parents? "And what did they do?" "And what did you beg them?" "You clung to their boots?" "And didn't they listen to you?" "Did they also take the second family?"* Yael is crushed by the humiliating image (her big, strong father is kneeling, clinging to the boots of the police and pleading), and she lets slip, "That's terrible," and after a silence, "I have a lot of questions." Now, once again as her father, he takes over. At the right moment, and perhaps with the right intonation, he only says three words: "I am here," as if telling her, "It was the little helpless boy there in that situation; now I am here again by your side, with everything that you know about me since then." Is he trying to calm her; perhaps trying to calm himself?

In a certain sense, the interview reaches a climax at this point. Yael can feel the greatness of her father at his weakest moment. Now she knows the memories with which her father has struggled all these years and also the source of his exaggerated worry about her – why he accompanied her home from school every day when she was 6 (he was 9 at the time of the trauma in Budapest), even when she preferred to go it alone; why he prevented her from going through Hebron on the class trip. The father, having shared with Yael some of the most difficult moments of his life, can now acknowledge her maturity as a listener who responds adequately to his descriptions. As a crescendo of harshness builds in his descriptions, Yael allows her response – "That's terrible" – to reveal her emotions as a participant-listener.

Yael's momentary ability, with almost a cry, to join in the harsh picture of her father-child kneeling and pleading in the face of his parent's helplessness and his brother's fright, creates a new encounter between his memory and their shared awareness. From now on, father, you are not alone there (with your memories) and I am not alone here (with your silences). However, Yael also signals that she cannot bear to hear anymore about the period, at least not for the moment. It is her first encounter between her monolithic Israeli-Jewish identity construction and the "weakness," by Israeli standards, of the Diaspora Jewish identity that he avoided showing her until now. Yet Yael does not wish to end the interview here, perhaps fearing that she will be unable to reconstruct such an encounter.

Speaking to the class, she tells of subsequent discussion with her father about the long-term effects of those difficult childhood events on him and on his relationship with her, with her sisters, and with his own father. Perhaps this more than the interview symbolizes the beginning of the process of mutual acceptance between daughter and father. The discussion focuses on the usual issues of relationship and separation. Yael asks, "Your family is everything, right?" "How do you feel now that your daughters are no longer at home?" "Why was it important to you that I keep my last name?"

Her father answers her fully aware of the respect he has for her. He feels that she can now contain the parts of himself that he tried to conceal from her. Likewise, he wishes to receive some acknowledgment of her respect for him. "Your world is larger," he tells her. "It has much wider borders. You also have many more aspirations and goals that you set yourself . . . and perhaps, I want to make the name more famous. Even though it's not the name I was born with." It is as if he is saying, "You will go farther than I, and it is I who have a part in your achievement, even though I still have unsolved questions about identity (and name)." Yael is now leading the discussion:

> But father, I am asking you how you feel about your daughters leaving and you talk about whether it's good for your daughters or not. I am asking you how you feel about grandfather dying and you talk about whether it's good for grandfather to live or not. Perhaps try and see how you feel?"

Her father tries to touch inside and reaches the source of his worry:

> I don't worry. I am at peace. Except for times, when all of a sudden, there is no contact. I need this contact. I always have to make sure that everyone is alive and at home. Well, I have no doubt that this is the result of uncertainty about a person returning home at all.

Now, after the spoken memories from Poland and Budapest, this sentence has a validity that transcends the feeling of suffocation that accompanied Yael in the past and that she presented in her opening monologue. A short exchange at the end reflects this combination of what was achieved and what was not achieved. The father tests a feeling of something "missing," but Yael states that the interview covered "as much as is possible." The father is happy about the interview with his daughter, yet he has a sad expression. She answers him:

> It doesn't matter how many details you gave me, it's what I do with them that matters.

> Good, listen. We can talk more. It is possible to elaborate, but now, what could be better than my daughter interviewing me today?

Perhaps as an echo to his anxiety, much more understandable now, comes Yael's final poem, in which he begs, "So don't leave me. Stay with me. And if you go . . . remember. Never forget." And she reassures him, "I will never forget, father . . . In my soul, I am all yours, even after you are gone." This seems like a return to the declaration of monolithic loyalty. But perhaps in the particular context of Yael and her father, it is a soothing declaration that goes with the words she used to sum up the interview: "[We covered] as much as is possible . . . it's what I do with it that matters." It is as if she is saying: "From here on, I, Yael, know you better than you know yourself." The dialogue started, but it is not yet completed.

4.2 DIALOGUE BETWEEN THE SELF AND THE ALIEN OTHER: ISRAELI JEWISH AND PALESTINIAN STUDENTS[2]

In 2000, we began workshops at Ben-Gurion University that we called Coexistence through Storytelling. Through interviewing family members from previous generations, participants saw and could relate to the complexity of their own collective identities. The process provided a glimpse into the complexity of the identity of the Other, beyond the dominant stereotypical mutual perceptions (Bar-On, 2004/2006; Bar-On & Kassem, 2004). These workshops followed previous workshops from 1994 to 1999 led by facilitators from Neve Shalom/Wahat al-Salam, based on a more confrontational model. Jewish and Arab students were led to confront each other and

---

[2] This section was written partially in collaboration with Shoshana Steinberg. We thank Dr. Shifra Sagi from the Department of Education at Ben-Gurion University and Michal Zak and Rabah Halabi from Neve Shalom, facilitators of the workshop, for their help in creating the dialogue. The workshop was supported by research grants from the Abraham Fund and the Hertzog Center for Diplomacy and the Middle East.

themselves through empowering the less dominant side. The absence of
the usual asymmetry of power that controls the relationship outside the
seminar room changed their perceptions of each other.

In everyday language in Israel, many Jewish-Israelis would call such a
workshop an encounter between "Arabs and Israelis." As we will see, however, this expression is problematic. Even though "Israeliness" is so often
identified with being Jewish, the Arabs in the workshop are not residents of
the West Bank and Gaza; they are Israelis. Some of these Arabs prefer to be
called Palestinians. They claim that "Arab citizens of Israel" demonstrates
Israeli hegemony, conferring an identity on them of Israeli and minority,
without consulting them. We tried calling the workshop "Encounters
between Jewish and Palestinian Israelis," but it sounded convoluted.[3] Moreover, we appeared to be taking a political stand. Many Israeli Jews are unwilling to acknowledge the Palestinian identity of Arabs living in Israel, or they
perceive such identification as affiliating with the "enemy" with whom we
are still in conflict. In addition, this name implies redefining them as Jews
first and foremost, which is not how predominantly secular Israelis of Jewish origin identify themselves. In this sense, already inherent in the issue
of a name for the workshop are some of the problems that emerge in the
group encounters themselves.

The dialogue between Yael and her father took place within a Jewish-
Israeli family. It entailed redefining aspects of the family members' mutual
identity as Israeli Jews with the Holocaust and the Diaspora in the background. At the workshops, in contrast, we bring together people who perceive themselves as representatives of two rivalry collectives. They do not
know each other very well, or they have only met across the stereotypical
barriers of hostility and force. From the moment they meet, they relate to
each other through the lens of the collective, the self versus the Other. Avner's
previous encounter with Arabs was working with them on a building site.
Nasser, his dialogue partner, knew Jews during his studies in Beer-Sheva and
generally experienced the encounter as humiliating and infuriating. Just as
the dialogue between Yael and her father was "prearranged" (initially the

---

[3] For a more explicit and thorough discussion of the questions concerning labels ("Israeli-
Arabs" and Palestinians in Israel") and their wider significance, see articles by Bishara
(1993) and Rabinowitz (1997).

result of a requirement for a class at university), so the encounter between Israeli-Jewish and Palestinian students is not a matter of spontaneity. It begins as a university workshop assignment. Even then, without appropriate facilitation, the students may well direct the discussion to cultural behavior, food, or soccer.

Our workshop discusses the conflict between Jews and Palestinians head-on.[4] For some years now, sixteen to eighteen participants from each "side" have spent three hours each week for an entire year confronting questions that concern the conflict between the two nations. They divide their time between regular binational encounters and uninational ones that take place once every three weeks. Once a year, they meet at Neve Shalom for a weekend and meet similar student groups from other universities. The weekly encounter serves as an opportunity to get to know each other. Each side tries to examine questions of personal and group boundaries, specifically looking at the question of who they are when no longer defined by the Other.

The two groups are by no means symmetrical: The Jewish group represents the dominant group in the Israeli population and the Palestinians represent the minority. Though the workshop is structured to provide the two groups with equal representation, the ostensible symmetry within the group and the uneven power relations outside it create an immediate tension (Maoz, 2000). These power relations have a double significance: Each side perceives itself as a minority and the victim of its fellow. The Jews perceive Israeli Arabs as being part of the larger Middle Eastern context and feel surrounded by a sea of hate. The Palestinians perceive themselves as a weak minority in the face of the Jewish-Israeli power with which they have grown up, and they also may feel at a disadvantage among the Arab states, which, for many years, did not recognize the Palestinians as an independent nation. In this sense, the workshop demonstrates the problem inherent in Contact Theory (Allport, 1954; Amir, 1976) and its assumption that in encounter situations a bubble of symmetry and cooperation can be created that endures despite the conflict and asymmetry in the reality outside of the

---

[4] The workshops were designed by facilitators from Neve Shalom and held first at Tel Aviv University and then, from 1994 to 1999, at Ben-Gurion University. Lately, I developed a different model, based on family storytelling (Bar-On, 2004/2006; Bar-On & Kassem, 2004).

encounter (Maoz, 2000). Experience gained in these workshops indicates that the encounter does not resolve problems that draw their energy from the asymmetry outside the context of the workshop. These continue to nourish the conflict in the light of past and present events or the absence of a promise of a solution in the future. Janet Helms (1990) views the problem that arises in the encounter between majority and minority as one of vagueness in the definition of self among the people of the majority (the white majority in the case of the United States) – a vagueness that stands out in the face of an oppressed minority's clearly strengthening identity (the black minority in the case of the United States). Moscovici (1976) and Mugny and Perez (1991) similarly maintain that in the encounter between the hegemonic group and the minority group, the latter's social representations confer an advantage: A minority knows how to differentiate between self-representation and the representation of the majority with which it is often in disaccord, while the hegemonic group usually has no such complex representation but merely a vague self-representation. Therefore, during the first stages of encounter, the minority group has a relative advantage, and it is members of the hegemonic group who must examine the vagueness and possible internal contradictions in their self-definition (Bar-On, 2004/2006).

It sometimes appears that groups in a workshop proceed along independent axes with no meeting point. According to one theoretical model,[5] the Jews move along the axis of fear-indifference-sympathy, while the Palestinians move along the axis of antipathy-justice-empathy. Although the Jews are trying to preserve some distance and even maintain indifference in their contact with their fellow participants, the Palestinians are trying to show them – even at the price of incurring an openly antagonistic response initially – that Jewish discourse is ethnocentric (Steinberg & Bar-On, 2002), concerned only with Jewish issues. These are the motivating forces when various people talk in the group: each side tries to tip the scales toward its own axis, thus keeping its identity "intact," as it was before the encounter, so that it will not have to examine its validity, discover internal tensions, and

---

[5] This theoretical model was a subject of Shoshana Steinberg's doctoral thesis. The encounter groups of Israeli Jewish and Palestinian students saw a process of change, from ethnocentric discourse to dialogical moments (Steinberg & Bar-On, 2002).

make cardinal changes. Later on we will see how, in the process of group discussion between Jews and Palestinians, the monolithic construction in group identity disintegrates. The very awareness that the components of the collective identity are no longer compatible with a single rule helps create a dialogue about questions of identity. In the course of the workshop, this dialogue changes in quality from a rather routine ping-pong between self and alien Other to a simultaneous internal and external dialogue.

It is difficult to discuss a group process because, with many individuals participating, various dynamics happen simultaneously. Likewise, it is difficult to use the biographical methods presented in previous chapters to analyze group dialogue. The analogy between groups that structure their life story according to a hidden strategy and individuals who do the same is a problematic one (Bar-On, 2004/2006). Our solution here is using one individual to represent each of the collectives, choosing excerpts from Avner and Nasser's discussions in the workshop of 1997–98. Both were key figures in their national groups. They became friends during the observation assignment they carried out together at the end of the first semester. More than once, the extreme opposing standpoints they expressed at the workshop were in sharp contrast to the friendship developing between them. The extracts from their dialogue throughout the first semester are representative of part of the broader group process (Maoz et al., 2002). Obviously, the dynamic between the two could not always represent the entire group and the extracts chosen do not necessarily represent everything that happened in the group or even between the two protagonists. The advantage of this mode of presentation is that it illustrates the interpersonal processes that take place at the workshop without the need for a more detailed presentation of multiple participants and the structure of connections between them.

Personal backgrounds: Nasser and Avner

Nasser was born in Acre and raised in an Arab neighborhood. His parents are originally from Jenin, today part of the Palestinian Authority. When he was seven years old, his family moved to Beer-Sheva. He studied at Tel-Sheva, a Bedouin town, as it was important to his parents that he study Arabic and his cultural and religious heritage. He transferred to a Jewish high school in Beer-Sheva with higher educational standards to increase his chances of success in the matriculation examination. Despite having Jewish friends and a very good relationship with his teachers (he emphasizes the fact that he received help in his studies and personal support and encouragement), he felt out of place – among Jews, as an Arab from the north among the nomadic Bedouins of the south, and, ultimately, as an Arab student at a Jewish university. He did not develop a sense of discrimination on a personal level.

> I always felt I was in a minority although everything usually worked out for me. When I came to study with the Bedouins, they regarded me as a *fallah* [peasant]. I learned the Bedouin and city accent. When I transferred to the Jewish school, I didn't have an Arabic accent. I studied Jewish history, tradition, language – everything. I know it hurts Arab parents when the children don't know Arabic... because of [my studies] I got into university. I matriculated, considered chemical engineering but was not accepted, registered for economics, and met Arab students at the university. I was glad to know them and to feel I belonged. Jews don't appreciate what they have. We acknowledge its importance because we don't have it. They have friends, festivals... I had to study during my festivals. I experienced this feeling for the first time when I visited Bir Zeit University. I was suddenly a different Nasser. I had never been in a place where everyone was an Arab. Maybe it's too late to erase; even if I go and live in Palestine, deep inside I won't belong because this is something that is hard to erase. People are always telling me there is an advantage in growing up in Israel with all the technology and economic advantages, but I don't think so. What worries me the most is that I blame my parents for my being in a minority, but they are also a minority. It may be too late for me, but not for my children; I can't blame my parents and not do something for my children. I write a lot of poetry, I believe that the wars and casualties are part of the peace process, and that, in the end, there has to be peace. The fact that we are living together means there will be peace.

This monologue was part of the initial interview with Nasser, conducted by Shoshana Steinberg during the first weeks of the workshop. This is also the context of the following excerpts from an interview with Avner.

Avner was born on Kibbutz Yad Mordechai. Named after Mordechai Anilewitch, the commander of the Warsaw Ghetto uprising in 1943, the kibbutz was put under Egyptian siege during the 1948 war and suffered heavy losses. Thus, one can say that Yad Mordechai represents the monolithic construction of Israeli-Jewish heroism in its most extreme form. However, it also belongs to the left-wing political party, and, as such, its members are largely in favor of Palestinian statehood.

Avner was exposed to the Holocaust at a very young age:

> On my kibbutz, you more or less live the Holocaust. When I was growing up, all the adults without exception, and many of the second generation, had been in the Holocaust. There is a large Holocaust museum on the kibbutz, a very big statue; the President comes on Holocaust Day. You must understand that when I was growing up on that kibbutz, a child of 3 or 4, I was already visiting a very large Holocaust museum.

Apologetically, he adds: "You can't expect me to reach the age of 10 or 11 without the Holocaust coming to mean more to me than the massacre at Kafar Kassem.[6] It's only natural."

Avner's army service was an important component of his Israeli-Jewish monolithic identity. Despite great difficulty and the dilemmas evoked by his service in the Occupied Territories, his loyalty to the army and the obligation to serve constituted a central, irrefutable value. He defined himself as a secular Israeli with left-wing political views who aspired to peace with the Arabs. Before participating in the workshop, he had met both Israeli Arabs and Palestinian Arabs from the Territories while working on a building site. He admitted to having limited knowledge of them. During his work in Perach (a guidance program for pupils), he had met an Arab counselor and played basketball with him, but no friendship developed between them. He chose to participate in the workshop to meet Arabs and know more about them because of the ongoing conflict, and he hoped that the encounter might draw them closer and help resolve the conflict between Israelis and Palestinians.

---

[6] In the village of Kafar Kassem on the opening day of the 1956 battle against Egypt, Israeli border police, who enforced the curfew then in effect in Arab villages, slaughtered forty-nine Arab civilians who returned late from their fields. It is known to be one of the worst massacres in the history of the Israeli-Arab conflict.

I worked together with them on a building site. Working together was a very positive experience. We worked and ate together; things like that. Once we traveled in a car together and Arabic music was playing. One of the laborers said that one day there would only be Arabic music on the radio and everything would be in Arabic. It didn't annoy me; both of us knew that this was not what was going to happen, but I was glad he could dream like that. The experience in Perach is also positive. We work together in "Havayeda."[7] We present the program in the Bedouin community . . . over and above this, I had no contact with Arabs. They had no significance in my life. Whenever there is a terrorist attack, there's a lot of anger, a feeling that something must be done, but even in the most difficult moments I believe there is a solution. There are feelings of anger at the situation and the people who do these things, and I can't understand them. I understand that, from their point of view, this is the way; I can't agree with it, but even when I felt the most pain, I believed that there was another solution. I came to the workshop in order to meet and understand them. If, after the workshop, I am better acquainted with the problems, if I can say I have some sort of solution because I talked to the other side and reached some sort of compromise, then the workshop will have achieved its purpose. We have to talk. I think these dialogues are very important. Such forums are worthwhile. If we talk, things will come out and no one will remain indifferent. Both sides need positive experiences.

An analysis of the dialogue between Avner and Nasser could begin with their personal frames of reference, as seen in these interviews. Nasser experiences being born to a rejected minority and is making his way in Jewish society by virtue of his intellectual ability. The first few sentences reveal a tension between his somewhat romanticized view of Palestinian Bir Zeit University on one hand, and on the other, his feeling of alienation both there and in Israel, though obviously for different reasons. In contrast, Avner immediately emphasizes the complex emotional burden passed on to him by a kibbutz with both a monolithic tradition of Holocaust memorials and a tradition of a positive regard for the political claims of the Palestinians. Avner approaches the encounter with naiveté: "if we talk . . . no one will remain indifferent." Before further analysis, we will look at the first interaction between Nasser and Avner.

---

[7] Haveyeda is a small, hands-on science museum at Ben-Gurion University with a support program run by students for children with learning disabilities.

The first encounter

Avner, in class:

> If they [the facilitators] relate to us as two groups, discussion will take place between one group and the other and not among individuals. In a group, a dynamic develops between individuals, and so following the path of the facilitators will be rather difficult for me.

Avner is one of the first in the class to speak after the Arab facilitator's introduction. He is proposing that the students relate to the subject of the relationships between the two groups on a personal basis rather than as one group to another, as the facilitators suggest. Polite requests for group dynamics between individuals while blurring their national identities are typically made by Jewish participants to Palestinians in the beginning. "We are all Israelis," they say. The hidden, unwitting message: We, members of the dominant group, do not need to emphasize our national characteristics here. If you are also willing to put yours aside, our dominance will be preserved and we will then be happy to relate to you on a personal basis.

Nasser, however, replies, "I am a Palestinian. There is a difference between national and political affiliation. I will never feel Israeli."

These two opening sentences indicate a full-scale drama. Nasser, with his authoritative assertion of identity, is trying, at this early stage, to say several things:

1. I will not consent to your suggestion, Avner; I am telling you straight out who I am, defining myself through my group identity.
2. In terms of group identity, I am a Palestinian and not an Israeli Arab – you should have no illusions about this.
3. Since I differentiate between nationality and political differences, I do not feel (and more than this, I will never feel) Israeli. That is, whatever develops here will not change my views. (At this stage, Nasser does not choose any specific example but remains on the generalized level at which Avner began the discussion.)

Avner: I want to know about everyday life. I'm not really interested in where your loyalty lies, with Arafat or with Peres. Why aren't you comfortable here? What's so bad about it?

For the first time we feel the parallel axes along which Avner and Nasser are moving. Avner is trying to "be nice" to Nasser, but, in fact, ignores his answer. While challenging Nasser, Avner is also contrasting his own political "openness" to most of the Israeli population, those who demand knowing whether Nasser's "loyalty" lies with the Palestinian or the Israeli leader. Trying to turn the discussion back to personal, daily problems, Avner is not at this point aware of the paternalism inherent in his words or his lack of direct response to what Nasser has said.

Nasser replies:

> I think that when someone has something, he doesn't appreciate it. This is why it is very hard for you to understand. I have been living here for twenty years now; on Fridays and Saturdays the shops are closed; there is nowhere to go. I stay here for the holidays and there's nothing for me to do. A mosque – to go and pray – it's been turned into the Beer-Sheva Museum. I miss a lot of things here. You don't feel this because you have it all. There's folk-dancing, discos, films. Not one film in Arabic, no Arab music.

In Nasser's words, there is a sharp transition from the initial, general level to a more concrete level. There is, however, no personal statement to Avner. Nasser's reply can be interpreted in various ways. On one hand, he ostensibly responds to Avner's suggestion and begins to describe what is "so bad" for him: not finding any place in Israel for Palestinian culture or the Muslim religion. On the other hand, Nasser opens with a strong statement ("when someone has something he does not appreciate it; this is why it is very hard for you to understand"). Nasser uses the example of the mosque in Beer-Sheva to illustrate the insult to his people and the brusque disregard for their feelings on the part of Israeli Jews. Additional examples ("no films in Arabic, no Arab music") reinforce the feeling of disregard and obliteration.

Avner: That's because of your own [dis]organization.

Does this response show Avner's lack of regard for Nasser? Or might this attack already show the beginning of his defense? Avner is still talking in the plural, ignoring Nasser's more personal address. Avner emphasizes "your" responsibility, presenting here for the first time the assumption of symmetry prevalent among Jewish participants at this stage of the discussion: If you changed, you'd get these sorts of things, just like us. You're just not organized enough. In majority-minority relations, this diversion by attributing blame to the minority is characteristic: "Your tough situation doesn't stem from external forces but from your own lack of effort." Nonetheless, without noticing, Avner has now responded to Nasser's need to communicate on the level of the group and not the individual.

> *Nasser:* Students' Day is a day for Jewish people.
> *Avner:* You've got representatives on the students' committee; they should do something. Take your complaints to your representatives. I understand the facts, but the question is whether this situation cannot be resolved. I ask you why you feel uncomfortable. You tell me you have no leisure activities. It stems from your own actions; you aren't organized.

Again Nasser and Avner are moving along parallel axes that don't meet at this stage. Nasser takes up another challenging point, brusquely charging that Students' Day is only for Jewish students. He thereby exposes – for the first time – the Jewish meaning of "Israeliness." Jews organize Students' Day for Jews, and as far as he is concerned, this is not "Israeli." There are other "Israelis" like himself whom the Jews disregard.

Avner is now clearly defending himself while trying to ignore the "Jewish" challenge presented by Nasser. Although Avner again momentarily approaches Nasser personally, asking why he feels uncomfortable, it appears that this is a rhetorical question: He answers the question himself, in the same vein as before: the problem is inaction; lack of organization.

This ends the first part of the encounter between Nasser and Avner. Each has defined his own frame of reference and is testing out the other. At this stage, Nasser is more adept in his responses and Avner must defend himself, trying the usual approaches to a discussion between Jews and Palestinians. They confront each other again toward the end of the session when the discussion in the group turns to the establishment of a Palestinian state. The monologue begun by Nasser expresses typical Palestinian arguments:

> The Jews get very sensitive and hurt when they are criticized for being racist. We are Palestinians who live here; we are one people. We have relatives there

in the West Bank and Gaza. We paid a price in order for the Jews to have a
state. There are many sad stories. We are one people, but we live all over the
world. What happened to the Jews is now happening to us because of your
desire to establish a Jewish state; because of this we live in the Diaspora.
We have feelings, and we want to establish a state. I don't want one uncle
to live in the U.S., one in Jordan, another in the Territories. A Palestinian
state threatens you. The name of this country is Palestine – this is why I am
known as a Palestinian.

In contrast with his laconic expressions at the outset of the encounter,
Nasser's present narrative is not only more explicit. For the first time,
he dramatically and movingly presents his own version of the Palestinian
narrative: You Jews don't feel so comfortable about being defined as racist,
and you don't feel comfortable about acknowledging that you have racist
tendencies. We, the Palestinians, paid a price for you to have your state.
What was done to you is now happening to us.

> *Avner:* Tell me, d'you want Haifa and Tel Aviv?
> *Nasser (laughing):* I do, but I can't have them.

Avner appears to have experienced Nasser's words as a threat and reacts
accordingly. Although he asks a direct question, he is nonetheless expressing
fear: Is it true that you want major Israeli cities as a part of your Palestinian
state? On one hand, his response to Nasser's saying, "The name of this
country is Palestine – this is why I am known as a Palestinian" enables him to
ignore the entire Palestinian narrative preceding that sentence. Nasser, who
may be enjoying the immediate effect he has elicited, answers laughingly, as
if doing so to reawaken the previous effect of strength, eliciting Avner's fear:
If I could, of course I would take them, just as you did whatever you wanted
when you could. It is here that Nasser responds to Avner's assumption of
symmetry: It is the strong who determine matters, and I too have ambitions
of being strong like you, though I cannot fulfill these ambitions right now.
Here surfaces the fear among Jews that if the Palestinians could, they would
take Jaffa and Tel Aviv.

> *Avner:* I would like you to answer a question. I more or less know what is
> happening with my people. My ideas are based on the Israeli consensus,
> or whatever you want to call it, but I don't know about you; this is truly

an innocent question: At what point in history, as you see it, does your definition of a Palestinian people begin?

Here there is an interesting turnabout between the two: Nasser has co-opted the assumption of symmetry, and Avner in turn accepts the definition of collective identity. He has stopped relating to the other side in the plural (as he did in relation to Students' Day) and begins to speak directly to Nasser. Fear that the Palestinians are too well organized and suspicion of their intentions toward the Jews have now replaced the claim that the Arab students are not sufficiently organized. But as Avner continues, he is not clear. Is he trying to understand the extent of the Palestinians' territorial ambitions, in another manifestation of the fear expressed previously, or has the fear faded, to be replaced by the initial sense of superiority as he asks an "innocent" question, underlying which is a challenge: In contrast to our long tradition and presence here thousands of years ago, the "Palestinian people" came into being during this century.[8]

> *Nasser:* I don't know anything about history.
> *Avner:* I'm just asking, I'm trying to understand . . .

Nasser does not respond, perhaps because he feels there isn't enough time to develop the subject or because he neither knows nor wants to continue in that direction. It might be that the very presentation of the Palestinian

---

[8] At the first Jewish uninational encounter two weeks later, Avner revisits his question:

> The first time I asked them, I really wanted to know the origin of the Palestinian people. I meant, is there something mentioned in the Koran or some date, even an inexact one, from some period, that can tell us that the Palestinian people was born at such and such a time? An ostensibly innocent question, but one which, when I thought about it at home, might be interpreted as provocative. What do you mean by it: that we Palestinians don't have a right to be here, that we are a people without national rights? The whole thing might stem from this paranoia, which is entirely legitimate. We say and mean the most innocent things in the world, from an honest desire to know and find out, but they're heard as provocative, because the Palestinians are so sensitive. I don't go around everyday with a feeling that I am a Jew, a Zionist, and an Israeli. I know it exists, but before that I am a student, I work, and so on. I think that with them, they take in Palestinian identity and a sense of deprivation and the occupation with their mother's milk. That's why they are so busy and sensitive; everything is interpreted as provocation.
> This bears witness to how quickly Avner understood, in retrospect, the possibility of how Nasser might interpret an "innocent" question.

narrative is more important to him than going into the complex maze of "who was here first."

The second conflict between the two ends in a stalemate, as if they have learned to appreciate each other's strength. Toward the end of the encounter, Avner again tries to divert the discussion between them, perhaps out of a last-minute desire to restore a personal, rather than a group context to the discussion; to "locate" himself and Nasser as closer than has been expressed in the discussion itself.

> *Avner:* I define myself according to my political views and according to my perceptions . . . I don't think we are so far apart, you and I. I hope I am right, but you understood the things I said, during the break too, very differently, and you related to them in a very hostile manner. I don't know where it's coming from, but it definitely has to do with the atmosphere, which isn't pleasant.

Avner is using a strategy that is well known in processes in which the groups are not symmetrical: a strategy of claiming a sense of justice together with an attempt to create feelings of guilt in the other: We are, in fact, quite close (in our viewpoint) but you have a problem in how you interpret what I say and you answer in a hostile manner and create a disagreeable atmosphere. Had Nasser accepted Avner's complaint and asked himself why Avner felt hurt, Avner would have ended the meeting with the moral advantage of creating guilt in Nasser. But Nasser seems quite practiced and ready for such attempts to "put him in the corner":

> *Nasser:* We came here to argue, to talk about things, and it isn't at all personal.
> *Avner:* You haven't hurt me and I'm not having a hard time, I don't have a problem with being attacked, I can take it . . . You attack me for things I didn't mean. I meant that things sound completely different.
> *Nasser:* You aren't in touch with what you're saying. You don't know how things come across – how we understand you.

For the first time, Nasser defines the purpose of the workshop as he sees it, while reemphasizing the group connection. But he also emphasizes that he did not intend to hurt Avner, thereby perhaps clarifying that Avner is important to him. Avner attempts to use Nasser's first expression of closeness in order to engage his help against one of the Arab-Palestinian women whom, he claimed, "didn't understand him at all." But Nasser remains loyal to the collective that he hitherto represented, with great success: "You are not in touch with what you are saying. You don't know how things come across – how we understand you." Avner, not to be outdone, ends the discussion by returning to the less specific level of the beginning. He tries to reestablish his superiority by using the claim of "debate culture."

> *Avner:* The question is why? Perhaps what we have been doing for the last half an hour reflects the natural situation of the Jewish-Arab conflict. We argued, confronted each other, and so on. But I think that in order to make the discussions more fruitful and operative, it would be more effective for both sides to adopt some sort of debate culture, something that might be more valuable than society as it is today.

THE FOURTH ENCOUNTER

This encounter took place following the Palestinian group's visit to Bir Zeit University, under Palestinian rule. The students arrive excited from the visit and make particular note of conditions that are lacking at Ben-Gurion University. At Bir Zeit University there is Arab music; lectures are held in Arabic. Members of the Jewish group ask if the Palestinian participants would go there to do master's degrees. Following is the discussion of this subject between Nasser and Avner.

> *Nasser:* I would like to clarify this point. I would study there if they had an M.A. in my subject. Someone who hasn't been there can't understand it . . . in short, the problem is one of conditions. We would like to study there.
>
> *Avner:* All your considerations are practical. The question is whether you are deciding not to study at a university where you feel at home for these practical reasons; if so, why not do the same when the Palestinian state is established? Why go on living here? It's impossible for you to feel at home here. You're saying something that sounds very odd. You're saying, in fact, that when the Palestinian state is established, you won't go and live there.
>
> *A few answer simultaneously:* Why should we go? Our land is here!

This time, Nasser expresses some ambivalence: On one hand, he identifies with Bir Zeit University (and, accordingly, perhaps, with the Palestinian nationalism of which it is a symbol), and on the other hand, he presents practical considerations, giving the reason why he will not study there. Avner immediately identifies Nasser's ambivalence and asks why, since it is impossible for him to feel comfortable as a minority in a Jewish state, he would go on living in it once the Palestinian state is established.

The Jews in the group are amazed at the Palestinian reaction: that they will not move because what is now Israel has been their land and home for generations. The Jewish students respond to this effect: Our forebears yearned for generations and some traveled vast distances to live in a Jewish state; to get away from living and raising children as a minority among non-Jews – and you are not willing to travel fifty kilometers so that your children can be raised together within the majority of your nation and religion – because of your connection to your parents' land? This amazement reveals the greatest gap so far between the two nations' monolithic belief systems. The Jews believe in Zionism, and they are willing to dislocate themselves from a tradition of hundreds of years of Diaspora. The Palestinians believe that their bond with the land is more important than the possibility of participating in the creation of their own nation-state. Naturally, the Jews fear that staying on the land is only the first of many stages. A familiar theory is that the Palestinians are still striving to gain control over the whole of Israel as they had intended in 1948. They are biding their time, with the intention of driving the Jews out step by step. Sharp transitions in the dialogue, between direct individual appeal and indirect general ones, characterize the doubt and unease and also perhaps the demagoguery prevalent among both parties.

> *Avner:* The question is how you, Nasser, a man who has no intention of moving to a Palestinian state, can say you have demands. I just want to know [turns to the Jewish group]; I want to understand their point of view, how can they make demands for an independent state they have no intention of living in. You, Nasser, have you no intention of moving there? As things stand now? He [referring to Nasser] isn't answering me [looks round in triumph].
>
> *Nasser [uneasy]:* I can't live there.

Avner: Why not?

Nasser: Because there is Man and Land. My land is here. Most Palestinian
people, should a state be established, will feel they belong there. But there
are those who won't leave their land to live with their own nation. Do you
understand? There are two separate issues here. Why didn't you agree
to go to Uganda?[9] You said that you differentiate between the nation
and the land. So why didn't you go to Uganda? As long as the nation is
together [that's what counts]. [Some of the Jewish participants call out.]
After all, you wanted a Jewish state. Had you gone to another country,
you would have felt comfortable with each other and you would not have
felt anti-Semitism. [But] another place has no meaning for you; it's the
same for us.

Avner enjoyed Nasser's distress. Turning from him to the group, he takes
advantage of the unusual lack of an immediate answer. Nasser tries to answer
in two ways ("there are two separate issues here"): He attempts to differentiate between the right of the Palestinian majority to realize its national
identity in a state and Israeli-Palestinians like himself who are connected to
land and are therefore willing to give up that affiliation. Second, Nasser gives
the example of the failed Uganda plan to try and explain the parallel Jewish
need to realize aspirations to nationhood on a particularly meaningful piece
of land ("Another place has no meaning for you? It's the same for us").

Avner: So, this means that the establishment of a Palestinian state,
even with Jerusalem as its capital, will not resolve the Arab-Jewish
conflict . . . Now, if I have an argument with some right-wing extremist
and he says to me, 'Listen, they want the Territories, they want Jerusalem
and tomorrow they will want Haifa and Jaffa,' I won't be able to tell
him it isn't true . . . You are fighting for a state you have no intention of
living in. In my opinion, you are wrong, for once the Palestinian state
is established and you come along with complaints, the first thing you'll
be told is, 'You have a state, so go there.' You are only making your own
situation worse.

Nasser: I think that once there is a Palestinian state, it will be easier for us
to define ourselves as Palestinians living in Israel.

---

[9] Theodor Herzl, in the early days of Zionism when he was not sure about the feasibility
of realizing his plans in Palestine, proposed Uganda (then a British colony) as an
alternative location for Jewish settlement.

Avner's contention (you are making things worse for yourselves because you are in favor of a state you don't want to live in) is political and pragmatic. In contrast, Nasser's claim ("it will be easier for us to define ourselves") is an emotional-social one.

> *Avner:* Speaking for myself, I identify with the struggle to establish a Palestinian state. Today I admit that the idea that the conflict will not be resolved when the Palestinian state is established came as a complete surprise to me.[10]
>
> *Nasser:* So the solution is to throw us out . . .
>
> *Avner:* That's not true! You just want to be a minority, that's all. If I didn't have a state I would go anywhere I could to live in my own state, never mind the land . . . Your attitude to land makes things very difficult for you. You're divided among yourselves, you cannot resolve it.
>
> *Nasser:* You want to resolve our problem and you tell us to leave. Maybe things could be good for us here?

This is the first time that the new balance between Nasser's ambivalence and Avner's aggressive tone has been disturbed. Nasser maintains that what Avner really means is that he doesn't want the Palestinians in Israel. Avner is outraged ("That's not true!") and passes the buck back to the other side, insisting that the problem is of their own making. And then Nasser suggests that things could be good for the Palestinians in Israel. But it seems that Avner doesn't grasp the real meaning of this – that he and his collective

---

[10] During the second Jewish uninational encounter, Avner referred to this discussion, showing signs that his monolithic construction is cracking:

> What frustrates me the most at this workshop is that I came here knowing exactly what I want, and what is good for them, and with each meeting that passes I leave the workshop agreeing less with them. Not because of the idea they present, but because of how they present it. And I am angrier with myself than I am with them. Sometimes I'm angry with myself because I don't have the courage to say "such and such is important to me." Right, it might sound primitive; maybe I sound like some member of the right-wing Likud party. But it's important to me. Why can't I say so? That's the feeling I have at this workshop. Personally, I didn't know I had such fantasies, [but] now I can say that I am afraid of what will happen. The idea of the conflict not ending after the establishment of a Palestinian state – I told them this at home; they said, "So what's new? Everyone knows that." And I couldn't explain to them why I was so shocked when they [the Palestinians] said it. I couldn't explain what disturbed me in their words or in the way they spoke.

could make things easier for the Arab minority – or he cannot deal with it. The cat is out of the bag in Avner's later remarks during the uninational discussion (see also last footnote). He says he is frustrated by the discussion because he discovers that he is more politically right wing than he had thought. He had believed that he knew what was "good for us" and what "was good for them" (separation) and during the discussion with Nasser he was surprised to discover otherwise. Avner is now torn between his monolithic construction and his neo-monolithic backlash.

> *Avner:* You cannot persuade me to agree with the concept that we live in conflict and also want our children to live in conflict. I don't understand the logic of that. This concept of land isn't clear to me.
> *Nasser:* You don't appreciate it because you have it. You want to get rid of us. Do you want me to convert? Soon you'll want us to celebrate Independence Day.

Nasser's initial complaints to Avner are repeated: You have land and therefore you don't appreciate what you have. You would like me to erase my national uniqueness in order to live among you. The gap between the two does not lessen, for there is no mutual, open acknowledgment of the fear behind their words. The Palestinians fear losing their identity as a result of living as a minority in Israel. The Jews fear the demand that they give up the Jewish character of their state, which is fundamental to their sense of security and identity.

> *Avner:* We are now aware that the conflict will continue even when a Palestinian state is established. This is acceptable and legitimate. What I don't understand is: What status do you perceive for yourselves once there is a Palestinian state? Will you be Israeli citizens? Will you be first and foremost Palestinians or Israelis? Or will you create some sort of synthesis? What obligations will you take upon yourselves? You'll really have a problem. The question is, are you are willing to take on the status of a minority?
> *Nasser:* We have been here all the time so how can this be a Jewish state? Any Russian Jew who has recently immigrated to Israel has more rights than I do . . . This is racism, the Jews are a racist nation.

Several Jews answer simultaneously: The Jews here don't see themselves
as living in a state that isn't Jewish.
Nasser [smiling]: We'll change you.

With this powerful statement, Nasser ends the encounter; new possibilities and implications cannot be examined at that moment because the class period is over. What direction will the effort to change the Jews take – one in which they would be able to encompass the reality of the minority as well? How can a minority change a majority? Or, does Nasser wish to transform the Jewish majority into a minority?

THE ELEVENTH ENCOUNTER

At this encounter, Jewish-Arab student pairs report about an observation assignment. Avner and Nasser observed a Jewish-Arab workshop at Kay Teachers' Seminar. Following is their report:

Avner: Nasser heard about a forum similar to ours and he persuaded me
to go, although at first it really didn't seem relevant . . . I understood the
purpose of observation in the field and going to this forum seemed a bit
artificial. I was wrong . . . I discovered a lot about Nasser at this forum.
You go on, Nasser.

Nasser: We arrived and sat down. We were introduced as guests from the
university . . . Two girls started lecturing about superstitions; they had
brought a *hamsa* [a hand-shaped amulet] and they tried, as I understood
it, to understand each other [Nasser and Avner both laugh]. In time, as
I talked to people, I understood that they were trying to get to know
each other through experiences. Last week they brought Arab foods.
We compared it to the dynamic that takes place here, but everything
seemed all right . . . They seemed to be old friends. At first we began to
ask questions, talk to people in between activities. They told us that at the
first encounter they had talked about politics. There was such an uproar –
people hurt each other – and they decided to drop that and do other, less
painful things. They were just like little kids; they played group games
and, at first, when we talked with people, Avner was convinced it was
a good method and I said it was "playing at" being friends. Tomorrow,
something will happen, someone will be killed and all their friendship
will collapse.

Avner: It didn't seem artificial to me at first; it seemed rather odd, as we were caught in our notion [from] here that it's good to let your painful feelings out first. At a certain stage we began talking to people and they explained the rationale behind it. And I thought: maybe this is the right way. It was during one of my more difficult times in our workshop. I thought it might be a good way because they weren't looking for discussions, they were looking for subjects of mutual interest to both national groups. For instance: superstitions and so on. On the other hand, Nasser raised a point; they said that in the first semester they tried to get closer and look for what they had in common, and in the second semester they would discuss the more difficult issues. This seems problematic – when you get closer it's harder to say things, as you perceive them differently. On the other hand, there is an advantage in knowing the other nation . . . Coexistence is achieved within the workshop itself. It's difficult to believe that any of these students will meet at a restaurant afterward or have coffee together.

Nasser: I felt they were trying to impose things and become friends and I saw that what was happening to them happens to many people: They think they are friends and suddenly, in a second, it can collapse, because they don't talk about what they are feeling deep inside. I think it is better to hurt one another than just sit around playing games . . . At first we didn't know what was happening there, if it was good or bad, but they clearly did not address the conflict – the approach [was] that one doesn't say anything and just goes on . . . I think that order is a good thing. Maybe they could have been friends, but they would not have been able to be honest with each other . . . If we had begun this workshop differently, I don't think I would have been able to talk to anyone here . . . I would have thought twice. I came to this workshop to learn new things; I also came to voice my opinions, so that people would be able to see things the way I do.

Avner: We leave the arguments here. I mean things don't go beyond the break or the workshop. We talk in the cafeteria; our arguments don't affect interpersonal relationships. So maybe this is a higher level, but maybe this is also a game. Maybe when I talk with Nasser here, I dare tell him "you are such and such." When we leave here it's different, as if I hadn't said it, or as if it weren't Nasser, meeting with me now, who heard what I said. There's a difference between Nasser-the-participant-in-the-workshop and Nasser meeting with me outside the workshop.

There is an issue here that I think is very individual. When I look at myself... there was a time when it was very difficult for me to relate to the workshop and to other things as well... when I listened to the news I didn't have the energy to hear those things. As time goes by I feel these things differently: Nasser can say things to me, visit me in my home, talk and express all sorts of things, to some of which I can say "O.K." That's Nasser's provocation, and he does provoke, saying things to raise consciousness, not for the sake of the things themselves. I don't know if he does it on purpose, but that's my interpretation. I might reach a stage where I'd say: Enough, I don't want to hear anymore. There's also a risk involved in opening up these things.

Nasser: If a right-wing extremist were sitting next to me, I would have no problem becoming his true friend, in spite of his views. It's not that there are two Nassers. It's that I can't reject his friendship just because he thinks that way about me.

Their joint observation assignment has made the two examine the way they have encountered each other at the workshop. They feel that the tough things they said to each other enabled a mutual closeness, in contrast to the process they observed at Kay College. Nasser maintains establishing a place for serious confrontation facilitates closeness outside the workshop. Courtesy in the workshop (without any expression of negative feelings when these arise) might lead to distance outside the workshop. Avner is still skeptical. Maybe this is also a game: Is Nasser in the group the same Nasser who smiles at him outside the group? Avner also admits that at first, when he was having a hard time in the workshop, he tended to prefer the idea of avoiding confrontations during the first semester. But he maintains that Nasser convinced him that this process does not really facilitate friendship. Avner can now define Nasser's extreme statements as "provocation." But he still fears that it can lead to losing control of the dialogue process. Nasser, for his part, maintains that even if Avner were a right-wing extremist (does he perhaps think that Avner is not too far from this?), he could still be his friend. It would appear that carrying out the joint assignment has allowed them to become friends in every sense of the word. This can be seen in the following encounters.

FINAL ENCOUNTER OF THE FIRST SEMESTER

Nasser: They've signed the Hebron[11] Agreement. I think Bibi [Netanyahu, then the Israeli prime minister] is quick [smiles] . . . Say "congratulations." Maybe there'll be peace with all the Arab states, and there'll be no need for this workshop next year? [Laughs. Everyone laughs.]

Another participant: What has each one of us learned at the workshop?

Nasser: Hard to say. Maybe I've learned to listen at the workshop.

Avner [smiling]: You've become quite human, in fact. [Everyone laughs.]

Nasser: I think we should be photographed and the picture exhibited in the Students' Hall, so everyone knows. These encounters are very important, but there aren't enough; a small group like this out of thousands of students at the university. If the photographs are seen, even more students and lecturers will come next year. So much money is invested in the university. Why don't they invest in things like this? All of us will raise a family, children, a lot of people want it. This place gets to a lot of people. This group should be written about in *Panim* [the students' bulletin]. We should do it. [He speaks seriously until this point, and adds with a smile:] We'll get money, go on trips.

The final encounter (and perhaps also the signing of the Hebron Agreement that day) creates a euphoric atmosphere. Nasser shows his "soft" side to the group in appreciation of what he has been willing to give and receive ("Maybe I've learned to listen").

A (POSITIVE) INTERIM SUMMARY

Avner has gained insight during the encounters with the other side and this is perhaps most clearly expressed in what he says during the final Jewish-only encounter of the group:

From the last meetings and discussions I've had with Nasser, I can understand the source of their frustrations. I feel it's because of the way he expresses himself; he said a lot of things to make us think. I feel a lot less disconcerted. They're angry. There's something about the label "leftist"

---

[11] In 1997, an agreement between Israeli Prime Minister Benjamin Netanyahu and Palestinian National Authority leader Yasser Arafat was signed at the Wye River Plantation (in Maryland) to provide the Palestinian Authority some control over the city of Hebron.

that goes beyond a political viewpoint. [It's] someone who really does want peace. What was a shock for them, and maybe for me, is that we don't want peace; we want an absence of violence. Nasser asked me: Tell me the truth, if you could get up in the morning and find there were no Arabs in Israel, wouldn't you be happy? It's true. He's disappointed in the enlightened among us. If we don't know what peace is . . . for us it's not an existential issue, for him it is. This greatly disappoints them. Obviously, one wants peace for its own sake, but they want something over and above what we want. It's a process. At first I felt threatened, which is why I wanted to say things like, the homeland is important to me. It was a reaction. I'm more immune now and can understand better. I used to say that I want peace and don't care about stones, and it's a pity that a soldier should lose even a finger for some place. Today I know the value of land for them [and] I have no problem saying that the land is important to me too, and I don't want to give up Jaffa and Haifa. I'm willing to confront each and every one of them and feel I have the right to do so. At first I felt weak. These rows have somehow given us a balance. I can even take the shouting with humor. The one-to-one interactions with Nasser were a lot more significant for me. [Responding to a Jewish participant who says that Muslims are "naturally" violent:] How can you create a dialogue, how can you progress if you say that genetically, biologically . . . if you make statements like that? Statements like that lead to a dead end. They freeze the minute you say to someone: You are inherently violent. You can't tell someone: You are different from me; you are violent, and it's in your genes, your father and grandfather's – not mine . . . I just don't think like that.

The uninational encounter indicates that Avner has gained insight: Although thinking of himself as left wing, he too would be willing to wake up one morning and find the Palestinians gone. However, Avner has learned that land is genuinely important to him and he has overcome his "weakness" about stating it openly, engaging the Other on a one-to-one basis. This insight leads Avner to rebuke a Jewish group member for attributing violence to Muslim teachings. This is an untenable claim. It prevents examination and progress in the dialogue.

This is the change in Avner's definition of himself: He is no longer a smug leftist who is offended by Nasser's accusations, but one who is willing to acknowledge the contradictions in his own identity construction and, therefore, in someone else's. The disintegration of his monolithic identity amid the neo-monolithic backlash has created an opportunity for him to acknowledge various irreconcilable aspects of himself and, through this awareness, establish a more significant dialogue with the Other, accepting him too as a multifaceted. Obviously, the process is incomplete, but this extract is sufficient to indicate what takes place in a binational encounter of this nature, with members of each side examining their own contradictions in identity as they confront one another.

FROM MONOLITHIC CONSTRUCTION, THROUGH DISINTEGRATION AND NEO-MONOLITHIC BACKLASH, TO DIALOGUE

The time has come to examine how well we have been able, with the help of our case studies, to substantiate the hypothesis outlined in the introduction to the book. We hypothesized that the Israeli collective "self" was initially constructed monolithically, in opposition to a number of "Others", including the Jewish-Diaspora Other, the Jewish-ethnic Other, and the alien, hostile Other. The latter Other, familiar for centuries in Europe, took its most extreme form in the mid-twentieth century with the Nazis and was later projected onto the Arabs as a whole and the Palestinians in particular.

I suggested that a monolithic construction was necessary for the early phases of the emerging Israeli "collective self," so the collective could distinguish itself from its predecessors. Contrast to the Other was key to the construction of Israeli-Jewish identity. Tension within the monolithic construction was already apparent in the symbiotic nature of the relations between the Israeli-Jewish self and the Diaspora Jewish Other. We further maintained that disintegration of the monolithic construction has accelerated in latter years, reaching a peak with the murder of the late Prime Minister Rabin, who, upon his death, became a symbol of the heroic Israeli *sabra*.

Different parts of the Israeli-Jewish population interpret this disintegration in different ways. Some view it as beneficial development, part of the maturing process of a collective. Others perceive it as regression from the romanticized ideal of the past. These differences in interpretation herald what outcome people foresee as the result of disintegration. The first group does not expect a new monolithic construction but rather aspires to maintaining multicultural diversity and to dialogue among the parts of identity that do not fit easily together (Kimmerling, 1998). The second group would prefer restoration of a neo-monolithic construction of Israeli identity after a period of crisis. I termed the phenomenon that exacerbates the special difficulties of our times "the whirlwind": disintegration continues amid a neo-monolithic backlash to the outbreak of violence and terror attacks. These two dynamics pull to opposite directions, creating disorientation and more chaos. Though hope for tranquility seems faraway, the exhaustion caused by the whirlwind may in fact bring about some forms of dialogue among the disintegrated parts.

In different chapters in the book, we saw various aspects of the phases in the development of collective Israeli-Jewish identity: monolithic construction, its disintegration, neo-monolithic backlash, and the beginnings of a dialogue between the parts exposed during the disintegration. With the aid of the case studies, we can now examine these stages one by one.

I chose to represent the monolithic construction through interviews with a former partisan, the Holocaust survivor Ze'ev, and his grandson Yoav, who was about to join the army. There are many examples in Israeli literature of the monolithic construction, from *He Walked through the Fields* by Moshe Shamir (1947), to the various "Hasamba" stories by Yigal Mosinson or Ka-Tzetnik's books about the Holocaust. However, I do not wish to suggest that such monolithic constructions characterize all Holocaust survivors. (Monologues by Genia and Olga in my 1995 book *Fear and Hope* are sufficient to show that this is not the case.)

In Chapter 1, Ze'ev describes the Germans entering the town and his revenge against the locals who had slaughtered Jews even before the Germans came. This taught him to believe that it is the strong in the world who are in control and thus he explains joining the partisans. Today, he views the family unit as a defense against an evil world. He is proud of his grandson who is joining the army, something that also allows him to express concern for another person for the first and only time during the interview. Yoav's words indicate a more complex capacity for identity construction. Like the grandfather he adores, he discusses the question of strength as opposed to weakness. It figures significantly in his experience of the pre-army program and his anticipation of army service.

Ze'ev's words and, to an extent, Yoav's as well faithfully represent a power-ful masculinity, a "black-and-white" viewpoint: "win-or-lose, everything-or-nothing." In today's world, those who continue to describe the world in terms of clear, unequivocal polarities struggling for control are perceived as fundamentalists. Innocently, they continue to believe that these polar-ities represent all of nature and human nature in particular, as if nothing new has happened in the history of mankind. In a crisis, this worldview enables people such as Ze'ev and many others to struggle for survival. The price is the reduction of all new life situations to emergencies to justify the monolithic construction.

Thus, this worldview enabled the generation of 1948 to endure the dif-ficult circumstances of the 1948 war and the establishment of the State of Israel. It is difficult to imagine how people could endure crises such as the Holocaust or that war without dividing the world into polarities, plac-ing themselves on the positive side in order to maintain hope for a better future once the crisis was past. However, today psychologists know that, parallel to the dominant process of locating oneself on the side of virtue, an internal process begins: identification with the oppressor. The words of Herzl and Nordau, quoted in the introduction, reveal their internalization of anti-Semitic images, projected onto the Diaspora Jew. When I first read of the antithesis of this Other, their new Jew who would be reborn in the Land of Israel, I was horrified by the similarity to Nazi descriptions of the ideal Aryan: blue eyes, healthy body, a blond crest of hair. Elsewhere I have speculated that internalized Nazi aggression was later collectively displaced and practiced against the Palestinians (Bar-On, 2001).

Three inteviewees illustrated the disintegration of the monolithic con-struction in Israeli identity: Alon, the son of a Holocaust survivor; C.R., who suffered shell shock during the 1948 war; and Shimon, a soldier during the 1987–92 Intifada. Another demonstration of the disintegration process is seen in the typology of moral argumentations presented by descendants of Nazi parents in Germany. In some of these examples, the intergenera-tional nature of the process stands out. Alon tried, unsuccessfully, to imitate the monolithic *sabra* façade of his father, an officer in the Israeli army: a façade – because his father had adopted the guise of a *sabra*, concealing his identity as a child survivor of the Holocaust. That part of his identity emerged in Alon's narrative, in opposition to the dominant social norm to which his father no doubt had to adjust himself. Here the feminine aspects of Alon's identity hidden within the masculine monolithic disintegration were allowed to surface, perhaps for the first time. In the interview with Alon, his grandmother, reading him frightening stories in her bed from a black book, represented the Holocaust. Alon burst into hysterical laughter when telling how she expressed her pain and sorrow. He did not find a way to combine this frightening "feminine" reaction with the dominant masculinity of his father, and his speech in fact broke down and disintegrated in the face of contradictory demands from inside and from without.

Although the Holocaust has meanwhile become a legitimate part of Israeli discourse (almost to the point of banalizing it, according to some), the notion of shell shock during the 1948 war is still taboo, at least in the eyes of most of that generation's fighters. The shell shocked of 1948 were called degenerates, cowards, and weaklings at the time. At best, if they ran from battle, they were said to be "disappeared." The words of Yehuda Amichai's poem *Ruchama*, recalling the war, attest to the cost of the monolithic construction (1969: 11).

> And now I do what any
> Male dog does, I whine in silence
> And mark in urine a male area about myself
> That no one can penetrate.

Amichai plays here on the relation between the Hebrew words for male and for memory (*zachar* and *zicharon*). Thus, the male area that "no one can penetrate" can also be translated as "area of remembrance." The sense of continuous legend created an enormous burden for those men who suffered from shell shock during that war. It was not permissible to ask for support from an estranged environment, either then or later on, as C.R. recounts in frank and painful words. We heard from other aging soldiers of the 1948 generation the belief that there was no shell shock in the ranks of the Palmach: "If at all, then among Gahal." (C.R. calls this charge disgraceful, having witnessed great personal strength on the part of Gahal soldiers who served in the war after enduring the torments of the Holocaust in Europe.)

From the monolithic Israeli-Jewish perspective of the 1948 *sabra* fighter, shell shock meant weakness, and this could only be attributed to "those weaklings" from "there." The number of distorted concepts still controlling so many people's minds more than half a century after the events is simply astounding.

It would be of academic interest to research the extent to which latent shell shock from 1948 correlated with shell shock in family members serving in later Israeli wars (particularly 1973 and 1982). What the present pilot study suggests is that a dense monolithic myth still surrounds the generation of 1948, particularly when it comes to the phenomenon of shell shock, and only a few have managed to escape and work through it.

The "recruited identity" for the purpose of war with the enemy is, apparently, the connection between struggles that are inherently different and chronologically distant, such as the war of 1948 and the first *Intifada* of the late 1980s and early 1990s. Yitzhak Rabin embodies such connections: a hero of the 1948 generation, he became the architect of the 1967 (Six-Day War) victory, managed to evade the fate of responsibility for defeat in the 1973 Yom Kippur War, and returned to us during the *Intifada* as defense minister with the unfortunate command to "break their arms and legs." Only in the nineties did Rabin choose to escape the vicious circle of the Israeli wars and take the brave and risky steps leading to the Oslo Accord, recognizing the Palestine Liberation Organization and the Palestinian Authority. His murder symbolized for me the fact that part of Israeli-Jewish society was unable to deconstruct its monolithic identity, especially the part that had been recruited to confront the "totally evil" Palestinian. Such Israelis could not grasp how a war hero could go so far in what they perceived as the wrong direction. Paradoxically, in an attempt to preserve the old construction, the murderer, Yigal Amir, hammered the last nails into the monolithic coffin of Israeli-Jewish collective identity.

Although Shimon, one of the *Intifada* recruits interviewed, was infuriated by the recruited identity and used his experience in order to shatter it and question its inner logic, Adi, the second soldier, still struggled with it. A junior but loyal officer, he shuttled between sincere, monolithic concerns about the deteriorating ethics of the army and a neo-monolithic backlash of contempt and suspicion of Palestinians, whose "mentality" he viewed as not only different but inferior. Only at one point during the interview did Adi abandon his recruited arguments, seeking a middle point between the polarities. In the scene he described, he wanted to avoid difficult situations that he understood were insoluble and that the army did not try to resolve.

As a final step in demonstrating monolithic disintegration, I presented some of my research on descendants of Nazis. The possibility of seeing these people as human beings, some of whom seriously struggle with the atrocities committed by their parents during the Holocaust, challenges the most sacred part of the monolithic construction in Israeli-Jewish identity. Many Israelis demonize any German as a Nazi and as the embodiment of "total evil" (Hadar, 1991).

This view is challenged by understanding the logic of the moral argumentations that the descendants of the Nazi perpetrators employ, and the stages in their processes of coming to terms with their family histories. It emerges that there are differences among them in terms of their moral coping, just as there are differences among Israelis. We can feel closeness to some of these Germans and even have empathy for them, while we have reservations about others and even loathe some. As my research indicates (Bar-On, 1989), even among the perpetrators themselves, we find – perhaps as in most of us – a capacity for evil and good, and one could not always tell which would determine their behavior at a given moment.

These four examples showed how monolithic disintegration can be identified, particularly with regard to the Other, sometimes an internal and Jewish Other, as for Alon and C.R., and sometimes an alien and imagined Other (but also in certain cases an external threat in reality, as for Shimon and Adi). Alternate examples could have represented the Jewish ethnic Other, religious Other, and Diaspora Other, all of whom assumed independent voices within Israeli identity, thereby deconstructing its monolithic pattern from within. As someone who lives within this disharmony, I do not claim it to be a particularly pleasant experience. However, I maintain that it is also depressing to persist in leaning on the ostensible harmony of a monolithic construction that belongs to the past and can no longer reflect internal or external social processes that have since taken place within and around us. It does not arouse hope for a better future.

What I could not foresee was the neo-monolithic backlash, as we have experienced it in the Israeli society since October 2000. This neo-monolithic backlash, as presented here through analysis of the interview with Adi and the work with Sami Adwan at PRIME and with Israeli-Palestinian facilitators at Ben-Gurion University, was especially confusing, as it could not stop the disintegration process. The analogy of the whirlwind describes the feeling of being torn between these two conflicting forces.

This final chapter of the book dealt with the possibility of a dialogue between bits and pieces of the disintegrating construction, though I have hitherto only identified this happening in "laboratory" settings that were relatively protected and secured from collective, polarized, and destructive discourse. I suggested in the introduction that at the dialogue stage the quality of the dialogue will become our identity construction, rather than this or that part of the previous monolithic constructions. In the interview by the daughter of a Holocaust survivor, the dialogue she initiates is her way of working through the monolithic construction of her childhood that excluded his Diaspora Jewish experiences. She is able to begin an open dialogue with her father, even if only to a limited extent. The dialogue between an Israeli Jew and an Israeli Palestinian participating in a student workshop at Ben-Gurion University is a different example of dialogue at the disintegration stage.

If this stage is not as clear-cut as monolithic construction on one hand, neither is it as chaotic as disintegration on the other. There is no control over the outcome of the dialogue stage, but it is more possible to evaluate the process. Inherent to it is communication between different components, communication that is difficult because no clear pattern can be predicted. This stage brings recognition that the harmony of monolithic constructions no longer exists. However, there is no comfort in the distance that has formed between the parts as a result of its disintegration and neo-monolithic backlash. The dialogue is the somewhat hesitant beginning of something else, but the direction is still unclear and certainly not linear. There is also the potential for neo-monolithic backlash – threatening and violent situations and the fear of losing stable ground may push participants of the dialogue to take the "armor from the hook," to use the metaphor I suggested earlier.

In the case of Yael and her father, we first see the loving and protective father of her initial remembrances. During the interview, Yael listens to his life story as he develops it. Her ability to do so is an achievement, a recognition of the "otherness of the Other," using the terminology of

Lévinas (1990), or a moral achievement, per Nussbaum (1990). But Yael is also fearful of this beginning because she knows neither where it will take her nor what she will have to give up. On the part of the father, we sense a tremendous effort to control her process of entering his story (particularly when he starts to tell about times when he, as a child during the Holocaust, did not have much control). Perhaps it was also his way of testing his daughter and the extent to which she truly was able to contain his difficult moments and experiences. They reach a critical moment when he describes to her how he knelt at the feet of the Hungarian fascist policemen who came to arrest his family in Budapest and pleaded for their lives. Yael could not continue with her concentrated listening after his description of this humiliating moment. This was, for the time being, the extent or quality of the dialogue they reached; the degree to which Yael was able to accept the weakness and vulnerability of the strongest person in her life up to that point, containing in her Israeli-Jewish identity her father's Diaspora Jewish experiences.

The dialogue between Avner and Nasser affords us a completely different view of dialogue, within a fierce, asymmetrical, and multidimensional conflict. In the atmosphere of suspicion and threat inherent to the conflict, Nasser tries to construct an independent, authentic voice that will reach those who, in fact, are used to silence or to looking at the alien Other through collective monolithic constructions. In fact, Nasser has the difficult task of creating an encounter, a possibility of dialogue that until then was suppressed by Israeli-Jewish hegemony. He does this through a combination of breaking the rules of the game dictated by the Jewish, dominant side, together with a fierce attack ("You are racist and don't want to see yourselves as such"). And he adds to this combination both charm and use of mannerisms adopted from the repertoire of Israeli-Jewish culture. Thus, an interesting friendship is formed between Nasser and Avner, despite fierce arguments between them. The friendship withstands tough tests within the group itself, against students from both groups who prefer to continue to represent the conflict in black-and-white monolithic images.

Since the encounter between Nasser and Avner, new events have occurred. Israel has faced a violent outbreak of hatred and terror and the Palestinians have faced renewed oppression and fierce military control. In light of these events, the dialogues presented here could be seen as poor and simplified alternatives to what is happening in daily life of Israelis and Palestinians. But I assume that at some point dialogue will become a preferred option, and therefore I suggest it in spite of our harsh reality. I know of many groups that even in these days of renewed conflict are using dialogue to explore identity vis-à-vis the Jewish ethnic Other or the religious Other. There is dialogue between new and veteran immigrants, between women and men, between generations. The examples here demonstrate rather than encompass or summarize the entire phenomenon. The future will tell the extent to which dialogue as internal and external form of communication will replace the monolithic and neo-monolithic constructions of collective identities in our society and in others.

Postscript

1. IDENTITY CONSTRUCTION IN OTHER CONFLICT-RIDDEN REGIONS

Israel is not the only country going through an intensive change in collective identity construction. The events of 9/11 in the United States, followed by the war in Afghanistan and Iraq, the disintegration of the Communist bloc in the late eighties, and the ongoing development of the European Union, created a fertile ground for change in many countries.

The early Communist regimes in the Soviet Union and other Eastern European countries had tried to create, through top-down indoctrination, a new collective identity construction through a monolithic negation of Others: capitalist America and the fascist Nazi regime. Similarly, they tried to create a negative sense of Otherness with regard to internal "anti-Communist" elements, such as the church, the farmers, or the merchants. This propaganda became quite anti-Semitic during the late Stalin era, suggesting that the Soviet regime needed more and more enemies, from within and from outside, to justify and defend its own monolithic collective identity construction.

In the late 1980s, this massive construction collapsed. Now it became obvious that Communist indoctrination had not been very successful – many citizens had maintained their original "tribal" identities, whether religious, ethnic, or cultural, beneath the Communist "mask." But with the "overriding element" of a unifying collective construction – shallow as it was – gone, the need for a new collective identity construction became apparent. In certain countries, alternative "enemies" were identified to recreate a monolithic construction to take the place of the old one. President

Slobodan Milosevitch's Serbia is probably the best-known case of this trend. In other countries, such as Hungary or the Czech Republic, old, pre-Communist national themes served as a unifying construction. In Poland, these had a strong, religious Catholic cast. In countries such as Bulgaria or Romania, Communism (defined now as "socialism") changed its external colors, but major parts of the old regime maintained their power, so that the new collective identity construction was a mixture of pre-Communist nationalist and Communist elements.

In all these cases, it became clear that the monolithic collective identity construction that had succeeded in maintaining at least a façade of unity during the Communist regimes was gone forever. Therefore, several "tribal" collective constructions competed for a new hegemony, without any serious questioning of whether a monolithic construction was needed at all and without a systematic dialogue phase. The dialogue around identity construction was accompanied by an economic crisis. The fall of the Communist bloc meant, among other things, the need to move from a planned economy into a competitive market in a very short time. This was done without the democratic tradition required to conduct such a change successfully (Dahrendorf, 2000).

In this sense, East Germany, the former German Democratic Republic, is especially interesting case study. First, though, we have to try to understand the processes that took place in Western Europe during the decades following the Second World War. Many Western Europeans were determined not to repeat the mistakes of the post–World War I period, when Germany was humiliated and made dependent on the big powers. However, the cold war context demanded some unifying construction pitting the "free world" against Communism. A kind of negotiation took place within each Western European nation as to how much to "unite" against the new enemy and how much to work through old, prewar rivalries employing a democratic process. In several countries, such as Italy and France, strong, internal Communist parties prevented an overly strong common anti-Communist front from developing.

The result of these deliberations can be seen in the development of a common European Market and later a more inclusive unification. A kind of a dialogical process developed, in which the specific conditions of each country had to be considered. Certain old rivalries have indeed been worked through. For example, special German-French and German-Polish commissions looked into textbooks and tried to develop a more positive mutual perception of the "otherness of the other" (Lévinas, 1990), thereby deconstructing old monolithic enemy definitions.

West Germany was very much in the center of these efforts. First, it tried thereby to wipe out the dark heritage inflicted by the Nazis of being feared as a dangerous paranoid neighbor, together with other shameful memories. The economic boom and the democratic regime enabled the creation of an alternate image – a "new West Germany" that aspired to unite Europe in a struggle together for a better world. However, because East Germany was Communist, some energy was perforce invested in the struggle with the dangerous Other behind the wall. Thus, when the wall came down in 1989, West Germans saw it as a victory for their own mode of thinking and behavior. As a result, unification was hastily arranged, mostly through subverting East to West, economically and politically. Many East Germans found themselves not only unemployed but also without any alternative "strong" identity construction, and with no preparation for a "softer" collective dialogical construction like the one that their neighbors in the West had accustomed themselves to over more than four decades. Therefore, many of their young people search for a strong monolithic collective identity construction that resembles the one they lost or which they find in neo-Nazi or other right-wing movements. These provide them with Others to hate and to be a foil for their identity construction.

Even in Western countries that did not go through an intensive transformation such as Germany's, European unification has not developed smoothly. We find a growing hatred of foreigners in Britain, France, Austria, and even Norway. In these countries, the disintegration of previous monolithic identity constructions and the replacement of a "softer," more complex collective identity construction (in the form of a "European" identity) is difficult for certain, usually less well-to-do parts of the population (Angvis & von Borris, 1999). They still seem to need a "strong" construction based on the negation of an Other, usually on ethnic or religious grounds. The present analysis could thus be useful to apply to processes of change, not only from the more common top-down political or economic angle but also from the bottom-up social-psychological perspective. Although political and economic perspectives emphasize the present and the future, social-psychological perspectives try to integrate the past into the present, thereby helping people make the necessary and difficult transition from a monolithic "strong" identity construction into a more complex and "softer" construction.

Our present psychosocial analysis may add to the conventional political thinking by noting that while conflicts may change on the manifest political level, this does not necessarily mean a weakening of hostile motives or prevention of new outbursts in the future. The best example of this is the ethnic conflict of the 1990s in Bosnia. To understand it, one has to dig deeper into the past, beyond that crisis. The Balkans were already in a civil crisis during World War I and World War II. The murder of an Austrian prince in Sarajevo was the catalyst for World War I. The partial collaboration of Croatian and Serbian fascists with Nazis and the struggle of Tito's partisans against them created a civil crisis during the Second World War. Have these crises been worked through? Was trust between the different ethnic components of the Balkan society reestablished after those dark periods? Probably not. Immediately after 1945, the cold war polarized the world anew, hindering a deeper reflection into the divisions of the past. The new Communist regime repressed old cleavages, trying to create a new future as if the broken social contract from the past had never occurred.

Psychodynamic psychologists must realize that repressed traumatic events do not disappear on the social level any more than on the individual level. On the contrary, they continue to broil under the surface, as silenced facts (Bar-On, 1999) that might burst out uncontrolled, when a political or economic opportunity is created. In the Balkans, this occurred after the fall of Communism in Eastern Europe in the early 1990s. It was almost predictable, even with a high rate of intermarriage between Muslims, Croatians, and Serbs. Neighbors and even family members suddenly turned against each other, not fully understanding the source of this "evil" energy in them. But even this grim chronicle is not the whole story. The Balkans were the "backyard" of all the empires: of the Ottoman Empire beginning more than five hundred years ago; of the Austro-Hungarian Empire during the nineteenth century; of the Nazi regime during World War II; and of the

Communist "empire" thereafter. Subjugation to a central power does not enable the development of positive self-image that is essential to the construction of a healthy multicultural society. When the aggression of oppressors has been internalized and repressed, it prevents both self-respect and respect for the Other. Balkan society might have become a positive example of a multicultural society had it not suffered this psychology of having been the "backyard" of empires in previous generations with an attendant failure to work through internalized aggression.[1] Instead of enjoying the beauty of diverse cultures that can enrich a population (as actually happened in Sarajevo and some small communities for short periods), many people continued to suffer, having internalized the aggression of their previous occupiers, with no legitimated or open access to the process, which is necessary in order to work through a history such as this.

To work it through, one first has to address where the internalized aggression comes from. In many cases (the Belgians in Rwanda; the Turks or the Nazis in Balkans), this is not easy because the original aggressor is no longer present and must be "reconstructed" artificially or symbolically for it to become clear that the tension did not originate between, using the latter example, the Croatians and the Serbs or the Muslims but was first kindled by outside agency. (In some cases, international tribunals have made this possible.) When many years have been invested in futile controversies, it is difficult to let them go in favor of another understanding of the source of that aggression, a source that is not present anymore.

We can also apply this analysis to the Jewish-Israeli case, as discussed earlier. Though Zionist identity was constructed to overcome the negative aspects of the Diaspora heritage, with its endless pogroms and persecutions and later the Holocaust, the internalized aggression of persecutions that have not been worked through reappear as displaced aggression toward the Palestinians or in seeing oneself as an eternal victim (Adwan & Bar-On, 2001; Bar-On, 2001).

[1] By "backyard psychology," I mean that when an external powerful society forcefully imposes itself, a weaker society will internalize the aggression of that imposition. Unacknowledged and never discussed or worked through, the internalized aggression remains dormant until an opportunity arises to externalize it against a group that is looked down on.

The internalized aggression, if not addressed and worked through, continues to work subliminally. When young people feel that negative collective self-image, even though they have no name for it, they tend to run away to another place where they can develop a seemingly more positive self-image, including a more positive image of themselves in relation to others. Lack of opportunity in their homeland (the natural place to develop a positive self-image) leads them to pay the price of being immigrants to alien cultures, giving up the collective feeling of belonging only their home setting can provide. This is reflected in the extended world travel common among young Israelis after army service, with the Far East and South America being popular destinations. Some settle abroad for many years.

What can be done to address and work through "backyard psychology" and the internalized aggression of the past? Some parties to conflict have no personal memories of the long-ago events that turned the aggression into silenced facts. This is always a more difficult situation to work through. Children of Nazi perpetrators have, in this sense, more opportunities to come to terms with the evil acts of their parents, as their personal experiences may lead them to acknowledgment and working through (Bar-On, 1989). Their own children or grandchildren will have a much more difficult time.

Elsewhere traumatic events have happened even longer ago, sometimes many generations earlier (for example, Native Americans, descendants of enslaved Africans, and former subjects of the Ottoman Empire in the Balkans all have bitter historical memories). Still, once an issue has been acknowledged, symbolic acts and reactivation of the past in artistic, educational, or literary form can try to enable the younger generation to access their repressed feelings and work through. Ron (2002) shows how doing this is a challenge for both Serbian and Israeli-Jewish societies: They have to acknowledge responsibility for their roles as perpetrators of other people's woes, relinquishing their perceptions of being solely heroic freedom fighters.

The following section describes group processes for addressing and working through such issues. They have one thing in common; regardless of economic or political perspectives, these group processes try to bring together unresolved issues of the past. They do not try to push the past away, charging that it is irrelevant, as do some politicians, thereby silencing unresolved issues from long ago. However, they also do not give in to the past (and its unresolved issues) without reintegrating it into the present and future perspectives. The group creates a relatively safe setting for developing trust and for reflection, prerequisites to moving away from monolithic constructions into more complex and less rigid ones. The difficulty is translating these processes on the micro-social level to the macro-social level. The Truth and Reconciliation process in South Africa[2] can serve as one example of creative construction of a macro process in the attempt to integrate the past into a new future. Though this process was not implemented without problems, it still demonstrates the basic social-psychological approach translated into a macro-social process.

2. PARTIES IN CONFLICT SHARING STORIES: ACKNOWLEDGMENT AND WORKING THROUGH

The TRT (To Reflect and Trust) group experience suggests a kind of bypass that can be used when the parties are not ready to forgive and reconcile. When the TRT group began in 1992, it brought together descendants of Holocaust survivors from United States and Israel and descendants of Nazi perpetrators from Germany (Bar-On, 1995). The group process that evolved was based on sharing personal stories. In the context of the present discussion, the group rejected the concept of *reconciliation* and chose the terms *trust* and *reflection* to describe the group's work. Moreover, the issue of forgiveness never came up in the group discussions. One explanation is that reconciliation and forgiveness have to be worked through, rather than talked about. Reconciliation and forgiveness are terms that have been loaded, over the generations, with deep religious meaning; they are constructions that promote differences and social exclusion rather than the bridging of differences and social inclusion. Therefore, these concepts had to be bypassed rather than addressed in intercultural peace-building

---

[2] A compromise, as part of the agreement between F. W. de Klerk and Nelson Mandela, the TRC process in South Africa provided a framework for the perpetrators during the apartheid regime to tell the truth about their actions, for the victims to tell about what was done to them, and for the perpetrators to receive amnesty, based on their confession and remorse (Boraine, 1994).

activities (Bar-On, 2000, 2006). Another interpretation is that the Christian members of the group gained insight into the differences between Christian and Jewish assumptions about forgiveness and the special sensitivity of the Jewish children of survivors who did not feel entitled to forgive on behalf of the dead.

THE FIRST PHASE: DEVELOPING AN EMOTIONAL AND CONCEPTUAL LANGUAGE ACROSS A DEEP ABYSS

My years of intensive work with descendants of Holocaust survivors in Israel (Bar-On, 2000) and the interviews with descendants of Nazi perpetrators in Germany (Bar-On, 1989) were followed by establishing a group setting so that both these groups could face one another and initiate an open dialogue. Could they face each other genuinely? Could this meeting help each party work through aspects that could not be worked through in their own "tribal ego" setting? Through such an encounter, would a common agenda emerge over and beyond the separate agendas of each side?

Six encounters took place over six years, between eight descendants of Holocaust perpetrators and nine descendants of Holocaust survivors (five American and four Israeli), as well as a Jewish child-survivor who lives in Germany. Rotating between Germany, Israel, and the United States, the meetings usually lasted four to five days. The first encounter was devoted to getting acquainted, mainly through listening to each other's personal accounts and stories. Subsequently, the group did the scheduling. The content of the meetings all along continued to focus on the stories. Many issues were discussed intensively during these encounters.

During this joint working-through effort, a kind of shared emotional and conceptual language developed, beyond the separate "languages" that characterized the communities from which these people originated. This development created a dilemma for the two groups of descendants. They had to struggle with the question of whether to become an isolated "sect" (as the communities to which they belonged could not yet cope with their mutual experience) or else forgo their common experience. The important point about this group was that they chose to reject both of these directions and were willing to pay the price of holding onto the tension between them, using the group's support, while hoping that their communities would slowly move closer to each other. This may explain why the TRT process is slow and intense.

To try and tell the story stepwise, members of both groups first shared all of their own experiences – how, when, and in what ways they could trace the aftereffects of the Holocaust within their own lives. This was a daily struggle for some, accompanied by sleeplessness, fears, and uncontrollable reactions. Often this reflected silence, repression, or other difficult reactions on the parts of their parents. In many cases, acknowledgment of a personal relationship to the Holocaust was accompanied by a strong feeling of estrangement, from themselves as well as from their social milieu. It took many years to clarify and comprehend how these aspects of estrangement were associated with an individual's personal relationship to the Holocaust.

The Jewish members of the group suffered, first of all, from physical uprootedness, as their parents had immigrated to the United States or to Israel after the Holocaust. This physical uprootedness was usually accompanied by psychological uprootedness, associated with the fact that their parents could not overcome the loss of so many family members and had difficulty integrating themselves into the new society. The German members of the group shared this feeling of psychological uprootedness, but for other reasons: They felt that atrocities committed by their parents had poisoned their origins and they could no longer use them as a base. Like the descendants of the survivors, they too had to develop new roots.

Struggling with the feelings of estrangement and uprootedness brought up other questions. A major one for members of both groups was, Can I allow myself to live my own life, neither dependent nor counterdependent on that of my parents? Although for the Jewish descendants, separation from parents was more difficult because the parents leaned on them emotionally, descendants of Nazi perpetrators tended to counterreact and distance themselves from their parents, thereby suffering from an emotional void (Danieli, 1998). This problem became more acute over time, especially when the parents aged and their need for care became a daily reality.

Members of both groups struggle daily with dreams of death, with bearing names of dead people (especially Jewish descendants of survivors), and with fantasies of sacrificing themselves for a human cause (especially descendants of perpetrators). As one member of the group said: "We talk about our feelings, emotions, and ideas, but they all concern the dead people who are in the back of our minds." Perhaps not by coincidence, several members of the group belong to the helping professions. Perhaps they are trying to give a special meaning to their lives under the shadow of death.

Members of the group could, quite easily, establish an open dialogue with the victim in themselves. This was easy for both descendants of Jewish victims and descendants of Nazi victimizers. But it was much more difficult for both groups to identify and enter into an open dialogue with the victimizer within and to let the two "figures" talk with each other. Eventually, it became clear that we all have this role as a potential within ourselves, and only by openly acknowledging and entering into a "dialogue" with it may its uncontrolled potential be reduced in future, unexpected situations. After this realization, a new issue arose: Once we accept and let go of these two roles of victim and victimizers within ourselves – what is left? Who are we, if not defined through these roles? This actually suggested the beginning of a new process of identity construction that was not built on negation of the Other (Bar-On, 1999).

The issues associated with identity construction brought up the question of "who suffered more?" and hierarchies of power, suffering, and heroism. In the group context, it became evident that we all tend to create a scale of suffering, judging who suffered more and who suffered less. Perhaps, faced with extreme suffering, we gain a sense of control by doing this. It is much more difficult to relate to the experiences of the Other as just being *different*, not more or less. As we cannot grasp our parents' experiences during the Holocaust, assigning them a rank helps us to live with it. Something similar happened around the subjects of heroism and power. It became an issue for the group – how to maintain the legitimacy of grasping the difference without ranking it, as this creates unnecessary pain and humiliation.

Members of the group developed a common feeling of mutual trust and respect, suggesting a new symmetry between parties in the dialogue. However, this by no means erased the asymmetry that still existed in people's minds between their parents as victimizers or victims during the Holocaust. These two types of relationships were difficult to maintain simultaneously, but it was very important to find a way to navigate between them. This was associated with the relationship between the past and the present.

Through the group experience, it became clear that the goal of the process was not to forget or be done with the past, once and for all, but to find new ways to live with it, perhaps in ways that are more conscious but also less threatening and self-destructive. This suggests that by working through such massive trauma, one does not end it or let it go; one can find new ways to live with it. The trauma will always have a presence, but its negative impact on our lives and the lives of others can be reduced through such conscious working-through processes by groups, as well as by individuals. In a way, these issues were the group's main "product," the group's own way of working through forgiveness and reconciliation, rather than talking about them.

THE SECOND PHASE: BRINGING IN PRACTITIONERS FROM CURRENT CONFLICTS

In 1998, the group decided to invite practitioners who work with victims and victimizers in current conflicts (South Africa, Northern Ireland, and Palestinians and Israelis) and test whether the TRT group process was relevant for their settings. As in the original process, the larger TRT encounters (1998–2000) employed storytelling that promoted trust, reflection, and inclusion of the Other, rather than explicit discussions concerning reconciliation and forgiveness.

The question that remained open was, To what extent can one generalize from the TRT group process to other, current conflict settings that see reconciliatory efforts taking place between populations (after or within conflict)? It was clear that each conflict setting had its special "biography" that had to be carefully studied and taken into consideration. Nonetheless, we wanted to test the relevance of the TRT group storytelling approach for those who struggle with the peace-building process in the regions noted previously. We assumed that this sort of dialogue between members of opposing sides could be a necessary step toward reaching the deeper, underlying issues that political, legal, or financial steps, or even time alone, may not help to heal. The TRT experience also suggested that the process of reconciliation is an intergenerational process and cannot be achieved, at least in the case of severe conflicts, within the life span of one generation.

The detailed account of this experience is presented elsewhere (Bar-On, 2000). For our present discussion, it is valuable to cite the writing of Julie Goschalk, a Jewish member of the original TRT group. In what she called "my personal journey," she reflected on the process and what happened when she was confronted with the Palestinian stories after having worked through her relationship with the Germans (Goschalk, in Bar-On, 2000).[3]

> This summer my belief system underwent a major challenge. I am still trying to digest the events which took place during a four-day workshop involving Palestinians, Jews from [North] America and Israel, and Germans, sons and daughters of Nazi perpetrators. This is the account of my personal journey as a daughter of Jewish Holocaust survivors. This journey has taken me from a place of deep hatred of all Germans to a more differentiated view of the heirs of Nazi Germany, and from a simplistic view of Jews, Germans, and Palestinians to a much more pained, compassionate, and thoughtful position. I have had to struggle with my ideas about victims and perpetrators, as well as the meaning of historical events and their impact on an individual's view of himself and his people.
>
> During the first encounter in Hamburg, I was shocked by the vehemence and anger with which the Palestinians spoke of their plight. It felt almost like a personal attack and I was annoyed by what I perceived to be their attempt to use every possible opportunity to speak from a "soapbox." By the time we got into our small "conflict groups," I was incredibly anxious. I was fearful that the differences and the palpable anger were too great [for us] to begin to bridge the gaps. When the first Palestinian spoke about his life, his past, his current painful, daily realities living on the West Bank, I found myself feeling defensive, embarrassed, shocked, and annoyed. I did believe what he was describing, but I found it really hard to believe that this was anything but an unacceptable mistake, that maybe he was just an unlucky exception and that it was unfair for him to pretend that this was "normal" life for Palestinians. Of course, I did not dare to voice any such thoughts.
>
> By the time the next Palestinian spoke, I was beginning to squirm. Again there were tales of persecution, fear, loss, and unbearable humiliation. I

---

[3] Goschalk wrote her essay one year after the first large TRT seminar (with the new members from the current conflicts(. It took place near Hamburg in August 1998, funded by the Koerber Foundation.

couldn't believe what I was hearing. How was this possible? The more I heard, the more I cringed. I felt embarrassed to be Jewish. I could not bear the thought that my fellow Jews were inflicting such pain and horror on these people. I wanted to defend their actions as being driven by a need for security for Israel and Israel's need for protection from terrorism, but I could not even persuade myself that those were good enough reasons, let alone make a good case for anyone else's benefit. I felt exhausted and did not want to be there.

But as the days went by and we heard more and more horrible stories on all sides, I felt my barriers beginning to break down. We cried together, comforted each other, and it felt like we were beginning to build bridges, the way the original TRT group had done in 1992. On the last day but one, after another Jewish person had told her story, and just moments before the lunch break, one of the Palestinian women suddenly asked what the truth was about the Holocaust. She said that she had heard a French professor state that the Holocaust was a lie. Well, you could have heard a pin drop. I felt as though this woman had just slapped me in the face. I was utterly speechless and furious. Where had she been during the last couple of days? Had she been listening at all? Did she not hear the other children of survivors and me talk about our parents' horrible experiences? What was wrong with this person? I felt as though this whole workshop was a total waste of time, and I wanted to pull away. But then, just at the edge of my rage, there was a tiny little awareness that this Palestinian woman had only asked for information. She was not making a political statement. She obviously was confused about what she had been taught and what she was now hearing from the sons and daughters of Holocaust survivors in this group. I actually think her confusion was a direct result of her liking and trusting us; otherwise she would have simply dismissed what we had shared, rather than ask about it. However, even though I knew this in my head, my emotions were unable to catch up . . . In spite of the fact that I really understood that the question had come from a place of ignorance, I was too hurt and felt too betrayed to accept this. I had felt very close to this woman, in part because she and I were the only religiously observant people in the whole group. I had also tried to learn more about her outside of the group sessions, and I had been so very touched by her story. Yet here she was showing me that she had apparently not listened at all to my story and, worse than that, she was apparently implying that my parents never went through their living hell. In an effort to explain her lack of information, she asked whether there were any books which had been written about the

Holocaust. Several of us volunteered to provide her with literature, but she requested material "not from the Jewish perspective."

Now that I have had time to reflect on all the events of the workshop, I can see some of the parallels between the Palestinian woman's feelings and my own, when I first encountered Germans in dialogue. Similar to the way [in which] I was unable to accept that the descendants of my own family's oppressors might have suffered as a result of the second world war, so this woman and probably many other Palestinians rejected the idea that Jews may have been victims. They get angry when they hear this. It challenges their worldview, just as mine was challenged by what I was learning about Germans. And for Palestinians it is even worse, because their pain is current and ongoing.

So once again my worldview has been turned on its head. In my view, Jews had always been in the victim category, but this view no longer holds in such a simple way. Through the workshop in Hamburg I was definitely tossed out of this category, and I was struggling to find a new place for myself. I am very grateful to all the members in our little conflict group for their courage to open up, share their pain, struggle with uncomfortable realities, and begin to let in new, challenging information.

I am more convinced than ever that something almost magical takes place when individuals from the opposite sides of a political and socially fueled divide meet with an open, honest, and caring attitude. I had already experienced this with TRT, but I believe that the workshop in Hamburg has much greater implications than the original TRT work, since it deals with current conflicts. Besides hearing each others' stories and learning about the "other side," the healing that can take place is much greater than any that could be achieved by only listening to the stories of others who share one's history. Supporting each other through this learning process has proved to be tremendously helpful and may well be the only way to prevent the trauma from being passed on to the following generations.

It was difficult for this participant to take in the suffering of the descendants of the Nazi perpetrators through the initial TRT process and to let go of her fury toward the German people as a whole (Goschalk, 2000). Here she describes how much more was demanded of her in listening to the suffering of the Palestinians, knowing that it was connected to the wrongdoing of her own people. We see this as an example of how difficult it is to move from the role of the victim (in the context of the Holocaust) into the role of the victimizer (in the Palestinian–Israeli context). The TRT provided a safe enough social framework and a method of storytelling that enabled Goschalk to accomplish this transformation. The German members played a positive role in a moment of crisis by letting the Palestinians accept the Holocaust in its wider perspective, not just as a "Jewish-Israeli manipulation."

The TRT group in its wider format met four times after Hamburg: in Bethlehem, in October 1999 (Adwan & Bar-On, 2001); at Stockton College, in July 2000; in Derry/Londonderry (Northern Ireland), in August 2002; and in Barcelona, Spain, in June 2004. Several initiatives came out of these encounters that tell us how the TRT approach can be relevant for other conflicts:

1. In Northern Ireland, Catholic and Protestant TRT participants from Derry/Londonderry initiated a three-day seminar, in November 2000, composed of former British soldiers who fought in Northern Ireland during "the Troubles" and bereaved parents of British soldiers, together with Sinn Fein ex-prisoners and Unionists who were involved in the Troubles. It was the first seminar of this kind organized in Northern Ireland. Seven TRT members from there co-facilitated the process as people told their own stories in small groups. Ground rules designed for the groups and facilitators were very much in line with the experience of the TRT group. The summarization of the seminar was published (Hetherington et al., 2001). In a follow-up session, the seminar organizers met in Britain with representatives of the ex-soldiers' organization and decided to cooperate in conducting additional seminars and in struggling for the acknowledgment of posttraumatic stress disorder affecting all parties during the violent conflict in Northern Ireland.

2. A group of ex-prisoners from South Africa came to Israel in March 2000, through an initiative of the Van Leer Institute in Jerusalem, meeting with a Palestinian group of ex-prisoners. Sami Adwan and Dan Bar-On designed and facilitated a two-day workshop in the spirit of TRT at which the two groups shared their life stories (Adwan & Bar-On, 2001). The facilitative presence of the South Africans aided

the Palestinians in working through their frustration and anger and confronting the new life problems they had to struggle with after detention. As a result of this seminar, several ex-prisoners from the Palestine National Authority and one from South Africa joined the Stockton TRT encounter. A special session was designed so they could focus on their common problems, together with an ex-prisoner from Northern Ireland.

3. Fatma Kassem and Dan Bar-On (both members of the TRT seminars in Hamburg, Bethlehem, and Stockton) initiated a new seminar for Jewish-Israeli and Palestinian-Israeli students at Ben-Gurion University in 2000–01. As described in Chapter 4 (Yael's interview of her father), the students were asked to interview one member of their parents' generation and one member of their grandparents' generation and bring the transcribed interviews to the seminar. The process that evolved was very powerful, requiring members of both groups to address the Other's personal narratives for the first time.

4. PRIME also managed to continue some of its activities after the outbreak of violent events in October 2000. In many ways, its ability to do so can be associated with the commitment of a few of its members that was established through the mutuality of the three expanded TRT seminars.

These few examples show what has been learned from the TRT process and how it has been implemented in the various conflict settings. They may be not more than a drop in the sea of hatred and frustration that still prevails in painful and conflict-ridden social contexts. However, they demonstrate a way to establish bonds and test new ideas through intensive and systematic work in a secure environment, implemented carefully through a trial-and-error process, since each conflict has its special "biography."

PERSONAL WINDOW 6: FROM THE MONOLITHIC CONSTRUCTION TO DIALOGUE

"Objective" writing by Israelis about processes of change in Israeli identity cannot be expected. This genre of contemporary writing is particularly taxing as its writers are part of the very processes they are trying to describe. As researchers they attempt to observe both what is happening to themselves and to their surroundings. This can have significant disadvantages: If a researcher's subjective viewpoint is biased or frozen, his or her examination of social processes may – to use navigational terms – "impose the map on reality" (Bar-On, 1999). Likewise, what may be relevant to the writer's way of thinking might be irrelevant to some readers who have completely different experiences or views. This might be so particularly when the monolithic construction is disintegrating. The writer still preserves a sense of hegemony – a sense of there being only "one truth" concerning a definition of identity – his or her own truth – while a multiplicity of voices around him or her are redefining what constitutes authentic Israeli identity.

As we open the debate, we should keep in mind the story about four blind people who try to describe an elephant. Each touches a different part of the elephant – an ivory tusk, the curving trunk, a heavy leg – and, generalizing on the basis of that limited personal experience, claims knowledge of the characteristics of an elephant. Each of us is holding onto what little we know and claiming that it constitutes the "elephant" as a whole. This is perhaps one of the difficulties in the dialogue between social scientists who deal with this subject. It is a difficulty that stems from the process of disintegration within our own system of concepts, formed during a scientifically monolithic period, and the need to create a new dialogue between various conceptualizations, asking what Israeli identity is and how one debates it. This is one reason that I gave up an attempt to define these processes using "objective" tools and statistical tests. The results would indicate a single general direction that could be assumed to exist only during the period of monolithic construction. The confusion stemming from the monolithic disintegration is so great that it is impossible to assume the existence of one "general direction" intrinsic to Israeli identity. In order to see the variety of directions, we must attempt to find out where they are developing and to try and give them an expression or "voice." This is the difficult role of a social scientist endowed with intuition with regard to social processes developing around him and not limited by the concept of "what has been is all that shall be."

I have chosen the method of presenting extracts from interviews that, in my opinion, reflect processes of social change, while trying to give expression to "voices" hitherto unexpressed in the Israeli canon. Obviously, responsibility for the choice of voices is mine. This method also enables other researchers to join in the debate. One can, naturally, give other meanings to the interviews or present examples from other interviews or "voices" in order to demonstrate directions that differ from those identified here.

Unlike some of my colleagues, I insisted on the need to anchor my own theoretical conceptualizations in an examination of authentic dialogue between people who live in Israel, observing themselves therein, while relating to real problems in their lives. There is a story, maybe a thousand stories, behind every person in this country. Sometimes I feel I should just walk the streets and collect these stories with a tape recorder or a video camera. However, this is not so simple: one also needs to know what to look for. The interview with C. R. would not have been possible without the initial hypothesis that there are still people suffering from shell shock incurred in 1948. In order to talk to Adi about his experiences in the Intifada, I had to assume ongoing stress caused by the Intifada, though it has "disappeared," so to speak, from current Israeli debate and awareness. Facilitating the dialogue between Yael and her father required that a context be constructed that was both safe and open and could contain her first attempt to encourage him to talk. The dialogue between Avner and Nasser could not simply have taken place in the street, certainly not in the way it developed during the Jewish-Arab workshop with the facilitators from Neve Shalom.

But the writing of this journey involves a bit more than intuition about changes or social processes. A great part of the work preceding the interviews was done internally – in a transition from the monolithic construction in my personal, young identity, through its disintegration in various ways and stages, toward a relatively new situation of containing an inner "multiplicity of voices." These voices are disharmonious, in contrast to the harmony of my monolithic days. It is important to me to note aspects of myself that are still part of the monolithic construction as I experienced it in my youth. For example, not long ago I went to the Beer-Sheva Theatre to see Moshe Shamir's play, *He Walked through the Fields*. During the play, I was overcome with yearning at the mention of places in the Carmel mountains that I knew as a child. I used to go eat *sabras* with my brother and my mother on the way back from Ein Hashofet, where my father was a doctor who rode a donkey to take care of patients in the *kibbutzim* of that area. I longed for the romantic atmosphere of those times, when, at least in retrospect, everything seemed so simple: evil was evil and good was good.

Thus the monolithic construction does not disappear; traces remain in one's feelings and consciousness. So it was when, one day, someone phoned from the unit in which I had served during the 1973 Yom Kippur War, inviting me to a memorial evening for our commander, who had died of a heart attack. It was to be an evening of stories and memories with his family. Participation in such an event, even if it is not only about nostalgia, evokes again all the old feelings associated with experiences that were mine when my identity as an Israeli Jew was monolithic. From my present perspective, however, this identity appears to me as "made up"; artificial in some way. This year I decided not to go to the cemetery on Memorial Day, as I had all the previous years, but I still stood at attention when the siren "froze" the entire country on that day.[4] The same old feelings are evoked when I visit the cemetery on personal days of mourning and cannot resist pausing for a moment at the grave of a friend who fell in one of the wars. That is to say, the process of collective conscription of personal feelings, until now the pillar of collective Israeli-Jewish identity, doesn't end even when one appears to have matured and, in the middle of one's sixth decade, wishes to see oneself immune to the continued intrusion of the collective into one's personal life.

At the second stage, as my eyes were opening, I had to cope with the pain of disintegration and inner contradictions in my identity. For instance, sitting for four years behind a one-way mirror and observing Jewish-Palestinian student groups, I discovered the limitations of my supposedly heightened awareness. I came to observe the group process sharing the assumption of most of the Jewish participants that I myself was "enlightened." That is to say, I was willing to "accept" the other side and acknowledge its existence. However, rather quickly it became clear to me that I suffered from "conditional enlightenment." I was expecting my Palestinian colleagues to show gratitude for my enlightenment and not ask me for anything else (Golan, 1998). I realized how hard it was for me to listen to the pain of the Palestinians, to their doubts as to our willingness to live with them and to accept them and change for their sake.

I found it disconcerting to periodically discover the innate comfort of the patronizing male Ashkenazi hegemony I was a part of. How difficult it was to relinquish it for someone else who was different from me, or "less" than I, according to standards that did not seem to be my own. It no longer matters if challenges

---

[4] Israel's Memorial Day observance includes two minutes of silence at a standstill while sirens blare. Most of us have relatives who fell in the wars, and it is common to visit their graves after the sirens go off.

came from my son who began (fortunately for him, at a young age) to question my "leadership," or from my wife who insisted on her right to be a partner in determining family life according to her preference and belief, from my daughter who wrote about her childhood in the kibbutz, omitting my role in it, or from a Bedouin neighbor who insisted on his right (which did not fit in at all well with my rights) to live his life in a way that seemed strange and even frightening to me. Each of these experiences chewed off a piece of me: from what had seemed to me to be common to "us." But, in a process of many stages and painful misunderstandings, I have realized that these things only served my "ego."

The difference between the liberal, "enlightened" atmosphere in which I grew up, and the process I am describing here, is mainly in the suffering that accompanies change. If enlightenment describes a multiplicity of voices as being desirable, as would be birth without pain, the disintegration process of the monolithic construction is difficult and painful. It involves a struggle and conscious or unconscious unceasing attempts to restore the glory of one's hegemony and monolithic identity. When one learns to surrender, or listens to "voices" that are different from one's own, no gratitude is forthcoming. The voices that one has acknowledged or liberated burst forth, their power bearing witness to the time and extent to which they have been suppressed and silenced. One is left rather alone by the wayside, feeling irrelevant and even slightly hurt. The external gains of this process are few: One continues to be "relevant" in the sense that one flows along with reality rather than losing touch with it. Perhaps by virtue of this your spouse and children sometimes listen to you, your students occasionally take an interest in the subjects of your lectures, but not much beyond this. The main short-term gain is internal: Proceeding otherwise is not an option, and when this becomes difficult, there is no choice but to confront aspects of yourself that have hitherto prevented others from achieving an independent voice.

In the process of dialogue – of acknowledging an internal and external multiculturalism – there is also long-term gain: an increased ability to endure difficult processes taking place around one. When I had to cope with the crisis of Rabin's murder or with the halt in the peace process; with the outbreak of the second Intifada, with the phenomenon of ultra-religious domination, or with the power struggle between the old elite and the new, I felt I had a perspective that diminished the pain or jolt experienced by those of my friends who still yearned for the monolithic; for the lost days of hegemony. I felt they were not sufficiently prepared

Bibliography

Adwan, S., & Bar-On, D. (2001). *Victimhood and Beyond: The Bethlehem TRT Workshop in October 1999*. Beit Jala: PRIME publications.

Al-Haj, M. (1995). *Education, Empowerment, and Control: The Case of the Arabs in Israel*. Albany: SUNY Press.

Allport, G. (1985). The historical background of social psychology. In G. Lindzey, E. Aronson (Eds.), *Handbook of Social Psychology* (vol. 1, 3rd ed., pp. 1–46). New York: Random House.

Almog, O. (1997). *The Sabre: A Profile*. Tel Aviv: Am Oved. (In Hebrew.)

Almog, S. (1984). From "Muscular Jewry" to the "Religion of Labor." *Zionism: Studies in the History of the Zionist Movement and of the Jewish Community in Palestine, IX*, 137–146. Tel Aviv: Hakibbutz Hameuchad. (In Hebrew.)

Amichai, Y. (1969). *Poems*. New York: Harper & Row.

Amir, S., Yitzhaki-Verner, T., & Bar-On, D. (1996). "The recruited identity": The influence of the Intifada on the perception of the peace process from the standpoint of the individual. *Journal of Narrative and Life History, 6*(3), 193–223.

Amir, Y. (1976). The rule of intergroup contact change of prejudice and ethnic relations. In P. A. Katz (Ed.), *Towards the Elimination of Racism* (pp. 245–308). New York: Pergamon.

Angvis, M., & von Borris, B. (1999). *Youth and History*. Hamburg: Koerber Foundation.

Arendt, H. (1958). *The Human Condition*. Chicago: University of Chicago Press.

Aulagnier, P. (1994). *The Violence of Interpretation: From Pictogram to Statement*. Philadelphia: Taylor & Francis.

Bakhtin, M. M. (1981). *The Dialogic Imagination: Four Essays, by M. M. Bakhtin*. M. Holquist (Ed.); C. Emerson & M. Holquist (Trans.). Austin: University of Texas Press.

Bar-On, D. (1989): *Legacy of Silence: Encounter with Children of the Third Reich*. Cambridge, MA: Harvard University Press.

213

Bar-On, D. (1993). A testimony of the moment before the (possible) occurrence of a massacre: On possible contradiction between the ability to adjust and the maintaining of human moral values. *Journal of Traumatic Stress, 5*(2), 289–301.

Bar-On, D. (1995). *Fear and Hope: Three Generations of the Holocaust.* Cambridge, MA: Harvard University Press.

Bar-On, D. (1998). The Israeli society between the culture of death and the culture of life. *Israel Studies, 2*(2) pp. 88–112.

Bar-On, D. (1999). *The Indescribable and the Undiscussible: Reconstructing Human Discourse after Trauma.* Budapest, Hungary: Central European University Press.

Bar-On, D. (2000). *Bridging the Gap.* Hamburg: Koerber.

Bar-On, D. (2001). Who counts as a Holocaust survivor? Who suffered more? Why did the Jews not take revenge on the Germans after the war? *Freie Assoziazionen, 4*(2), 155–187. (In German.)

Bar-On, D. (2004). *Erzaehl dein Leben! Meine Wege zum Dialogarbeit und Politischen Verstandigung.* Hamburg: Koerber. (In German.) In English (2006): *Tell Your Life-Story: Creating Dialogue between Jews and Germans, Israelis and Palestinians.* Budapest: CEUP.

Bar-On, D., & Charny, I. (1992). The logic of moral argumentation of children of the Nazi era in Germany. *International Journal of Group Tensions, 22*, 3–20.

Bar-On, D., & Kassem, F. (2004). Storytelling as a way to work through intractable conflicts: The German-Jewish experience and its relevance to the Palestinian-Israeli context. *Journal of Social Issues, 60*(2), 289–306.

Bar-On, D., & Mor, Y. (1996). The ostensible "sabraness" of second-generation Holocaust survivors: A biographical and narrative analysis of one interview. *Sichot, 11*(1), 36–48. (In Hebrew.)

Bar-On, D., Sadeh, M., & Triester, D. (1995). The psychological perspective of immigration and resettlement in Israel: Separation vs. severance. *Refuge, 14*(6), 18–24.

Bar-Tal, D., & Antebi, D. (1992). Siege mentality in Israel. *International Journal of Intercultural Relations, 16*, 251–275.

Bernstein, D. S., *Pioneers and Homemakers: Jewish Women in Pre-State Israel.* New York: SUNY, 1992.

Bishara, A. (1993). On the Question of the Palestinian Minority in Israel. *Theory and Criticism, 3*, 7–21. (In Hebrew.)

Boyarin, D. (1997). *Unheroic Conduct.* Berkeley: University of California Press.

Comaroff, J. & J. (Eds.), (1993). *Modernity and its Malcontents: Ritual and Power in Postcolonial Africa.* Chicago: University of Chicago Press.

Dahan Kalev, H. (1997). The dialectics of ethnocentrism in Israel. Lecture at the Humphrey Center, Ben-Gurion University, March 18, 1997. (In Hebrew.)

Dahrendorf, R. (2000). A critical view on globalization. Lecture at the Israel Academy of Sciences, Jerusalem, April 2000.

Danieli, Y. (1998). *International Handbook of Multigenerational Legacies of Trauma*. New York: Plenum.

Erickson. E. H. (1968). *Identity: Youth and Crisis*. New York: Norton. In German (1970): *Jugend und Krise. Die Psychodynamik im sozialen Wandel*. Stuttgart: Ernst Klett.

Fischer-Rosenthal, W. (1995). The problem with identity: Biography as solution to some (post)-modernist dilemmas. *Comenius, 3,* 250–266.

Gal, R. (1990). *The Seventh War: The Impact of the Intifada on Israeli Society*. Tel Aviv: Hakibutz Hameuchad. (In Hebrew.)

Garber, J., & Seligman, M. E. P. (1980). *Human Helplessness: Theory and Application*. New York: Academic Press.

Gergen, K. J. (1991). *The Saturated Self*. New York: Basic Books.

Giddens, A. (1991). *Modernity and Self-Identity: Self and Society in the Late Modern Age*. Cambridge: Polity Press.

Gluzman, M. (1998). Longing for heterosexuality: Zionism and sexuality in Altneuland. *Theory and Criticism, 11,* 145–162. (In Hebrew.)

Goffman, E. (1959). *The Presentation of Self in Everyday Life*. Garden City, NY: Doubleday.

Golan, S. (1998). *The politics of depression in Jewish-Arab encounters*. Department of Behavioral Sciences, Ben-Gurion University. (In Hebrew.)

Goschalk, J. (2000). A challenge to my world view. In D. Bar-On (Ed.), *Bridging the Gap* (pp. 41–47). Hamburg: Koerber.

Grossman, D. (1987). *The Yellow Time*. Tel Aviv: Sifriat Hapoalim. (In Hebrew.) In English (1988): *The Yellow Wind*. New York: Farrar Straus Giroux.

Guri, S. (1995). *The Impact of Social Support on the Risk of Getting Combat Shock*. Unpublished master's thesis, Tel Aviv University. (In Hebrew.)

Gur-Zeev, I. (2003). *Destroying the Other's Collective Memory*. New York: Peter Lang.

Habermas, J. (1971). *Erkenntnis und Interesse*. Frankfurt Am Main: Suhrkamp.

Hadar, Y. (1991). Good and evil in the eyes of Holocaust survivors and their descendants. Lecture delivered at the eighth Family Therapy conference, Bat Yam Conference Center, Bat Yam, Israel. (In Hebrew.)

Helms, J. (1990). *Black and White Racial Identity*. Westport, CT: Greenwood Press.

Herzl, T. (1928). Moishel [Moses] facing the nation and world. *Alef, 1,* 151–155. (In Hebrew.)

Hetherington, M., Deanne, E., Irvine, T., O'Neill, J., & Lindsey, J. (2001). *Toward Understanding and Healing: An Evaluation Report of the Lusty Beg Residential.* Derry/Londonderry: Derry City Council.

Horowitz, D., & Lissak, M. (1989). *Trouble in Utopia: The Overburdened Polity of Israel.* Albany: SUNY Press.

Izraeli, D. N. (1997). Gendering military service in the Israel Defense Forces. *Israel Social Science Research, 1,* 129–166.

Izraeli, D. N., Friedman, A., Dahan-Kalev, H., Fogiel-Bijaui, S., Herzog, H., Hasan, M., & Naveh, H. (1999). *Sex, Gender, Politics: Women in Israel.* Tel Aviv: Hakibbutz Hameuchad. (In Hebrew.)

Kimmerling, B. (1993). *Zionism and Territory.* Berkeley: Institute of International Studies, University of California.

Kimmerling, B. (2001). *The Invention and Decline of Israeliness.* Los Angeles: University of California Press.

Kimmerling, B., & Moore, D. (1997). Collective identity as agency and structuration of society (the Israeli case). *International Review of Sociology, 7*(1), 25–49.

Langer, L. (1992). *Holocaust Testimonies.* New Haven: Yale University Press.

Lanir, Z. (1990). *A Young Kibbutz in a Conceptual Crisis.* Efal: Yad Tabenkin, Hakibbutz Hameuchad. (In Hebrew.)

Lerner, M. (1974). The justice motive in social behavior. *Journal of Social Issues, 31*(3), 1–19.

Lévinas, E. (1990): *Totality and Infinity: An Essay on Exteriority.* Pittsburgh: Duquesne University Press.

Lomsky-Feder, E. (1994). Patterns of participation in war and their impact on the construction of war and life: The case of the Yom Kippur War veterans. PhD diss., Hebrew University, Jerusalem. (In Hebrew.)

Maoz, I. (2000). Power relations in intergroup encounters: A case study of Jewish-Arab encounters in Israel. *International Journal of Intercultural Relations, 24*(4), 259–277.

Maoz, I., Bar-On, D., Steinberg, S., & Farkhadeen, M. (2002). The dialogue between the "Self" and the "Other": A process analysis of Palestinian-Jewish encounters in Israel. *Human Relations, 55*(8), 931–962.

Maoz, I., & Buzaglo, M. (1997). *The Approach of Oriental Israeli Jews toward Arabs: Attitudes of Values, Images, and Willingness for Closeness.* Hebrew University, Jerusalem: Department of Communication and Philosophy.

Margalit-Stern, Bat-Sheva. (2006). Redemption in chains: The women workers' movement in Eretz-Israel, 1920–1939. Jerusalem: Yad Ben Zvi & the Schechter Institute of Jewish Studies. (In Hebrew.)

Morris, B. (1999). *Righteous Victims.* New York: Knopf.

Moscovici, S. (1976). *Social Influence and Social Change.* London: Academic Press.

Mugny, G., & Perez, J. A. (1991). *The Social Psychology of Minority Influence.* London: Cambridge University Press.

Nordau, M. (1960). "What is the meaning of gymnastics for us Jews?" In *Political Essays* (vol. 2). Jerusalem: Zionist Library. (In Hebrew.)

Noy, S. (1991). *"I can't take it anymore": Combat Stress Reactions.* Jerusalem: Ministry of Defense. (In Hebrew.)

Nussbaum, M. (1990). *Love's Knowledge: Essays on the Philosophy of Literature* (pp. 148–167). New York: Oxford University Press.

Oyserman, D. (1993). The lens of personhood: Viewing the self and others in a multicultural society. *Journal of Personality and Social Psychology, 65,* 993–1009.

Peled, Y. (1993). Toward a redefinition of Jewish nationalism in Israel? The enigma of Shas. *Ethnic and Racial Studies, 13*(3), 345–367.

Potter, J., & Wetherell, M. (1990). *Mapping the Language of Racism.* New York: Harvester.

Rabinowitz, D. (1997). *Overlooking Nazareth: The Ethnography of Exclusion in Galilee.* Cambridge: Cambridge University Press.

Ram, U. (1993). *The Israeli Society: Critical Aspects.* Tel Aviv: Brerot. (In Hebrew.)

Raz-Krakotzkin, A. (1994). Diaspora in statehood: Criticism of the negating of the Diaspora in Israeli culture. *Theory and Criticism* (Jerusalem), 4, 23–55, and 5, 113–132. (In Hebrew.)

Ron, J. (2002). *Frontiers and Ghettos: State Violence in Serbia and Israel.* Berkeley: University of California Press.

Rosenthal, G. (Ed.) (1998). *The Holocaust in Three Generations. Families of Victims and Perpetrators of the Nazi Regime.* London: Cassell.

Said, E. (1979). *Orientalism.* New York: Vintage Books.

Sarup, M. (1996). *Identity, Culture, and the Postmodern World.* Athens: University of Georgia Press.

Segev, T. (1992). *The Seventh Million.* Jerusalem: Keter.

Shamir, M. (1947). *Hu Halach Basadot.* Tel Aviv: Sifriat Hapoalim. (In Hebrew.) In English (1959): *He Walked in the Fields.* Jerusalem: World Zionist Foundation.

Shapiro, D. (1965). *Neurotic Styles.* New York: Basic Books.

Shasha-Beiton, Y. (2002). Negative and just peace: Perceptions of Israeli and Palestinian students about the peace process. PhD diss., University of Haifa, Israel.

Shavit, A. (1997). The hatred toward Bibi. *Ha'aretz,* December 27, 1997. (In Hebrew.)

Shenhav, Y. (2003). *The Jewish Arabs: Nationality, Religion, and Ethnicity.* Tel Aviv: Ofakim. (In Hebrew.)

Sherif, M. (1966). *In Common Predicament: Social Psychology of Intergroup Conflict and Cooperation.* Boston: Houghton Mifflin.

Sichrovsky, P. (1988). *Born Guilty: Children of Nazi Families.* New York: Basic Books.

Smooha, S. (1992). *Arabs and Jews in Israel. Vol. 2: Change and Continuity in Mutual Intolerance.* Boulder, CO: Westview Press.

Solomon, Z. (1993). *Combat Stress Reaction – The Enduring Toll of War.* New York: Plenum Press.

Spence, D. (1982). The paradox of denial. In S. Breznitz (Ed.), *The Denial of Stress* (pp. 103–123). New York: International University Press.

Steinberg, S., & Bar-On, D. (2002). An analysis of the group process in encounters between Jews and Palestinians using a typology for discourse classification. *International Journal of Intercultural Relations, 26,* 199–214.

Stryker, S., & Serpe, R. T. (1994). Identity salience and psychological centrality: Equivalent, overlapping or complementary concepts? *Social Psychology Quarterly, 57,* 16–35.

Tajfel, H. (1982). *Social Identity and Intergroup Relations.* London: Cambridge University Press.

Tajfel, H., & Turner, J. C. (1986). The social identity theory of intergroup behavior. In S. Worchel and W. G. Austin (Eds.), *Psychology of Intergroup Relations* (pp. 7–24). Chicago: Nelson-Hall.

Taub, G. (1997). *A Dispirited Rebellion: Essays on Contemporary Israeli Culture.* Tel Aviv: Hakibbutz Hameuchad. (In Hebrew.)

Tetlock, P. (1987). A value pluralism model for ideological reasoning. *Journal of Personality and Social Psychology, 50*(4), 819–827.

Wiztum, E., & Levy, A. (1989). Combat reactions in the Israeli wars, 1948–1973. *Sichot, 4,* 60–70. (In Hebrew.)

Wiztum, E., Malkinson, R., & Rubin, S. (1993). *Loss and Bereavement in Israeli Society.* Jerusalem: Ministry of Defense.

Yiftachel, O. (1998). Challenging ethnocracy: Protest among the Israeli peripheries. Lecture at the seminar, Europe in the Middle East: Civil Society, April 1998, Van Leer Jerusalem Institute, Jerusalem.

Zizek, S. (1989). *The Sublime Object of Ideology.* London: Verso.

Zerubavel, Y. (1994). Facing memory and the memory of death. *Alpayim, 10,* 42–67. (In Hebrew.)

Index